A Theory of Literary Production

A Theory of Literary Production

Pierre Macherey

Translated from the French by

Geoffrey Wall

Routledge & Kegan Paul

LONDON, BOSTON AND HENLEY

This translation first published in 1978
by Routledge & Kegan Paul Ltd
39 Store Street,
London WC1E 7DD,
Broadway House,
Newtown Road,
Henley-on-Thames,
Oxon RG9 1EN and
9 Park Street,
Boston, Mass. 02108, USA
Set in 12 on 13 Bembo by
Kelly Typesetting, Bradford-on-Avon, Wiltshire
and printed in Great Britain by
Page Bros. Ltd., Norwich, Norfolk
Reprinted in 1980
Translated from Pour une théorie de la production littéraire

British Library Cataloguing in Publication Data

Macherey, Pierre

A theory of literary production
1. Fiction
I. Title
801'.953 PN3331 78-40559

ISBN 0 7100 8978 3 (c)

ISBN 0 7100 0087 1 (p)

Contents

II Some Critics

Translator's Preface

> To deprive the bourgeoisie not of its art but of its concept of art, this is the precondition of a revolutionary argument.

Pour une théorie de la production littéraire was published in Paris in 1966, bringing together six essays on various authors and critics – Barthes and Lévi-Strauss, Lenin, Jules Verne, Daniel Defoe, Borges, and Balzac – with the addition of a systematic theoretical exposition (written at the suggestion of Louis Althusser) for its inclusion in the series *Théorie*.

Several works in this series have already appeared in English translation, and the reader who is familiar with *For Marx* and *Reading Capital* will have no difficulty with Macherey's specialised use of certain concepts and categories. I have tried as far as possible to follow the terminology proposed by Althusser's translator, Ben Brewster, in the excellent glossary appended to *For Marx*. The complexity and difficulty of theoretical discourse is not gratuitous, not a perverse ingenuity. The words of Marx and Freud are conscientious and unspontaneous precisely in order to accomplish that negative, critical work upon the natural representations of the world which constitute ideology.

Pierre Macherey writes as a Marxist philosopher, from within the French Communist Party, working inside the problematic of the 'early' Althusser, and addressing himself to the question of literature as a part of the larger enterprise of rethinking and recovering the very categories of historical materialism in the aftermath of de-Stalinisation. The title of this work, *A Theory of Literary Production*, is (in the best sense) a slogan: a mobilisation of certain ideas in order to capture a particular ideological terrain (literary criticism). For, unlike other texts in the Marxist canon (say Trotsky's *Literature and Revolution* or Brecht's writings on theatre), this is not a political intervention in a specific historical conjuncture; it is a theoretical intervention which attempts to restate the relations between the literary text, ideology and history, as well as to criticise mistaken accounts of that relationship produced within bourgeois idealism and structuralism alike.

It does not fall within the scope of this brief introduction to offer a summary of Macherey's arguments, nor to attempt to revise and supplement his theory in the light of the later Althusser (a task which has already been attempted in Terry Eagleton's *Criticism and Ideology*). Readers may, however, wish to refer to Macherey's more recent work:

'A propos du processus d'exposition du *Capital*' in *Lire le Capital* (Paris, Maspero, 1968), vol. IV.
'De la littérature comme forme idéologique' in *Littérature* (Paris) 13 February 1974.
'Présentation' (with E. Balibar) in R. Balibar's *Les Français fictifs* (Paris, Hachette, 1974) pp. 7–49.

There is also a usefully self-critical interview with Macherey in *Red Letters*: Communist Party Literature Journal, no. 5, Summer 1977, pp. 3–9.

In his account of the complex materiality of the literary text Macherey draws rather reticently upon the Freudian theory of the unconscious, and in particular upon the concept of a 'symptomatic' reading which enables us to identify those gaps and silences, contradictions and absences, which deform the text and reveal the repressed presence of those ideological materials which are transformed in the labour of literary production. If we are to use Macherey correctly, if we are to reach a true judgment of the value of his work, this 'symptomatic' reading must be attempted in his own case. Such a reading might begin from some of the following questions: His detailed examples are all drawn from the nineteenth-century novel; does the theory apply to other genres and to works from a different historical period? Would a historical account of the elaboration of the category of 'literature' substantially modify Macherey's epistemological scheme of theory-fiction-ideology? What are the theoretical problems involved in the incorporation of psychoanalytic concepts into historical materialism? Is the critique of structuralism relevant to developments since 1966: to Barthes' *S/Z*, for instance; to Lacan's reading of Freud?

Acknowledgement

The publishers would like to thank Lawrence & Wishart, Ltd, London, for permission to reproduce extracts from *Lenin on Literature and Art*, 1978, and *Collected Works*, Vol. 16, 1963.

I

Some Elementary Concepts

Chapter 1

Criticism and Judgment

What is literary criticism? The question is deceptively simple. If we answer, 'Criticism is the attempt to know a work of literature', we have given the enterprise of criticism a domain of research but not – properly speaking – an object. On the other hand, we are doubtless using the term 'knowledge' prematurely. We ought to be asking about the meanings and usages of this word 'criticism', which has been used ever more exclusively since the seventeenth century to denote the study of literary works. Even the expression 'literary history', once so much in favour, has failed to supplant 'criticism'. It was soon felt necessary to distinguish between literary history and literary criticism, to posit them antithetically. Yet the term 'criticism' is ambiguous: it implies, on the one hand, a gesture of refusal, a denunciation, a hostile judgment; and on the other hand it denotes (in its more fundamental sense) the positive knowledge of limits, the study of the conditions and possibilities of an activity. We pass easily from one sense to the other as though they were merely aspects of a single operation, related even in their incompatibility. The discipline of criticism is rooted in this ambiguity, this double attitude. The disparity between the negative judgment of criticism-as-condemnation, and the positive knowledge of what can be provisionally termed criticism-as-explanation, requires that we make a positive distinction between criticism as apprecia-tion (the education of taste), and criticism as knowledge (the

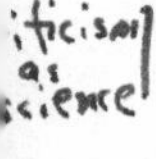

'science of literary production'). The former is normative and invokes rules; the latter is speculative and formulates laws. The one is an art, a technique (in the strict sense). The other is a science.

Will it be possible to practise both at once? Or must we choose between them? What will their respective methods involve?

Chapter 2

Domain and Object

If we say that literary criticism is the study of works of literature we have established a domain rather than an object. We have already chosen an art or technique rather than a form of knowledge. Such a temptation is easily understood, for the domain of a technique is 'given', inevitably and empirically (or at least it is held to be). Thus it becomes easy to make a beginning, to find a point of departure; for every rational activity has a natural tendency to offer itself *initially* as an art. But in theoretical practice, as the history of the sciences demonstrates, the object is never given but is progressively discovered. There are no immediate data of knowledge; reality – in a very vague, very inadequate sense – is the only horizon. This reality will certainly be the final object of our knowledge, but there is no *a priori* limit. It is elaborated, superimposed upon the entire field of the real, so that a knowledge can be inscribed within that limit. We are thus confronted with two different propositions: a science has a real domain and it also has an object. Science begins *from* the real, moving away from it. We have posed the whole problem of the institution of a form of knowledge once we begin to ask: To what distance and by which path?

This means that a rigorous knowledge must beware of all forms of empiricism, for the objects of any rational investigation have no prior existence but are thought into being. The object does not pose before the interrogating eye, for thought is not the passive perception of a general disposition, as though the object should offer to share itself, like an open fruit, both displayed and concealed by a single gesture. The act of knowing is not like listening to a discourse already constituted, a mere fiction which we have simply to translate. It is rather the elaboration of a new discourse, the articulation of a silence.

Knowledge is not the discovery or reconstruction of a latent meaning, forgotten or concealed. It is something newly raised up, an addition to the reality from which it begins. Remember that the idea of the circle is not itself circular and does not depend on the existence of actual circles. Remember that the emergence of thought institutes a certain distance and separation, thus circumscribing the domain of the real, rendering it finite as an object of knowledge.

This distance is irreducible. The empiricist typically attempts to reduce all rational activity to the general form of a technique: he believes that the real object is a kind of pillar on which the truth is to be displayed; he expects that the distance between thought and its objects will gradually be reduced as knowledge advances. Thought is thus an unfolding, a description or translation, an assimilation of the unknown into the known. The field of knowledge is reduced to a single point: the emergence of truth. This truth is instantaneous – merely an accurate glance cast over the order of things. The enterprise of thought is inherently provisional, culminating in its own abolition when it is reassimilated into an unmodified, merely interpreted reality. When thought is thus reduced to an art (perhaps merely, as we shall see, an art of reading) it has been stripped of its history, its past, its future and its present. Distilled to a technical and universal function, it evaporates.

If we are to preserve the value and potency of thought, we must no longer think of it as a provisional stratagem or artifice, an intermediary or means through which we approach truth and reality in order to take possession of them. We must, in other words, restore it to its rightful autonomy (though this is not the same as independence), its proper dimension. We must acknowledge its capacity to generate novelty, to actively transform its initial data. Thought is not an implement but a task. Such a definition will at least offer three distinct categories: material, means and product. In Bachelard's words, we have to identify the discursiveness characteristic of true knowledge.

The statement can now be formulated: either literary criticism is an art, completely determined by the pre-existence of a domain, the literary works, and finally reunited with them in the discovery of their truth, and as such it has no autonomous existence; or, it is a certain form of knowledge, and has an object, which is not a given but a product of literary criticism. To this object literary criticism applies a certain effort of transformation. Literary criticism is neither the imitation nor the facsimile of the objects; it maintains a certain separation or distance between knowledge and its object. If knowledge is expressed in discourse, and is applied to discourse, this discourse must by its nature be different from the object which it animated in order to talk about it. Scientific discourse is rigorous because its chosen object is defined by a different order of strictness and coherence.

This distance or gap, large enough to accommodate an authentic discursiveness, is the determining characteristic of the relationship between literature and criticism. What can be said *of* the work can never be confused with what the work itself is saying, because two distinct kinds of discourse which differ in both form and content are being superimposed. Thus, between the writer and the critic, an irreducible difference must be posited right from the beginning: not the difference between two points of view on the same object, but the exclusion separating two forms of discourse that have nothing in common. The work that the author wrote is not precisely the work that is explicated by the critic. Let us say, provisionally, that the critic, employing a new language, brings out a *difference* within the work by demonstrating that it is *other than it is*.

Chapter 3

Questions and Answers

There can be no adequate empirical description of the enterprise of criticism. There ought rather to be a rational justification, a demonstration that it can take a specific deductive form, applying an appropriate method to the object under consideration. Obviously, though, neither method nor object is given *a priori*. They are mutually determining. The method is necessary to construe the object, but the authority of the method is itself derived from the existence of the object.

This is the issue: the form of rationality proper to any activity can only be described by the determination of its object and its method. But, in its turn, this determination depends on the exercise, and thus on the knowledge, of this form of rationality. How do we escape from this circle?

I shall be insisting that the object and the method make possible the identification of a form of knowledge after the event, in so far as it is a doctrine presenting a coherent knowledge, but not in so far as it is an act of discovery. Object and method clearly define the knowledge that has already been produced, but they cannot demonstrate directly *how* it has been produced, or *the laws of its production*: in other words, the actual conditions of its possibility.

Thus, in order to identify a form of knowledge, rather than its quantitative content, we must seek the conditions which make the emergence of this knowledge possible. Instead of considering it as a doctrine, a system of answers, we shall attempt to formulate the initial question which gives meaning to those answers. It is when the answers are mainly explicit that the question which gave rise to them is most often ignored; concealed under the answers, the question is rapidly forgotten. To discover the theory of a form of knowledge, that concealed central question must be rendered explicit. So rather than taking an inventory of critical doctrines, the questions which they are supposed to be answering must be disclosed. The first question must be: What is literary criticism?; and it must be formulated with great precision, otherwise it is only a false and empty question, an empiricist question.

But because an entire sequence of answers stands in the way, it is never easy to reach back to these first questions, which in themselves are never simple. Actually, there is not one question but several. A speculative activity is not neatly organised around a single problem, though we may have been led to think so by the projected image of a specific doctrine. On the contrary, a real history of questions reveals that they are scattered and intermittent. The present state of a question, if we are using the expression in its true sense rather than to denote an inert, definitive, supra-historical vagueness, is actually the conjunction of several questions. There is no definitive question, and probably there has never been an isolated question.

When the question is thus animated by a history which endows it with meaning and necessity, it is not reduced to the linear unfolding of *a given question*, the progressive development of an initial state. The question which initiates a history is neither simple nor given. It consists of several terms used to generate an inevitably complex problem, a problem which cannot be abolished by a single answer. In an important text, Jakobson has shown that 'synchronic is not the same as static': a historical question (and we might call such a question a 'structure') not only implies the possibility of change but is the incarnation and real inscription of this possibility. 'Inscribed' should certainly not be confused with 'written' (in the traditional and impoverished sense of 'recorded'). The question of structure is not the delayed materialisation, the late incarnation, of a pre-existing meaning, it is the real condition of its very possibility. The history depends on the question and the manner in which it is formulated. Though it brings together two simultaneous terms, the question is neither a token of the instantaneous nor the sign of a linear continuity. Once the question has been posed, a real history can be traced, undistorted by a mythical anticipation. This has been convincingly demonstrated in the history of the sciences; it should also be possible in the history of literary criticism.

Nevertheless we must be clear about the meaning of these terms: on the one hand, condition; on the other, complexity. When it is proposed to trace a history by formulating it as an *initial* question, such an *initiation* should not be given the sense of a beginning or an origin. In this case, the opposition of before and after is obviously inadequate: the question is not given before the history, for it too must be historically constituted. The question is initiated at the same moment as the history, though at a different level. The *condition* is not the empirical cause of a process, preceding it in a relationship of cause to effect; it is in fact the principle without which this process could not become an object of knowledge. This, the knowledge of the conditions of a process, is the true programme of a theoretical investigation – the demonstration that change and simultaneity (the terms of the question) are not incompatible, but are in a necessary alliance.

The 'condition' is thus a theoretical object; but not, for all that, the product of mere speculation. In particular, its *complexity* is real. It is not articulated by those *ideal* distinctions of which the Hegelian contradiction supplies both the best example and the perfect caricature. The proposition that the critical question is not simple but complex does not mean that it contains an internal conflict which, by intensification and deformation, by an internal development and resolution, generates its own history. The theoretical principle which will enable us to produce the theory of real history, to formulate its text, does not exist (as we have already seen) either before or after the history. Equally, the history is not contained in the question, nor the question in the history. This question is separate without actually being independent; it remains on a level of its own. Experience, very relevantly, demonstrates that a history can be made without its theory. The Hegelian interpretation of the historical process tends to confuse history and theory; in the guise of theorising experience (presenting it as the manifestation of the idea) it paradoxically makes theory empirical.

To recapitulate, the history of critical doctrines can only be understood when we have determined the complex question which is the condition of that history.

Chapter 4

Rule and Law

A writer's work does not present itself in terms of a knowledge (this point will be developed in due course). But the act of the writer, on the other hand, can become the object of a certain knowledge. The two can at least be disentangled. Thus, if it is accepted that critical discourse brings the new exigence of a rationality to bear on the discourse of the writer, it becomes essential to define the proper status of criticism, and in particular to renounce any claims to a position within literature.

This supposes a new purpose for literary criticism: it will no longer be satisfied with describing the finished product, preparing it to be transmitted and consumed; rather it will elaborate this product, explaining rather than describing. In a radical departure from all the active tendencies of previous criticism, a new critical question is proposed: What are the laws of literary production? One can see what a large price must be paid for returning criticism to the sphere of rationality: it must be given *a new object*. Unless criticism can make this change, unless it can break definitively with its past, it is condemned to being merely the elaboration of public taste, no more than an art. A rational knowledge is concerned, as we have seen, with the establishment of laws (both universal and necessary within the limits defined by the conditions of their formulation). An art, empirical and practical rather than theoretical (the first characteristic of rules which merely govern the use of an empirically *given* reality), formulates general rules which have only an approximate or average value. Hence the expression 'as a general rule'. For rules, despite their restraining function, do not demonstrate any true necessity. The exception proves the rule, but it overturns the law. *As a general rule*, those critics who have adopted the role of the technician of taste are never mistaken; but in the attempt to define the average realities of taste they are always and inevitably mistaken because their work evades rationality and does not produce a knowledge in the strict sense of the word. The rule guarantees an activity which is both normative and approximative (they mean the same thing); this activity could be termed contradictory in that it is unable to produce its own justifications, thus it *receives* its norms from elsewhere. The art of criticism is distinguished by its *borrowed* attitude, its acquiescence in the use of external principles for which it can offer no explanation. Obviously a criticism which pursues an activity based on rules treats literature as a commodity, as a set of objects for consumption. It organises and controls the uses of a given reality which has offered itself empirically to the attention. Such a criticism resolves the question of its own existence by an appeal to the inevitably mysterious nature of creation, a new sanctuary for ignorance.

It is no accident that the art of criticism proposes only rules of consumption; a rigorous knowledge, on the other hand, must elaborate from the beginning the laws of production. We might begin from the proposition that reading and writing are not equivalent and reversible operations. Let us avoid confusing them.

The preceding pages have identified a fundamental problem in the method of traditional criticism: its tendency to slide into the natural fallacy of empiricism, to treat the work (the object of the enterprise of criticism) as factually given, spontaneously isolated for inspection. The work thus exists only to be received, described, and assimilated through the procedures of criticism. Dependent entirely upon its object, the critical judgment is required only to reproduce and imitate it by tracing its obvious outline. This is the only possible displacement that the work can accomplish: to be consumed, to move out from the provisional container of the book into the minds of possible readers, minds in diverse states of clarity and readiness. The critical gaze is the model of such a communication.

Let us now consider another fallacy, apparently very different, even opposed: the normative fallacy.

Chapter 5

Positive and Negative Judgment

When posited in its broadest sense, the activity of criticism seems to involve a modification of its object. Criticism, if it is not active and effective change, evokes at least the possibility of change, and may, occasionally, provoke it. Behind the critical attitude there is an implicit but decisive affirmation: 'It could or ought to be different.' Criticism thus has both a positive and a negative aspect: by reference to an ideal norm it destroys that which is, substituting a revised, corrected and consistent version of an initial reality. It does not matter that this elaboration expresses an ideal and a wish; for not only is the possible preferred to the real, but the real itself is depicted as the possible form of a norm *given* at the same moment. It would be agreed, in general, that criticism can begin only from a desire for change.

Therefore criticism is never absolutely satisfied with what it has been given. If it were unable to make its own voice heard by reduplicating the work from a point outside it in the language of ambivalent praise, it would run the risk of abolishing itself in satisfaction. By its very nature, then, criticism immediately dissents from the empiricist fallacy; it aspires to indicate a possible alternative to the given. Conceivably, a certain type of criticism proposes a modest translation of a work, but even with this minimum of transformation, so scrupulous and restrained, it is seeking to replace what is by *something else*. The critical transformation, then, takes the form of a transposition. As will be subsequently demonstrated, this operation presupposes the permanence and autonomy of the site of these substitutions, and we lapse into a series of spatial metaphors: we talk of the space of the work and even of the space of literature.

Criticism first appears as a denial; its basic gesture is a refusal. Yet it intends to supply a knowledge, and the authority that it appropriates should be acknowledged as decisive. The true is to be announced while the false is being denounced. It expresses a knowledge, even though this knowledge may obey eccentric rules, even though it might be a subjective knowledge (that contradiction in terms). Criticism defines itself by a refusal to recognise that contradiction. Not only does it attempt to scatter and disperse that which cannot survive and resist its interrogation; it also wants to construct and produce. It covets creativity; and even in the expression of regret for not creating, the spectre of production is established. The critical enterprise takes the positive form of a valuation or revelation, an articulation of the affirmative power in the work, a restoration of its truth. Criticism demonstrates its power over the work, for in the space generated by that initial gesture of refusal and separation there is born a new and perhaps different object, something which only criticism could have brought to life.

Refusing to accept the given work as definitive, and emphasising rather its modifications, the critical judgment affirms the presence of the *other*, of the elsewhere which ratifies judgment. Submitted to an external principle of legality the work is deprived of its autonomy; its insufficiency is exposed. Even in its pretensions to constructive and positive judgment, normative criticism affirms its destructive power.

Its legalities are external, after the fact. They are applied to an already existing object to which they have not contributed. But aesthetic legality has a judicial rather than a theoretical status; at the most its rules merely restrain the writer's activity. Because it is powerless to examine the work on its own terms, unable to exert an influence on it, criticism resorts to a corroding resentment. In this sense, all criticism can be summed up as a value judgment in the margin of the book: 'could do better'. Glimpsing but never attaining this 'better', it looks beyond the real work to its dream image. There can be no doubt that this legality is merely reactive, valuable only as a defence, affirming this hypothetical distance between the fact and the law, the work and the norm, solely in order to secure and maintain its own function. But this is only a temporary defeat for empiricism. Both the 'taste' which asks no questions and the 'judgment' which dispenses with scruples are closely related. The naive consumer and the harsh judge are finally collaborators in a single action.

There is only one true difference between them, and this will appear later: the empiricist critic wants to be the author's accomplice, he believes that the work can only emerge under the pressure of participation; the judge, on the other hand, would set himself up to instruct the writer, claiming a clearer vision of his intention, pointing out his carelessness, evading the delays of a real production in his impatience for the *essential*.

The purpose assigned to the work by the rules of a prescriptive aesthetics is finally realised by means of relentless invocation; enfranchised and autonomous, the work can now give voice to its purpose, unless from modesty it is indicated without being named. This purpose is a model, a means of measuring conformities.

According to the normative fallacy the work should be other than it is; its only reality is its relationship to the model which was the very condition of its elaboration. The work can be corrected and effectively modified by continuous comparison with the model which has an independent, *a priori* existence. The critical judgment corrects the efforts of the author through prolonged and intimate participation. It becomes obvious how closely the empiricist and the normative fallacies are related. Criticism derives its authority from the model and is determined by the rules which govern access to this model. The complete and perfect work is one which has reabsorbed its own criticism, which has criticised itself to the very limit, reaching out to the model. The work itself is finally abolished, pushed aside by the marriage of criticism with its model.

Hypothetically, the work is *preceded*: the unfolding of its text is mere fiction. The work can only advance towards an identity already fixed in the model. Whatever the chosen route, it will always be possible to imagine one shorter and better. Any reading, any detour is legitimate. The critical reading is the most direct, and because it is guided by anticipations of the model, it can move faster than the narrative. The suggestion will perhaps be made that such a reading is prompted by a desire to grasp the content of the narrative directly, independently, immediately. The literal narrative is irrelevant because it serves only to hide a secret and can be cast aside once this secret is revealed.

The detective story offers the best example of this disappearance of narrative. It is constructed entirely around the possibility of this prophetic reading which completes the story at the moment of its abolition. We find in such stories, so manifestly concerned with the discovery of a truth, the temptation of a short cut which can lead us directly to the solution of the mystery, the temptation to read the last page first. It is typical of the normative fallacy to take the end for a beginning. This was precisely what Spinoza defined, in the appendix to the first volume of his *Ethics*, as the confusion of causes and effects. In like fashion, the critic begins from the model, ignoring the fact that the enigmatic narrative gives the solution and the problem in inextricable simultaneity. Besides, the distinction between before and after is only one element of the narrative. It cannot form the entire basis of our response.

If the purpose of reading were to *reach* the truth (and even a truth symbolically stored in the final pages), the test of a good story would be its *honesty*. When correctly and frankly stated, the problem could be resolved naturally and uncontrivedly from the means given at the very beginning. With nothing concealed, except perhaps provisionally, the truth might emerge independently of the narrative. The true and sincere story would gradually abolish its own contours, proclaim its own redundance, suggest that its linear progress was an avoidable detour. The object, hitherto concealed beneath the folds of the narration, would appear, after the delay required for the fulfilment of the text, at the merest glance.

By analogy, this is how a certain criticism succeeds in confronting the work with its own truth – a truth so corrosive and substantial that the work finally vanishes, an embarrassed spectre.

The narrative is merely a guide and a means of access, the hesitating companion of the effective content.

All the literature of the mysterious illustrates a similar doctrine. From the heroines of Mrs Radcliffe to Sherlock Holmes, one finds, in a degenerate form, though with unsurpassed clarity, this novelistic meditation upon the treachery of appearances, the very theme of the moral-critical judgment. Once the enigma has been resolved the real meaning leaps out from behind the screen of all the intermediate episodes. The artifices of narration are merely the vehicle for a procrastinated anecdote. But there must be two sides to this sort of literature. If the text is reproached for futile deviation from its real meaning, it is also displayed in motion on that long path which both divides it from and unites it with its eventual destination. The reverse side of the work is perhaps that model through which it confesses its own nothingness. But it could also be this nothing which – in the interior of the text – multiplies and *composes* it, leading it along the path of more than one meaning.

To summarise provisionally what has been said so far:

Criticism claims to treat the work as an object of consumption, thus falling into the empiricist fallacy (first in authority) because it asks only how to *receive* a given object. But this first fallacy is closely followed by a second, the normative fallacy, in which criticism proposes to modify the work in order to assimilate it more thoroughly, denying its factual reality as being merely the provisional version of an unfulfilled intention.

The second fallacy is no more than a variety of the first, a displacement of it. In fact only the empirical characteristics of the work are transposed, by being attributed to a model – that fixed and independent entity which exists alongside the work, guaranteeing both its consistency and its readability and making it accessible as an object of judgment. The normative fallacy proposes a transformation of its object only within certain previously defined limits. It is the sublimation of empiricism, its ideal image, but based ultimately on the same principles.

Later we shall examine a third and related fallacy, the interpretive.

Chapter 6

Front and Back

The normative fallacy, as we have just seen, releases a problematic of the end and the beginning. The model, being that towards which the work aspires, raises the issue of its teleology, its fulfilment within real or ideal limits. Though it may appear finite and closed, the work is perhaps torn and gaping. Perhaps it is that long corridor which leads to the Room, a pure introduction. Despite appearances, perhaps its manifest course is unsteady, its path interrupted and deflected. Through the violence that it does to the work the normative fallacy at least renders it mobile. As an approach, it is not entirely barren. Though it may not, in the strictest sense, teach us anything, it can at least show us something new.

The work is not what it appears to be. This proposition is worth considering, even though it may have no theoretical value (because it depends on an ideological distinction between realities and appearances): all the more so because, at a different level entirely, the idea may appear in the discourse of the writer himself, within the work, and not only in the discourse of the critic. The idea may thus be detached from its ideological context, receiving a different value and meaning, though never constituting a knowledge.

But even before considering any examples, there is one important objection: perhaps the works based on such a principle are false – critical works which attempt to put questions about the nature of discourse when they themselves are really discourse in disguise. They would be like those judges who venture secretly into the criminal underworld, the better to destroy it from a close knowledge. When Poe, in his famous essay 'The Philosophy of Composition',* states that the beginning is at the end, it is obviously the commentator rather than the poet who is speaking, and he runs the risk of digression and deviation. Like Valéry, who found success in introducing futility simultaneously into poetry and criticism, he pronounces judgment on what he does not himself undertake. Nevertheless, it is worth examining this text of Poe's: it will be seen that the statement in question is intended only in a poetic rather than a critical sense, so that it functions as an index of the challenging of the work rather than as a reason. And our interpretation is confirmed when we find an almost identical theme in the unreflecting work of Mrs Radcliffe.

There remains one important objection, for the themes immediately extracted from *literary* texts can have no initial value as concepts. As such, the 'front' (*endroit*) and the 'back' (*envers*) can legitimately be regarded as no more than suggestive metaphors. As 'ideas' they are contaminated by the normative fallacy from which they have been only artificially separated. In the argument that follows they are being used in parenthesis and should not be taken too literally.

The Genesis of a Poem

One of his favourite axioms was always –

'In poetry as in fiction, in the sonnet as in the novel, every element should contribute to the conclusion. A good writer has already foreseen the last line when he writes the first.' Thanks to this admirable method, the compositor can begin at the end, working as he chooses on any section. Those who believe in the frenzy of inspiration may be offended by such cynical maxims; but they can be

* Translator's note: Baudelaire's translation of Poe's 'The Philosophy of Composition' is entitled *La Genèse d'un poème* – hence Macherey's play on the word 'genesis' in the first part of the chapter.

> interpreted just as you choose. It will always be useful to convince amateurs of the advantage art may derive from deliberation, to show the wordly what labour
> is involved in the luxury commodity of poetry. (*Oeuvres en prose d'Edgar Allan Poe: traduites par Ch. Baudelaire*, Paris, Pléiade, 1951, p. 979)

The mechanism of poetic fabrication, as it is *exposed* by Poe, is evidently the verdict of the normative fallacy on the work of the writer. Concentrated around and towards an ending, the work as a whole is no more than an approximation, a preparation, all in relationship to that final term. Organised and reduced, it states its essence through an accumulation of appearances. As Baudelaire correctly observes, the implacable judge has become a guilty cynic. He pleads premeditation: 'Throughout the entire composition there should not be allowed a single phrase which is not also an intention, nothing which does not contribute, directly or indirectly, to the premeditated design.' The poet displays his methods of work, emphasising their intermediary and subordinate function, their role in the real purpose of the narrative. As merely the product of a technical secret, the work is by no means what it appears; it lurks, deceptively, *behind* its real meaning. Through this confession, the author leads us back to that initial reality which is the source and truth of all its remote and ulterior manifestations. Unlike the simple reader who faithfully follows the work, we can reach towards this truth by racing ahead and marking out the path; we no longer submit to the unfolding of the work, we participate in the systematic construction of its fiction.

As Baudelaire rightly said, the poet is a compositor, the poem is essentially composed and composite. The distinct elements of the text are only apparently placed end to end. There is an emphasis on the *diversity of the letter* – the text is saying several things at once, and hence it is composed of elements as different as they are instantaneous. Poe offers a psychological explanation of this multiplicity: 'by a psychic necessity, all intense impulses are short-lived.' It is possible that this explanation is merely a defence, but it does bring forward the important notion of *an uneven development of the text*, especially obvious in the long poem which is no longer *one* poem but a sequence of separate poems: 'For this reason, at least one half of the *Paradise Lost* is essentially prose – a succession of poetical excitements interspersed, *inevitably*, with corresponding depressions – the whole being deprived, through the extremeness of its length, of the vastly important artistic element, totality, or unity, of effect.' Poe considers that this unevenness is a defect, and proposes, as a law, that unity can only be preserved in a short text. But this idea could be developed to an entirely different conclusion; as we shall see, unevenness is characteristic of every text.

According to Poe, composition is construction. This large claim invites two preliminary observations. First, this myth of genesis involves an important separation between reading (in the ordinary sense) and writing. To read only with the eyes of a reader, says Poe, is to remain blind to the conditions which shape the meaning of the work, to see only effects. To really know the writer's intentions we must first establish these conditions and then follow the movement that they generate. Reading and writing are rival activities and could only be confused from a profound ignorance of the real nature of the work.

Second, Poe's thesis has no theoretical value: like all myths it serves an essentially polemical purpose. Baudelaire was aware of this when he assessed his own translations of Poe as 'A Grotesque and Solemn Work'. The primary aim of the story (for it is a story rather than a theoretical analysis) is to refute the fallacies about spontaneous creativity – commonplace fallacies to which it was essential to oppose a *fantastic* account of the work of the writer. A straightforward reading reveals only the banal surface, but behind the scenes is enacted the astonishing and controlled drama of *genesis*. The spontaneity of the reader contrasts with the rational calculation of the author. 'It is my design to render it manifest that no one point in its composition is referable either to accident or intuition – that the work proceeded, step by step, to its completion with the precision and rigid consequence of a mathematical problem.' The mathematical problem is a fanciful image of the work: the solution of the one corresponds to the conclusion of the other. But the work's solution also entails its disappearance, hence the work is sustained only by the question to which it must provide an answer.

Though this idea has an undeniable critical value it is not a knowledge. Once the satire on a popular error is recognised, we have not really been taught anything; the positive claims advanced merely reproduce the fallacy initially condemned. Reading and writing are opposites and we must beware of too facile inversions (see Louis Althusser, *For Marx*, London, Allen Lane, 1969). To invert is only to transpose, to say the same thing in a different and more acceptable form. Poe restores the diabolic double to the work (if the devil is merely 'Deus inversus') but leaves both aspects, the 'front' (*endroit*) and the 'back' (*envers*), related by an analogy which is even more deceptive because it seems to be definitive. However you trace the inside (*envers*) and the outside (*endroit*),* the work remains unchanged; having been constructed it is stable and continuous. Whether it be actively elaborated or passively followed it offers the same kind of unity, which can be indifferently considered in alternative ways ('in front' and 'behind', to vary our spatial metaphor). Casual appearance or rigorous deduction: these are two versions or aspects of the same reality. The ending unifies them both, and to perceive this unity we relate the work to its necessary conditions. Inside and outside have been only provisionally distinguished in order to demonstrate the principle of coherence in the discourse.

Poe then proposes to deduce the parts of 'The Raven' from a central and final intention which is also a parody of its meaning. Baudelaire was aware of this when he pointed out the 'wanton insolence' of the text. 'Poe was always magnificent, not only in his noble ideas but also in his practical jokes': he could be fantastic and serious at the same time. If we take Poe's proposition seriously, we miss the fact that it is actually preposterous. The author cannot deduce, from an initial intention, the means by which that intention shall be realised, as will be fully demonstrated hereafter. Such a procedure also ignores the fact that the curve of the text is neither simple nor continuous. Poe himself

* Translator's note: There is no single English translation of *envers/endroit* which fits Macherey's figurative usage. I have used both 'back/front' and 'inside/outside' according to context.

was aware of this, having affirmed elsewhere that the discourse of the text was unevenly developed, and that this development was not, therefore, deductive. On this occasion, however, the parody is poetic in that it sometimes manages to take itself seriously. The narrative is necessarily interrupted, though not for the reasons claimed by Poe. It is interrupted by factitious ideological considerations which guide Poe back to the terrain of traditional aesthetics, seduced by the comic-opera Platonism of 'the contemplation of beauty'. At this point there is a gap in Poe's account which betrays its untheoretical status. The construction of the poem, the disposition of means towards a certain end, is itself subordinated to an external end. Poetic discourse is directed towards the realisation of beauty, a mythical task which endows the poem with a unity and totality into which it vanishes. Every moment in the text announces the purpose which will consummate its annihilation, ironically enough in the phrase 'nevermore'. Thus the poem is a somewhat facile image of its own processes; the coincidence between the text and its object shows that Genesis is the correlative of the poem. Its immanent truth is analogously presented by the poem itself. This truth is accessible only because it is the image of a knowledge. In this ideological context, the normative fallacy interposes itself once again. It should also be noticed that the intrusion of a prescriptive aesthetics involves the argument in an embarrassing contradiction: the work is the product both of a certain labour and of a passive contemplation. Poe, similarly, proposes Platonic theories only to become a fantastic writer in actual practice.

Everything that appeared valid in Poe's text is now caught up in something beyond itself, in a different meaning and purpose. The ideas do not survive away from their context. All that Poe is finally saying can be expressed in the neo-classical notion that the text and the commentary which accounts for it are equivalent, even if they are inversely related. Or alternatively, that the text and the commentary occupy – though in a different fashion – the same space and are derived from the same principle of organisation. Far from being decentred, justified, the work is doubly fixed within the limits of a closed structure. Its conclusion, perverse and apparently disjointed, was also its stopping place.

Consequently the metaphor of the work's internal existence is only interesting as a caricature version of a knowledge which must be formulated elsewhere. Poe's text certainly does not propose an analysis of literature; it is a story which might appropriately be placed among the adventures of Dupin. 'The Philosophy of Composition' is written on the model of the famous analyses which are interesting as fiction rather than for their real content. It only makes sense if we are aware of the grotesque which sustains its seriousness. The relationship between the author and the work, as it is embodied in the first-person narrative, is thus deceptive. This author analysing his creation, as garrulous as the hero of a novel, is too ingenious to be telling the truth (to quote one of Poe's own ideas):

> Truth is not always in a well. In fact, as regards the most important knowledge, I do believe that she is invariably superficial. The truth lies not in the valleys where we seek her, but upon the mountain-tops where she is found. ('The Murders in the Rue Morgue')

There can be no other text like this one for having replaced its apparently simple line by a direct inversion of that line. This is why Genesis is an allegory or myth. But we can use this myth by relating it to a truth which myth cannot utter: a text can be read in more than one direction, and thus there can co-exist within the text a front and a back at least. The text derives a certain 'opulence' (to use Poe's expression) from its complexity and its density, in spite of the systematic thinness of its discourse, a mere line coiled on the book. It is neither so simple nor so direct that the bright side (revealed in reading) does not imply at least the presence of a dark side. Refusing the very ideology that Poe espouses, it is proposed that *diversity* is the principle of the text. Poe's text is important because, in a new myth of *clinamen*, it invokes the possibility of transformations in the text (though this is expressed in mythical terms of working backwards or in reverse), the possibility of turning or *slanting* (to borrow an image from another practitioner of the fantastic). By a kind of inward hesitation the text advertises the plurality of its voices. It is this diversity and multiplicity which will require elucidation.

The discourse of a work: sealed and interminable, completed or endlessly beginning again, diffuse and dense, coiled about an absent centre which it can neither conceal nor reveal.

Thaumantis Regia: Les Visions d'un château des Pyrénées

This next example does not duplicate the previous one, it presents the same image in a different way; after another fashion it illustrates the energy which impels the discourse of the writer. In this instance we are not faced with a critical text which challenges itself with a vague and wavering irony: this is a naive, spontaneous text, the most uncomplicated novel imaginable. The themes of the inside and the outside make their appearance, caught in the very movement of the book, endowed with their full poetic significance, exempted from that fatal suspicion of merely reduplicating the work by a factitious and intrusive commentary. In fact – and this must constantly be emphasised – there is no innocent work: the apparent spontaneity of the easy book pledged to an immediate consumption assumes the application of familiar methods which may often have been derived from the most subtle literature, and can be smuggled from one work to another. 'The Philosophy of Composition' and *Les Visions d'un château des Pyrénées** are simply different versions, the one as simple as the other is complicated (but which is really which?), of that same theme which is to be found at every level in the genre of the mystery story. But if there is no book which is entirely innocent, and here the second example is decisive, neither is there any book which is completely self-conscious, aware of the means of its own realisation, aware of what it is doing. Once again, this is why the themes of the inside and the outside, which we will rediscover in the work itself, are not so much concepts as clues. Unless we have relapsed into the empiricist fallacy, and by this stage we ought to be beyond that, we will recognise that when they are so obvious, so available in the thread of certain works, they are not reliable.

* Translator's note: This novel, of which no English original has been identified, is generally considered to be incorrectly ascribed to Mrs Radcliffe.

It is to be regretted that Mrs Radcliffe's work, once so popular, has now fallen into neglect. André Breton saw her as just a 'master of surprise' and he was careful to place her within the limits of the traditional Gothic novel in order to justify a preference for his own dark favourites, Walpole, Lewis, and Maturin. He castigated that victorious rationalism which made her 'set up shop', a shop that did such good business, on that forbidden ground of the 'truly miraculous'. In this judgment two quite distinct criticisms have been blurred together: she is accused of a narrow rationalism and of having capitulated enthusiastically to public taste. See how easily we move from a magical notion of great literature to another which is most traditional: Mrs Radcliffe is minor because her reductive imagination betrayed the truth of the real – a point that might just be conceded, provisionally at least – but also because she sought an audience beyond the small circle of connoisseurs. In her desire to please the crowd she betrayed a genre by popularising it. This is an astonishing accusation, for the notion of a popular literature is not intrinsically suspect. Also the stylistic distance between great literature and minor literature is not obviously and easily defined. It is not inevitably a matter of dilution and decline; more often it involves a new meaning, old tools modified to perform new tasks. Minor literature can inspire great literature: in the work of Poe there is more of Mrs Radcliffe than there is of Walpole.

The book in question is, as they say, unpretentious. This is not to our disadvantage; indeed, it is precisely why it has been chosen. Even among minor works it is of the second rank; probably it was not written by Mrs Radcliffe but is a forgery, a pastiche, published under her name after her death. This kind of text, the more or less accurate fake, is often the most characteristic of a genre or style. Here is to be found in a pure if not original state all that defines the type. The skilful imitation can be more revealing than the model.

This book – and let us remember that it belongs to the genre of the 'mystery tale' – is particularly interesting because in the development of the text there is emphasised the possibility of a double movement which reverses the direction of its apparent progress:

> 'I can tell you nothing more; I must respect the promise I have made to him; a moment will come when all these mysteries will be revealed to you. Until that time, which I cannot anticipate, I can at least tell you . . .' (*Les Visions d'un château des Pyrénées*, vol. 2, p. 227)

Here is that double movement: the mystery must be concealed before it is revealed. Until that crisis the secret must press upon the mind or the heart of the hero, and the entire elaboration of the narrative consists in the description and the organisation of this delay. To narrate is also to construct, to build this edifice of secrecy which coincides miraculously with the real architecture which initiates it, or which it initiates: the black abode of a castle.

We know from the beginning that knowledge is delayed rather than lost, we know that this folly which threatens is only temporary. We are constantly being promised an explanation of the prodigious. Those minor revelations which do not endanger the central mystery herald the conclusion in which illusion is to be abolished. We are aware that there is something behind the mystery and that it will be disclosed. We ought to be scrutinising what is there from the first rather than what we will know at the last, which will not be entirely mysterious. The depths are less fascinating than this frail and deceptive surface. The time of the novel separates the founding moment of illusions from the irruption of a truth which is also a promise of safety (the period of ignorance is also a period of danger). The narrative progresses only by the inhibition of the truth; its movement is an ambivalence, an effort to postpone rather than to hasten revelation. The novel lasts for as long as it can cling to appearances, and in this it displays its true nature: it arises in a parenthesis, it is a go-between, an interlude, a diversion.

The action of the novel intervenes in the unfolding of a life and divides it into two parts: a before, the prehistory of a former happiness or a childhood, and an after, which is its fulfilment. The plot emerges disguised as the interruption of a destiny; it takes advantage of something unfinished in order to perfect it. One day a life was suspended, and the narrative repeats this basic episode in a series of abrupt changes which echo that first surprise, that abduction, just as if no other fate could have played itself out in that precarious interlude of imprisonment amongst wonders: here is the beginning of an adventure. The continuity of a life is changed into the novelty of an endless series of encounters. Since the arresting intervention of chance everything recalls that persisting lapse. As Victoria is walking in the gardens of the château she comes across a statue of Apollo 'which was remarkable for being only half-finished'; she learns that the statue is the work of a young man who died suddenly. This episode is typical: the interrupted heroine encounters everywhere the signs of her own condition. The unfinished statue is the counterpart of a ruin, and thus it is nevertheless the token of a conclusion: it recapitulates ideally the processes of deterioration.

This waiting for destiny permeates the feelings with a radical indecision. An essential theme in the interpretation of the Gothic novel is this fact of the ambiguity of the characters and the emotions. Let us take the portrayal of Francisco, if we can justifiably talk of a portrayal, since he is never seen and is little more than an indeterminate presence. Francisco, 'whose life is full of mysteries and whose actions are so many indecipherable enigmas', dominates the plot; an inscrutable power, benevolent or malevolent, whose actions are determined by some higher scheme, or improvised in the absence of any scheme – we do not know which until after the event. By being so predictably devious he is a protector, he effaces the indecisiveness with which all the others judge him. There is hope of safety because every encounter is deceptive. The good pirate and the loyal bandit represent this universal duplicity. Happiness and virtue are temporary, but then so is misfortune, for anything can happen in the course of the story.

Hero and reader are not faced with the choice between appearance and reality, between falsehood and truth; they are not provided with such clear alternatives, but must work in that immanent zone between the bright and the dark side of truth itself. Everything is decisively exposed at the very beginning of the narrative. From this undertaking the mystery emerges secularised; inescapably surprise is made familiar. Evil is here rather than elsewhere – here in the confusion of the good. Everything wears a disguise.

In Mrs Radcliffe's version of the Gothic novel the protagonist confronts a vague diversity; he is pushed out beyond the comforts of dualism into a realm of endless transformations. The hero is not merely poised between misfortune and happiness, he is actually powerless to define his exact situation. Bewildered at the edge of the illusory, symbolised by the grounds of the château, he no longer knows who he is and cannot control his feelings. The enclosing château could be either a refuge or a prison. The one is frequently mistaken for the other, for it may be safe to shelter on the very threshold of danger except that the refuge may suddenly turn into a trap. The château is always changing, in a cycle of incessant novelty. The unfinished building and the inexhaustible scenery reflect the story played out in their midst. Even the settings are indeterminate: they break down into a series of autonomous trajectories in which the various interlacing episodes are enacted, often converging blindly in the same room. Every façade is hollow and deceptive, but never obviously so, as they come apart in self-contradictory ways. The only means of escape is to advance into the labyrinth, in the hope of eventually reaching the centre. Here, at the heart of the secret, reposes the mysterious desired object which will totally transform the structure of this world. The story, then, is an initiation: *The Magic Flute* is the opera of the Gothic novel. It is also a journey to that place at which ambiguities converge; by simple contrast it implies a unity. Here we find the transition from the picturesque to the horrific, unless mystery and anxiety are abolished by concealment in a secret valley.

> Having reached the opposite side of the glen, the road gradually descended the precipice for about half a mile, when it opened towards extensive prospects over plains and towards distant mountains – the sunshine landscape which had long appeared to bound this shadowy pass. The transition was as the passage through the vale of death to the bliss of eternity. (A. Radcliffe, *The Italian*, Oxford, 1968, pp. 63–4)

Until certain signs point to an unforeseen risk: nature, like the mysterious ruined form, is protean.

Moreover it is difficult to tell the difference between confidence and carelessness. If a character, in being torn from his former self, has changed to the point of becoming the hero of a Gothic novel, perhaps the others that he encounters have become what they are without ceasing to be what they were, by some strange deterioration or perversion. Certain men, in whom the signs of a former happiness are still visible, who are obviously not what they seem, will inspire a strong confidence (Diego, the stranger in the chapel). But there are others who display a thorough perversity (the duke of Vicence): 'From this moment, I know the perversity of your heart', and no explanation, no change, can revoke the judgment. Thus love can begin, since it requires an initial trust, once a certain discrimination is possible. Surrounded by wicked men, obscurely attracted to strangers, Victoria must constantly identify her own motives; her feelings are always being challenged. Has not the man she is beginning to love let her overhear that he loves another? Has she not seen her rival in a scene of strange happiness that adds fuel to her anxieties? But if she were to understand that image she would have to be able to decipher it. Every incident and every scene becomes a trial: every manifest presence brings with it an equivocal double: the most exposed shapes are ideally veiled.

> Victoria remained silent; her feelings were overcome by an irresistible spell, but her prudence did not desert her, and her heart was a prey to a thousand uncertainties. The more she felt her confidence being won over by the looks, the language and the accents of the stranger, the more she summoned reason to her aid. She had observed that beneath the most aimiable features, beneath the most seductive exterior, Don Manuel concealed a profound wickedness. Who knows whether this enchanter in whose words she took such pleasure was not formed in the same dangerous school? And yet if he were honest and sincere, as she so ardently hoped, as all the powers of her heart impelled her to believe him, what ungraciousness, what ingratitude in the very coldness with which she received his generous

> offers. Sensitive as she is, she knows better than another how an open and compassionate heart is cruelly wounded when its advances meet only with mistrust and unjust suspicions. Tormented, overwhelmed by this painful struggle, she raises her moist eyes in which are portrayed so clearly the tenderness of her feelings and the trouble in her soul, and glancing alternately at the friendly stranger and then upon the arches of the temple, she seems to be praying for a ray of light from the heavens to guide the choice she must make. (*Les Visions d'un château des Pyrénées*)

The discovery of the secret motives of the other is not the least of the mysteries in the house of illusions.

This hesitation in judging, as it is registered in the turmoil of emotion – for love does not at first know itself – is also expressed in the silence of the images. Of those who might be friends or enemies only an image is afforded, and judgment must rely on this alone. Typically, the potential lover first appears as a portrait to be deciphered:

> For the rest, that which we so admire is perhaps altogether ideal; the brilliant imagination and skill of the artist have alone been able to create that which seems so charming in this countenance, whereas the original has perhaps a merely ordinary face, or at least greatly inferior to the expression with which he has been endowed. (Ibid., p. 272)

It is a great contest of images, forms and symbols, so many ambiguous signs. The novel contains a whole machinery of apparitions, masked giants, ghosts, voices from inside the walls; the plot is a procession of profiles. The story finishes when the truth of these appearances is revealed, when they are dispersed. Until that moment, although they have remained enigmatic, it is still a question of whether or not they were actually seen, since they merely pass by and disappear.

> In any other situation, Victoria would have laughed at her mistake; but overwhelmed by extraordinary misfortunes and surrounded by unprecedented dangers, she was not

> surprised that her bewildered imagination made phantoms from all the objects about her. (Ibid., p. 226)

The mystery novel, as it is practised by Mrs Radcliffe, seems, then, to be the product of two different movements: the one establishes the mystery while the other dispels it. The ambiguity of the narrative derives from the fact that these two movements are not, properly speaking, successive (in which case they would cancel each other out only at the finish) but are inextricably simultaneous. The one (but which one?) endlessly opposes the other: and perhaps, contrary to Breton's notion, it is the revelation rather than the mystery which emerges reduced by this venture. Thus it is that the time of the narrative is like an interlude, after which everything can begin as before. But this interlude is actually interminable. There is no end to the birth and death of secrets. Moreover, the conclusion ('here finishes the third and last volume') which offers the final key to the mystery, is usually banal and uncertain and embarrassingly crude. In its fragility and gratuitousness it reveals that the time of the narrative acknowledges no before or after beyond its own development because, on the contrary, it includes them both. The text is both perfectly transparent (everything is finally resolved) and perfectly opaque (everything is initially concealed). The enigma carries the promise of its resolution, the principle of its nullity, only because it challenges all judgment: the enigma is temporary at the very moment when everything becomes enigmatic. The Gothic novel tells us that everything is both itself and something else; this is because it grows in two dimensions: simultaneously it has an inside and an outside.

The enigma implies its own resolution, a truth which dispels it; but this truth is not from outside the narrative. Those who would prefer to get straight to this truth, to make an easy guess, miss the point. By going directly to the model, the light (the way of the normative critic), by missing out the journey which leads to the destination and gives it meaning, we find it singularly dull, much less vivid for not having to chase any more shadows.

> Like all Holmes' reasoning, the thing seemed simplicity itself when once it was explained. He read the thought

> upon my features, and his smile had a tinge of bitterness.
>
> 'I am afraid that I rather give myself away when I explain,' said he. 'Results without causes are much more impressive.' (A. Conan Doyle, 'The Stockbroker's Clerk', in *Sherlock Holmes: The Complete Short Stories*, London, John Murray, 1928, p. 356)
>
> 'Quite so!' said he, a little nettled. 'Every problem becomes very childish when once it is explained to you.' ('The Dancing Man', ibid., pp. 611–12)
>
> 'Excellent!' I cried.
>
> 'Elementary,' said he. 'It is one of those instances where the reasoner can produce an effect which seems remarkable to his neighbour because the latter has missed the one little point which is the basis of the deduction. The same may be said, my dear fellow, for the effect of some of these little sketches of yours, which is entirely meretricious, depending as it does upon your retaining in your own hands some factors in the problem which are never imparted to the reader. Now, at present I am in the position of these same readers, for I hold in this hand several threads of one of the strangest cases which ever perplexed a man's brain, and yet I lack the one or two which are needful to complete my theory. But I'll have them, Watson, I'll have them!' ('The Crooked Man', ibid., p. 440)

Indeed, the text will not hesitate to produce them in order to give them to him.

More examples could be produced, but they would not add anything to these texts, which are absolutely remarkable in themselves: though provided, once again, that they are not taken too seriously, and that we see the trap which they represent. The book consists entirely of a distance which separates a beginning from an end, in this case a problem of its resolution. But this distance is not pre-established, otherwise the book would merely have to put itself into this given frame. First it must arrange this possibility, upon which all else will depend. Before the enigma and the key, it establishes the distances between them, without which it could not even take place. Does this mean that it is a detour or an artifice, a delay or a circumlocution? It must be realised that to follow this ideal line exactly would be to do away with it, to make it disappear into the obvious. Consequently, one of the genuine sources of the text is the initial incompatibility between its beginning and its end: in this way it can be read in two directions. But these two directions are not equivalent, or spontaneously superimposable. This is why they never succeed in cancelling themselves, why they in fact unite in the elaboration of the intricate line of a narrative. The book is not the embodiment of an external reality which is veiled as it is displayed. Its reality is exclusively in the conflict which impels it and gives it its ordinances. For this reason, not everything is made obvious at the beginning of the narrative, though nor is it concealed: otherwise nothing could actually happen. Otherwise we could only throw the thing down after having been misled for a while by its futility, in our disappointment at not finding something that was never there.

> Indeed, it is very important that the book itself include a secret. At the start the reader must not know how it will finish. There must be some change produced for me, I must know something that I did not know before, that I did not guess at, that others would not guess without having read it; and as might be expected this requirement finds its clearer expression in popular forms like the detective novel. (Michel Butor, *Cahiers de l'Association Internationale des études françaises*, no. 14, March 1962)

Furthermore, it seems that the movement of the narrative can only be compared with the detective's logical deductions in a spirit of parody (whether the deduction is direct, as in Sherlock Holmes, or indirect, as in Poe). In narrative there is no continuity, but rather a constant disparity which is the form of its necessity and the possibility of its existence. So, if we are to elucidate its development it will not be enough to follow just its apparent progress.

Within a narrative the contingent and the necessary conspire in the elaboration of the text – a point to which we shall return.

The real, as it is formulated in the discourse of the work, is always arbitrary because it depends entirely on the unfolding of this discourse. Although this knowledge is impossible, we ought to be able to know this Real immediately. This is because the enigma, in so far as it establishes the work – and there is something enigmatic at the bottom of every work – this enigma has nothing to do with a riddle. We are acquainted with those 'double' pictures in which the landscape conceals the form of a gendarme's hat; as soon as we recognise the hidden shape, all the others disappear in a new configuration of elements. In fact we forgot them and the hat is all that is left. What had once seemed to be real now disappears, cancelled by the new reality. In the same way, the pagan world of the Venusberg suddenly collapses as soon as the naive pastoral universe of revealed nature appears for the enlightenment of the knight Tannhäuser. In the same way, in Descartes' 'Second Meditation' the wax loses its old shape and receives another which cancels all the rest. In a *coup de théâtre* which distinguishes all the metamorphoses of illusion the idea of extension is produced like a rabbit from a hat. Like the hero of opera, the magician who controls the game of the 'Second Meditation' can only sing his song, cry his wares, astonish and enlighten at the same time, because he is depending on that sudden scene-shifting without which there could be no progress in the action and no sequence in the argument. Understood, released and discovered, the truth seems so dazzling that it pushes aside all the moments that heralded it. In a sudden flourish, its presence abolishes all previous disguises.

But unlike the riddle, the book could not – except ironically – abolish its unfolding in a conclusion. If it has a limit, whether it is a real limit denoted by the words 'the end', or an ideal limit in the model, this limit is not the proper form which shows up all the remainder as gratuitous illusion. The book is neither reality nor experience, but artifice. The artifice is not a riddle, but an authentic mystery which lives entirely in the trajectory of its resolution: the Sphinx's question has meaning only in the context of the determining allusions which link it to the story of Oedipus, and which themselves determine that story. For this reason it is somewhat futile to hold to the notion that the secret of every work can be deciphered (for there is a secret in every work, otherwise why would we need to explain them?). It is not enough to resolve the problem in a way that simply gets rid of it: we must show the process of its institution. The transparency of the book is always retrospective, and it is only ever a moment rather than a defining characteristic of the narrative. As Mrs Radcliffe says, everything will be explained when the time is right; we must be content to wait. In its substance and its truth, this delay makes the work possible. Other than its own unfolding there is nothing within or behind the narrative; thus it reproduces itself. The urgent need to understand, to achieve a transparent reading, paradoxically requires delay and opacity.

In examining the work, then, we ought not to be weighing it against an extrinsic or a concealed truth. Transcendent and immanent criticism are equally misguided, for both tend to divert attention from the work's real complexity.

Chapter 7

Improvisation, Structure and Necessity

The literary work is not a precariously prolonged adventure, a quest for its own vanishing point. The linear simplicity which gives it boldness and freshness is actually only its most superficial aspect; we must also be able to distinguish its real and fundamental complexity. And in this complexity we must recognise the signs of a necessity: the work does not move with the ingenuous freedom and independence that betoken pure invention; it is in fact sustained by a premeditated diversity which gives both form and content.

So it is that the work's apparent spontaneity is merely an effect and in no way a cause. The work does not develop at random, in undiscriminating freedom; it grows because it is precisely determined at every moment and at every level. And this is why chaos and chance are never excuses for confusion, but the token of the irruption of the real; they make the work what it is. In a work as obviously and explicitly a medley as Rameau's *Le Neveu* (The Nephew) the stable traditional elements of which it is composed are easily identifiable: portrait, speech, dramatic dialogue (though it would not be enough merely to enumerate forms). But over and above all that, it is true in a more general way that improvisation is itself a genre, a category of literary production.

It has been shown that the folk-tale, the most naive and least self-conscious kind of narrative, begins from a rigid convention without which it would be amorphous and impossible. The simplicity of the tale is the *effect produced* by a chain of invariable units which give the text its internal coherence. And this archetypal necessity derives from the work's relationship to a model – a model which is pre-established, complete and determining. But this is an external necessity, of a sort we have already identified as being unable to furnish an authentic knowledge of the work. But this inherent failing in Propp's method need not occupy us for the moment: it remains true that this method brings out the norm and the model even if it does depend on an ideology of the system. It emphasises that the work is not randomly put together, but depends on a set of finite combinations.

The work is determined: it is itself and nothing else. Here we have the beginnings of a rational method. Our discourse can be more than just a commentary because there is nothing that can be altered in the discourse of the work. Thus stabilised, if not, as we shall see, immobilised, the literary work becomes a theoretical object.

But it is not enough to state that necessity and adjust ourselves to it; we must seek to define it systematically. At first glance we might call it 'premeditation', the apparent expression of the unity of an intention or model which permeates and animates the work, giving it an organic life. Whether this unity is subjective (the result of an authorial choice, conscious or unconscious) or objective (the embodiment of an essential device – a key signature, frame or model) the assumption remains that it is the whole which is determining.

The problem thus posed is that of the structure – if we understand by structure that which makes it possible to think through the kind of necessity from which the work derives, its determinateness. But the notion of structure is misleading in so far as it pretends to show us, whether within or beyond the work, its intelligible image, falling thus into one of the fallacies already defined. If we are to make sense of the concept of structure it must be with the recognition that structure is neither a property of the object nor a feature of its representation: the work does not derive from the unity of an intention which permeates it, nor from its conformity to an autonomous model. This will be clearer when we have demonstrated that the hypothesis of the work's unity is yet another fallacy (the interpretive) which is as useless as all the others.

We have just seen, in Chapter 6, how the work is composed in more than one sense: in such a way that a real diversity accompanies its formation. As it develops before the reader's eye it may happen to unravel and take on a new form, revealing a real complexity in the place of a false simplicity. Thus, in the allegorical sense, it can be said that there is something happening in every book, that the adventure story is the very image of the literary work, because they both offer a surprise in relation to an initial situation. In all literary works can be found the tokens of this internal rupture, this decentering, the evidence of its subordinate dependence on precise conditions of possibility. Thus the work is never – or only apparently – a coherent and unified whole. It is neither improvised nor predetermined; it depends, as it were, on a free necessity which remains to be more clearly defined.

A literary work, then, is never entirely premeditated; or rather, it is, but at several levels at once, without deriving monolithically from a unique and simple conception. It would not be enough to say that the work is constructed, a deliberate and fixed arrangement, if we want to determine its form. We must not stop at *technique*, as did some of the Russian Formalists, especially Shlovsky, but behind the technique we must recognise the real process without which artifice would remain entirely factitious. The work is the product of a certain labour, and hence of an art. But not all art is artificial: it is the work of a labourer, and not of a conjurer or a showman. The power of this worker is not the false miracle of invoking an absolutely chosen form from nothing (this is why it is pointless to call the author a creator); and the scene of his labours is not a theatre – a stage for the presentation of some temporary decorative apparition. This is why he produces real determinate works. To speak of art as technique is to ignore its actual nature.

The writer, as the producer of a text, does not manufacture the materials with which he works. Neither does he stumble across them as spontaneously available wandering fragments, useful in the building of any sort of edifice; they are not neutral transparent components which have the grace to vanish, to disappear into the totality they contribute to, giving it substance and adopting its forms. The causes that determine the existence of the work are not free implements, useful to elaborate any meaning: as we shall see in the course of a very definite example, they have a sort of specific weight, a peculiar power, which means that even when they are used and blended into a totality they retain a certain autonomy; and may, in some cases, resume their particular life. Not because there is some absolute and transcendent logic of aesthetic facts, but because their real inscription in a history of forms means that they cannot be defined exclusively by their immediate function in a specific work. Later we shall be studying one such motif, that of the island, in one of the novels of Jules Verne.

The proposition that the work is necessary does not in any way imply that it is perfected, completed, or consonant with a model that is determined independently of it. The necessity of the work, if it is an objective determination, is not one of its natural properties, the index of the presence of a model or an intention. The necessity of the work is not an initial datum, but a product, at the point where several lines of necessity converge. The important thing is not a confused perception of the unity of the work, but a recognition of its transformations (its contradictions, as long as contradiction is not reduced to merely a new type of unity). The logical, the ideal contradiction – which we meet in its pure form in Hegelian logic – annuls the real complexity of the work and reduces it to the internal confrontation of a single meaning.

A theoretical and therefore rigorous knowledge of the literary work must depend on a logic, in the general sense of the word; to such a logic would fall the task of representing the form of necessity which preserves the real diversity which makes up the work. Obviously this logic could not be based exclusively on the study of literary works; it would have to derive from all those other forms of knowledge which also pose the question of the organisation of a multiple.

Let us take all this up again with the example of the adventure story, which is, as we have seen, an allegory of the literary work in general. By its nature it is a story full of events, full of surprises. If all were initially given it would violate the conventions of its genre: nothing would happen, the sequence of episodes would be factitious and to a practised eye entirely predictable. On the contrary, reading an adventure story ought to be a continuous encounter with novelty and surprise: the reader follows the development of the narrative and experiences all its shock and its infinite novelty; every moment is a thunderclap, a discontinuity, an advent. Let us take one of these tales, in order to keep the analysis at a general level, taking an example of a work which does not depend on the limited genre of the *récit*.

Victor Hugo used the image of an almost impregnable wall which surrounds the garden of the queen in order to represent concretely – even though the object is never actually revealed to the spectators – the distance separating Ruy Blas from his 'queen' (and here the cliché becomes the very cause of the plot); Ruy Blas, transgressing this boundary, leaves a flower within (i.e. he deflowers); but the enterprise is so hazardous that he is wounded (i.e. he inflicts a wound); and leaves a fragment of bloodstained lace caught on the wall (no need this time to suggest an interpretation), which will later be used as a token of recognition by the two lovers. This wall is not only a rather easily interpreted symbol but also a real component of the plot: the hero meets an obstacle in his journey. For whoever is watching or following him, whoever is gazing after him, a delay arises: he will either pass the obstacle or he will not. The reader following the same path meets the same test, save that he has only to turn the page to find the problem resolved. Inevitably the wall either will or will not be climbed over: and the solution proposed by the text will have the force of a law. To turn the page is also to climb over the wall, or to stop finally at its foot. This is why reading is an adventure in which we experience the inevitable as a surprise, and vice versa. The narrative compels, just as the protagonist is compelled by circumstances within the story.

This compulsion demonstrates that the language 'spoken' by the writer is not quite the same as that which we use ordinarily, where there is no such manifest necessity (even if its laws are hardly known). It would be a mistake to say that literature is a new language (there is, in the strict sense, only one language; it is the peculiarity of Hegelian aesthetics to reduce all forms of expression to a language). But, through a specific usage, it is just as though the nature of language had changed: language in disguise (*travesti*), embellished, transformed. One of the essential characteristics of literary language is that it deludes (*fait illusion*); we shall return later to consider the adequacy of this expression. For the moment, it is enough to have grasped that this illusion is constitutive: it is not added to language from the outside, conferring a novel usage on it; it changes language profoundly, making it into something different. Let us say simply that it establishes a new relationship between the word and its meaning, between language and its object. In fact, language as it is modified by the writer does not concern itself with distinctions between the true and the false, in so far as it establishes – reflexively but not speculatively – its own truth: the illusion that it produces is its own peculiar norm. This language does not express the existence of an order independent of itself, to which it claims to conform; it suggests itself the category of truth to which it is to be referred. Language does not designate; it begets, in a new form of expression.

The novelty of this language derives from its self-constituting power. With nothing apparently before or behind it, untroubled by any alien presence, it is autonomous in so far as it is, in effect, lacking in depth, unfolded entirely on its own surface. So it has no need to coin new words to differentiate itself from ordinary language; it transforms words by weaving them into a text; once the old bonds are broken there emerges a new 'reality'. We can go so far as to say that this transmutation consists entirely in the production of a tautology. Language reduced to its thinness, devising a meaning within the narrow trajectory of its development, opening a uniquely internal perspective; without an understudy, language repeats, reproduces, and prolongs itself, to the exclusion of everything else. Whether it is merely the combination of two words, or an expansion to the material limits of the book, the writer's work builds up its own horizon through the very labour that goes into producing it. The 'literary space' in which the work finds its place is, finally, nothing more than the line coiled in the text. And though this line excludes all profundity, it is not simple, but multiple and diverse.

It might be said that the language spoken by the work is not answerable to any external meaning or reality; however, it will later be seen that there is no first, independent, innocent language. To take an elementary example, the Napoleon in Tolstoy's *War and Peace* is not open to refutation by historians. If we are reading properly we know that the name is not quite being used to designate a real person. It derives its meaning only from its relationship to the rest of the text of which it is a part. The writer is able to create both an object and the standards by which it is to be judged. Uninhibited by customary usage and narrow definitions, language wins a remarkable freedom and power of improvisation which has wrongly been considered to be the monopoly of poetry but which actually defines all types of writing. On this issue the postscript of *Les Paysans* (The Peasants) is as good as a manifesto. Here Balzac is replying to an attack published in the *Moniteur de l'Armée*, in which he had been criticised for bringing dishonour to the army by his mistakes.

> Once and for all the author here states that his inaccuracies are conscious and intentional. Soon they will be asking us where to find La Ville aux Fayes, the Avonne and Soulanges in the geography books. All these realms and these soldiers occupy the same enormous world as the Tower of Ravenswood, the waters of Saint-Ronan, Tillietudlem, Gunder-Cleug, Lilliput, the Abbey of Thélème, Hoffman's Privy Counsellors, Robinson Crusoe's island, Shandy Hall, a world exempt from taxes, where the journeys are paid for by those who travel at 20 centimes a volume.

To say that the inaccuracies are 'conscious and intentional' is perhaps going too far, or not far enough, since it reduces the specificity of the writer's work to the systematic use of manufacturing technique. It is more to the point that inaccuracies are not perceived as such, because there are no available standards upon which to base such a judgment. 'Once and for all . . .' but in a typical shift of tone, this text proclaims the power that all books have of setting up their own world. It hardly matters that this world is written, a world of language: Balzac's desire to write a book which would be like a world does away with this problem.

So the language 'spoken' by the writer (and we have deliberately chosen our examples from among those writers whose principal care is to stay close to 'reality') is not governed by a conformity to any external rule. Line by line, he follows his whim, entirely free, and this necessary freedom defines his use of language.

However, this freedom, even if it seems to be improvisation and caprice, is not indiscriminate. In so far as it makes its own standards, the literary work establishes a certain kind of necessity, which is evident primarily in the fact that not a word in the text can be changed. As literature it ought to be convincing enough in itself to persuade us to recognise its validity. It would thus be absurd to insist that the book must be plausible if it is to be of any substance – a quality which would belong especially to its content. It depends far more on finding a compelling mode of expression. The work may indeed be implausible, weak, or gratuitous, and obviously these are three separate possibilities; but it cannot be transcended, and within its own limits it remains true, for otherwise it would actually be unreadable, a fake. Nevertheless many examples of such 'lacking' works could be quoted. Furthermore, the language established by the act of the writer, in the form given by his statement, is irreducible.

Debased literature – which also produces its books and its readers – might be defined precisely by its inability to produce the conditions for this kind of truth. It has to seek a basis and a pretext outside itself; unregulated by a specific form, this language makes its escape by sliding endlessly towards something else – tradition, morality or ideology.

This irreducibility, the guarantee of readability, defines all forms of writing – the fantastic, the poetic, or the realist. It might even be said that 'realist' writing, in its oft-proclaimed ambition to give a true equivalent of the real, finds the greatest difficulty in not over-reaching itself, so pursued is it by an ideal of conformity. The realist writer is most to be commended, for it is he who goes furthest in the enterprise of writing, even if he is not always successful, and it is he who has the greatest difficulty in remaining a writer when he settles in the domain where everything becomes hazardous.

Accordingly, the text has a truth, which it alone can express. Yet this truth is problematical because the object we encounter in our reading is not a real one. There is no natural necessity that governs whether or not the wall is climbed: it depends on the letter of the text. The narrative constrains the reader because it encloses the result in such a web of fiction. The intrigue is thus more striking the more cunning, uncertain and arbitrary it is: this is how the feeling of danger is established, without which it would cease to be adventurous. It must always seem that a new story with a different ending is possible. The narrative gives the impression of novelty in so far as it is a new story at every moment: other words might have been spoken, things might have happened differently. Novelty is just this continuous presence of possibility within the narrative itself. Constraint simultaneously implies a certain transparency: the narrative compels precisely because it *seems* that it might have been different.

But this transparency owes its existence and its power to the fact that it is combined with a certain opacity: one is not reading all possible narratives, but this particular materialisation, this specific writing. There is only one narrative: each of its moments is 'surprising', 'free', but also definitive. The plot-sequence, for all its apparent simplicity, is in fact constituted in a complex and contradictory way: it is both completed and changing. Freedom and necessity, coercion and relaxation – we are always surprised by the same opposition in our investigation of narrative; but it is this opposition which sweeps us along in the course of a simple reading when we surrender ourselves to the narrative.

The power of illusion – that is the issue. Where is the source of this openness within the closed circle of the narrative? But the question allows of two formulations: from the viewpoint of a simple reading (by the person who likes stories), and from that of theoretical knowledge (by the person who asks what narrative is).

In reply to the first we might say that the power of the narrative is the product of an intention, a decision, a will. It was the author who issued his decree: he allowed the protagonist, and subsequently the reader, to climb over the wall. The unexpected is the very token of the creative authorial presence. The finished text is the product of a series of choices to which the reader submits, as a spectator rather than a participant, receiving from on high.

This reply is obviously inadequate. The author certainly makes decisions, but, as we know, his decisions are determined; it would be astonishing if the hero were to vanish after the first few pages, unless by way of parody. To a great extent the author also *encounters* the solutions and resigns himself to handing them on. His narrative is discovered rather than invented, not because he begins at the end, but because certain directions are firmly closed to him. We might say that the author is the first reader of his own work; he first gives himself the surprises that he will hand on to us, he enjoys playing the game of free choice according to the rules. In this sense, writing is compelling – it forces us – to the extent that it is already reading. Thus it is that Propp's analysis, though it deals with collective works, demonstrates how the narrative is determined: the story follows a necessary path – not, as Poe would say, because everything derives from a final intention, but because it is the reading of a previously established model. The allegorical obstacle which we have just been discussing is always surmounted in analogous conditions. If we transpose the laws of collective production to an analysis of individual production, the writer's choice is indeed the illusion of a choice: the narrative sequence depends on something altogether different from that kind of empty decision. But it is not a question of taking from the authorial consciousness and giving to a collective consciousness or to a specific unconscious. This would be merely tinkering with our first reply whilst remaining within the same problematic. (The unconscious is not productive. At least, the unconscious does not produce the work, it produces effects.) It might indeed be said that it is the narrative as such which is determining: it produces its own development on its own terms. It retains the function of saying something new, of articulating it into legibility.

The disadvantages of this theory are obvious: the author, an individual subject, only ceases to be lord and master of his work because the work has been exiled from itself. Defined exclusively by the structure which limits and begets it, the work becomes a second reality, the mythical product of a process it can never mention. This kind of structuralism is closer than is generally recognised to a mechanical theory of reflection. A new question must obviously now be asked: What produces the model? Unless we are going to consider it as an absolute condition with all the necessity of a logical principle, we must isolate and define it and formulate the laws of its operation. We are otherwise imprisoned in a myth of writing as reading which ignores the relationship between knowledge and its object. (If writing is reading, then, inversely, reading is writing; the critic is a writer who simply practises a form of introspection.)

The worst defect of this logical formalism is that it tries to explain the work in relation to a *single* series of conditions: the model, by definition, is unique and self-sufficient. And here we have smuggled back the postulate of the unity and totality of the work; its real complexity has been abolished, dismantled the better to be ignored. This shows a profound misunderstanding of the notion of a *condition*. A condition is not that which is initially given, a cause in the empirical sense; it is the principle of rationality which makes the work accessible to thought. To know the conditions of a work is not to reduce the process of its production to merely the growth of a seed which contains all its future possibilities from the very beginning, a kind of genesis which is the reversed image of an analysis. To know the conditions of a work is to define the real process of its constitution, to show how it is composed from a real diversity of elements which give it substance. Nor must we confuse necessity with fatality: the work is not the product of chance, but it does involve novelty, which is inscribed in its very letter. It is this mobility which makes the work possible, and from which it emerges. Although it is not rigidly subordinated to a model, its progress is not random but becomes an object of knowledge.

Later I shall be studying Jules Verne's *The Mysterious Island*, which can be considered the supreme example of this kind of mutation: the opening pages announce the intention of exemplifying a certain *project* (a conception of the relations between man and nature); the final pages implicitly concede the failure of this undertaking, and a surprising transformation of the initial project. Paradoxically the work begins to swerve from the enabling model which it had adopted; it speaks with several voices at once, exhibiting the contrast between them even if it fails to express and account for this contrast. The change was certainly not part of the author's intention. One might even say that he had overlooked it: not because he had not noticed it – something we will never know – but because by the very logic of his work he had to let it happen. This surprise is not deliberately contrived; it is prepared and derives its significance solely from its place in the movement of the book, otherwise it would actually be imperceptible. To take up the image around which a contemporary novelist has constructed his entire work: at the heart of the book there secretly proliferates a *modification* which is due neither to chance nor to forethought. And it is this which we must account for.

In defining the necessity of the work we are not trying to demonstrate that all the components of its writing and reading are previously and extrinsically given. That sort of necessity would be a pure contrivance and the book would be a kind of mechanism. Before we know how the text works we must know the laws of its production.

Chapter 8

Autonomy and Independence

We have just seen that the text possesses and contains its own kind of truth, and that an extrinsic judgment involves an arbitrary distortion. But does this mean that this truth must be sought in the work itself, where it has settled permanently? If this were so, knowledge would simply involve a reading, a penetration of appearances in order to appropriate some secret; a negative *corroding* criticism by which the work is destroyed or dismantled to reveal the centre around which it had been built. Must we go over this again? For at least four reasons such a performance is completely spurious: it confuses reading and writing; it decomposes where it should be studying the laws of a composition; it limits itself to seizing hold of something already given; it confines the process of understanding the work to the search for a single meaning. And so the problem of the specificity of the work is not yet properly resolved, and several fallacies remain in our path.

What do we mean when we talk of the specificity of the literary work? First, that it is irreducible, that it cannot be assimilated into what it is not. It is the product of a specific labour, and consequently cannot be achieved by a process of a different nature. Furthermore, it is the product of a rupture, it initiates something new. If we have properly grasped this quality of novelty we will not *confuse* the work with what is extrinsic to it; we will want to *distinguish* it emphatically from what surrounds it. To take up a familiar example: it is said that the author's life will not teach us anything about his work, though it is not totally irrelevant, because it can show how a writer has modified his life in using it as literary material. George Painter's celebrated and paradoxical biography of Proust is an excellent demonstration of this process, showing how the writer's life illustrates the Quest, how it is governed entirely by the work; what better way to portray the life than to articulate it in terms of the work? Thus, for the purposes of theoretical analysis, the work is construed as a *centre* of interest although this does not imply that the work itself is *centred*.

The specificity of the work is also its autonomy: in so far as it is self-elaborating it is a law unto itself and acknowledges only an intrinsic standard, an autonomous necessity. This is why literary works ought to be the object of a *specific science*: otherwise they will never be understood. And though various disciplines such as linguistics, the theory of art, the theory of history, the theory of ideologies, the theory of unconscious formations, must all collaborate in this enterprise – for without them it would remain incomplete and would perhaps be impossible – yet they can in no sense replace this specific science of the literary work. It is important to recognise that literary texts make a novel use of language and ideology (perhaps the two are not so very different) by wresting them in a new direction and conscripting them into a project peculiar to them alone.

The work has its beginnings in a break from the usual ways of speaking and writing – a break which sets it apart from all other forms of ideological expression. This is why writing cannot be understood by analogy with some apparently similar activity that is in fact radically different. And yet this is exactly Roland Barthes' strategy in the preface to his *Essais critiques* (Critical Essays) when he defines writing in terms of the customs of polite circumlocution which govern the composition of a formal letter. This break is not the same as the difference which separates art and life, nor is it that *real break* between ideology and theoretical knowledge; rather it is that specific difference which is defined by the characteristic use of the means of representation. The autonomy of the work does not derive from an epistemological break in the familiar sense of the word; but it establishes in its own way a distinct and radical separation which forbids its assimilation into something different.

However, *autonomy must not be confused with independence*. The work only establishes the difference which brings it into being, by establishing relations to that which it is not; otherwise it would have no reality and would actually be unreadable and invisible. Thus the literary work must not be considered as a reality complete in itself, a thing apart, under the pretext of blocking all attempts at reduction; this would be to isolate it into incomprehensibility as the mythical product of some radical epiphany. Even though the work is determined by its own rules, it possesses no internal principle of elaboration. This notion of absolute independence generally characterises that mythical thinking which attests to entities already formed without explaining their origins and development. The difference between two autonomous realities already constitutes a kind of relationship. All the more so because real differences are dialectical rather than static; they are a continuously sustained, elaborated and recapitulated process, they display a very precise mode of relationship, non-empirical, but none the less real, because they are the product of a certain labour.

We shall not, then, be studying the literary work as if it were a self-sufficient totality. As we shall see, it is self-contained not in so far as it might be a totality: the arbitrary assumption of the unity and independence of the text is grounded in a radical misunderstanding of the nature of the writer's work. Through its relationship to the theoretical and ideological uses of language, the text is also influenced by the formal function of the writer and by the problems of his individual existence; finally, specific literary works are determined by the history of literary production from which they receive the means of their own realisation.

In short, a book never arrives unaccompanied: it is a figure against a background of other formations, depending on them rather than contrasting with them. It is, like all products, a *second reality*, though it does have its own laws. As will be seen later, it is this secondariness that truly defines the work of the writer, if it is true that his function is always parodic.

Chapter 9

Image and Concept: Beautiful Language and True Language

The activity of the writer initially presents itself as labour, as work, once we seek to *know* rather than to follow it. It is a work of language, on language, a form given to language, though none of these expressions adequately defines it. A public speech, a private letter, a conversation, a newspaper article, a scientific report – these are also uses of language; but they are quite distinct from that of the writer, because they adopt conventions of sincerity, persuasiveness or social elegance, whereas literature traditionally belongs to the realm of art, and acknowledges only the rather specialised aesthetic judgment. It makes no difference that the class of literary objects may be judged as 'beautiful', at least within the tradition which still theoretically prevails – (in fact, the aesthetic of the beautiful has perhaps been inverted and challenged – in the efforts of surrealism-romanticism to establish an aesthetic of the ugly – but it has not been replaced by a different *theory*. Though Baudelaire and the surrealists indisputably achieved a major artistic revolution, it was at the price of a considerable theoretical regression, in the return to an other-worldly Platonism. This regression might have been profitable, but it could in no way be definitive. The theory of the surrealist revolution has yet to be formulated, thought this is a task beyond the powers of the surrealists themselves) – and that this notion of beauty was formulated during the Renaissance, and that our theory of art is principally a theory of literature (as in Hegelian aesthetics). At a specific moment writers placed themselves under a certain set of laws, and we are still bound by that decision. Dedicated to the making of a beautiful language, where nature – language as it was given them – met the convention of the beautiful, they invented the literary work. But rather than analysing the act of writing in terms of language and art, let us look at the specificity of this activity.

The writer's language is new, not in its material form but in its use. Let us say provisionally that this language establishes an illusion: its first quality is veracity. It convinces all the more readily when it does not answer to any extrinsic standard. It is defined by its power of evocation; it constructs meanings. But this analysis is little more than a description: this evocative power is not unique to the writer's language, for the production of an *impression of reality*, which gives the literary work its *necessity*, belongs to language in general, and the particular use that the writer makes of it cannot be distinguished.

It is not enough to say that the literary work arranges a necessary language. There are actually many types of necessary language. Scientific discourse, by its rigorous form, also implies a kind of necessity, which sets precise limits to thinking, so that the learned agree on at least one point – that they occupy the same domain and speak the same language – and their discussions are governed by this shared assumption. A certain rationality forms the horizon of their discourse, a rationality of concepts solidly rooted in definitions; and the power of the definition is such that even in their most violent disagreements they know – because of the stability of their concepts – that they are disagreeing about the same thing. The necessity of such a rationality is not *any* necessity, of *anything*, but a determinate necessity: the language of science and the language of theory is fixed, though obviously it is not in a state of arrested perfection.

Now, the horizon bounding literary endeavour is not reason but illusion, and the surface of its discourse is the scene of an illusion. On this side or on that of the distinction between true and false is the text, a dense fabric which obeys its own logic (stylistics ought to be part of this logic). Notice in passing that once we have thus mapped out the site of the literary discourse it

c

becomes difficult to describe the work of the writer as a mystification which produces a pure illusion. If there is no line dividing true and false, how could we detect any deception, except in relationship to another truth – the truth of a world or an intention outside the text, and which has no jurisdiction over the text. If it is truly constitutive, the illusion that hides in, or contains, the text could not thus be isolated and reduced. Far from being opposed to a reality on the basis of which it would play a very precarious game, this illusion must have a certain reality of its own.

However, the rigour peculiar to the mechanism of illusion is initially defined by the nature of the objects that it assimilates into its progress. Let us say that it turns on compelling images rather than definite concepts. The element of *style* (word, turn or artifice of composition) asserts itself as a literary object by its obsessing quality first of all: literature exists only through repetition in the guise of variation; scientific discourse, on the other hand, avoids redundancy as far as possible, and tends spontaneously towards ellipsis. The components fused in the literary text can have no independent reality: unlike the scientific concept, which can be moved from one theory to another, they are bound to a specific context which defines the only horizon with respect to which they can be read. It is within the framework of the particular book that they gain their power of suggestion and become representative: they are impoverished by any kind of displacement. We can see how there is a specifically poetic – rather than logical – rigour which unites form and content: the image behind the word can obsess in isolation, but it has meaning and power only within the system of the text.

Thus, to take a simple example, the Paris of the *Comédie humaine* is a literary object only in so far as it is a product of an effort of writing; it has no prior existence. But the elements that comprise this object, the relationships that give them coherence, are reciprocally determined. They draw their 'truth' from one another and not from anything else. Balzac's Paris is not an expression of the real Paris, a concrete generality (whereas the concept would be an abstract generality). It is the product of a certain labour, dictated not by reality but by the work. It is not the reflection of a reality or an experience but of an artifice, which consists wholly in the establishment of a complex system of relations. Each component (image), therefore, derives its meaning from its position in the internal order of the book, rather than from its conformity to some other extrinsic order.

> In the big city Balzac discovered a source of mystery, and his curiosity is ever alert. Curiosity is his muse. He is never comic or tragic; he is curious. He enters an entanglement of things, with the air of one who scents and promises a mystery, one who dismantles the whole machine piece by piece with a harsh, keen and triumphant pleasure. Observe how he approaches his new characters: he scrutinises them like rarities, defines, sculpts, and annotates them, brings out all their singularity and promises miracles. His judgments, his observations, his tirades and his words are not psychological truths but the suspicions and tricks of an examining magistrate, blows of the fist upon this mystery, which, by God, must be elucidated. (C. Pavese, *Le Métier de vivre* (The Profession of Living))

Obviously this description of an inquisitive genius is no more psychological than the 'truths' it reveals: curiosity here acquires an allegorical value. The investigative impulse which guides the author as if in pursuit of an unpublished world, represents that process of *singularisation* by which the text is constructed (to take up the idea that Shlovsky applied to Tolstoy). The fictional object does not appear alone; it is entangled, inscribed in this text which uses it, a token for something else, to herald its next impulse, constantly extending it into something else.

Before this process of elaboration, the image has no substance, no self-identity; it slides, pours, overflows, seeks a purpose beyond itself. This exposition is to the image what demonstration is to the concept. Thus, Balzac's Paris is the analogy of the book: traversed, shifting in front of the gaze which fashions it, constantly hollowing itself out in front of it, for a new pursuit. This pursuit is a constitutive part, since it eventually creates its object. The fictional reality is bound up with, if not dependent on, this searching gaze. It is an object crystallised as far as the gaze can see, but never completed, always escaping from a fixed gaze, never completely grasped, mastered, or exhausted, because it must always be prolonged. The book, as we shall see later, *holds together* only because it remains incomplete; thus the object shown appears inexhaustible. The image presented in the book gives the illusion of the real by its endless need to multiply in itself or in others.

If the writer's discourse produces an effect of reality, this is because he consciously uses the very limits of the fascination by the image (far from being carried away by this fascination, he plays on it). In the impossibility of an ending he finds the opportunity for an endless *reprise* in which the line of the text is elaborated. So this line is not as simple as it seems; it retains something of the confusion which fashioned it.

The way the writer exploits both the negative and the positive qualities of images reveals the illusory character of his work, though it does not define that illusion. In fact if the analysis were to stop there, we would come to the point of considering literature as pure *artifice*, reducing it to merely a system of operations.

Now we must identify the system of production behind this purely technical reality. How does the work make use of these means? What use are they to it? In other words, what kind of rigour establishes this logic of images, this logic that fashions images into an illusion?

To summarise: the activity of the writer is realised entirely on the level of an utterance; it constitutes and is constituted by a discourse, it has nothing extrinsic; all its truth or authority is materialised on the thin surface of the discourse. But this definition remains unsatisfactory because it is empty and purely formal. Above all, discourse, even that of ordinary speech, implies the temporary absence of the object of discourse; the object has been put to one side, banished into silence. Speech is *par excellence* an act which modifies the reality of that to which it is applied. 'To name a flower' is the equivalent of picking it, creating 'l'absente de tout bouquet' with only the thin contours of the word, receiving its only depth from the transitivity which makes it possible to advance from image to image, never allowing any particular image to stand alone. The reality banished by speech to the black horizon of its manifestation is only spoken in its absence, in another place. It is characteristic of all language to constitute a special object which has no existence until the moment of utterance: the conformity between discourse and the world of things is always illusory. It is not that things seek out an appropriate discourse to attain expression; it is that language speaks of itself, its forms and its objects. The bias of things is the bias of language.

Thus it seems that the discourse of the writer has not, by choice, that privilege of illusion which would enable it to say something else. Discourse implies the absence of its object, and inhabits the space vacated by the banishment of what is spoken. This is as true of everyday speech as it is of literary discourse, and also of scientific propositions, the order of concepts is objectively constitutive, and defines an autonomous (though not independent) level of reality governed by specific laws. The literary discourse assembles images rather than concepts, and images by their nature defy definition. However, as we have seen, the fascination of the image is diverted from its usual function: it is *exploited* for purposes other than those which govern ordinary speech, and must permit the construction of an autonomous entity, a literary work. This modification is achieved by a rigorous use of images which order them within the limits of *a necessary text*.

This enables us to say that the autonomy of the writer's discourse is established from its relationship with the other uses of language: everyday speech, scientific propositions. By its energy and thinness literary discourse mimics theoretical discourse, rehearsing but never actually performing its script. But in that evocative power, by which it denotes a specific reality, it also imitates the everyday language which is the language of ideology. We could offer a provisional definition of literature as being characterised by this power of parody. Mingling the real uses of language in an endless confrontation, it concludes by *revealing* their truth. Experimenting with language rather than inventing it, the literary work is both the analogy of a knowledge and a caricature of customary ideology.

We always eventually find, at the edge of the text, the language of ideology, momentarily hidden, but eloquent by its very absence. This parody quality of the literary work strips it of its apparent spontaneity and makes it a secondary work. Through the diverse modes of their presence the different elements conflict more than they unite: the 'life' kidnapped by everyday speech, the echo of which is found in the literary work, confronts that speech with its own unreality (which is attended by the production of an effect of reality); whereas the finished literary work (since nothing can be added to it) *reveals* the gaps in ideology. Literature is the mythology of its own myths: it has no need of a soothsayer to uncover its secrets.

Chapter 10

Illusion and Fiction

We have defined literary discourse as parody, as a contestation of language rather than a representation of reality. It distorts rather than imitates. Moreover the idea of imitation, correctly understood, implies distortion, if, as Plato suggests in *The Cratylus*, the essence of resemblance is difference. The image that corresponded perfectly with the original would no longer be an image; it remains an image by virtue of its difference from that which it resembles. The aesthetic of the baroque merely takes this idea to its paradoxical extreme: the greater the difference the better the imitation, culminating in a theory of caricature. In this sense, all literature is ultimately baroque in inspiration.

But this remains a merely negative description; it would only be adequate if it could be shown that the function of literary discourse is itself essentially negative. We would be saying that the book, constructed by proven methods, produces an illusion, an artifice, rather than a positive reality. And until this moment we have been using this term 'illusion'.

This amounts to considering literature as a mythology: a manipulation of signs that takes the place of an absent reality. Literature is deceptive in so far as it is evocative and apparently expressive: its discourse has a shadow-life at the edge of a radical exclusion, the exclusion of its pretended object, which does not exist. Making us take the word for the thing, or vice versa, it would be a fabric of lies, all the more radical for being unconscious, preceding the act of writing just as the place precedes and lies in wait for the future event.

Then we would speak of a literary space, the scene of this mystification. All writing would be furrowed by this elision; at best, as in Mallarmé, it might manage to reveal the truth of its absence. Then the differences between the various types of writing finally reflect back to a common nature which constrains them equally: they speak and say nothing. The writer sends empty messages, whose only reality is the specific code in which they are expressed. (This is the argument that Roland Barthes puts forward in *Writing Degree Zero*.)

The only theory of literature would then be one based on denunciation and complicity, and as we have seen these two attitudes can be held simultaneously. In this instance, the writer and the critic submit to the same myth of language: critical objectivity is actually defined by its eloquent compliance with an *inevitability* which is also its *raison d'être*. The theoretical idea of necessity is thus degraded, literally caricatured: in an elegaic euphoria, literature proclaims the absence or vanity of all its works. The works are nothing; they are this nothing, and through it they are at most the manifestation of an essence (literature) whose mechanism can be studied for its own sake.

This conception of the nature of the literary work is inadequate largely because it misjudges the role played by *fiction* in the work of the writer. The text is not a tissue of illusions which has merely to be *unravelled* if we wish to understand its power. An illusion that has been *set to work* becomes more than just an illusion, more than a mere deception. It is an illusion *interrupted*, *realised*, completely transformed. To ignore this transformation is to confuse the non-literary use of language *from which* the text is made, and the labour of elaboration which produces the text from this initial state of language; it implies the belief that it is enough to dream in order to write.

The language of illusion, the writer's raw material, is the vehicle and source of everyday ideology – that thing we bear within us which turns us into things as we are carried along on the endless stream of this formless discourse in which one image is substituted for another, though the excluded middle term which might verify the argument is never to be found. To understand this ordinary condition of language, let us borrow from Spinoza's description of an ardent life: desire seeks an imaginary object and expresses itself fluently, lost in the pursuit of an absence, distracted from its own presence; an impotent, inadequate, incomplete, torn and empty discourse flinging itself into the quest for an excluded centre, unable to construct the complete form of a contradiction; a line endlessly extended according to a false perspective. Desire lagging behind its own emptiness, deprived from the first, never appeased. Language in flight, running after a reality which it can only define negatively, speaking of order, liberty and perfection, the beautiful and the good, as well as chance and destiny. A delirium, speech bereft of its object, displaced from its own manifest meaning, not spoken by any subject: bewildered, forsaken, inconsistent; despairing throughout its dim fall. Existence comes to the individual in the form of a very primitive illusion, a true dream, which sets up a certain number of necessary images: man, liberty, the will of God. It is spontaneously defined by a spontaneous use of language which turns it into a shapeless gaping text – a text that slides vigorously over itself, doing its utmost to say nothing, since it is not designed actually to say anything.

Spinoza's notion of liberation involves a new attitude to language; the hollow speech of the imagination must be halted, anchored; the unfinished must be endowed with form, determined (even though the indeterminate depends on a certain kind of necessity, since it can be known). To effect this change, two sorts of activity are proposed: theoretical activity fixes language and makes it speak in concepts as the means of acquiring knowledge – for Spinoza there is no other way; however, aesthetic activity, on which he is almost silent, also arrests language by giving it a limited – though unfinished – form. There is a profound difference between the vague language of the imagination and that of the text; within the limits of the text this language is in several senses deposited (fallen, forsaken and gathered). The literary work interrupts and *solidifies* the apparent motion of the former – in which words are moved to no purpose; in this space where language confronts itself, is constructed that true distance which is the condition of any real progression – the discourse of the book. Determinate reverie: a true and necessary fiction, making its way to a specific destination. This is why, once again, there is little point in denouncing the myth which would endow the book with a semblance of life. Since it is built from the formless language of illusion, the book revolves around this myth; but in the process of its formation the book takes a stand regarding this myth, exposing it. This does not mean that the book is able to become its own criticism: it gives an implicit critique of its ideological content, if only because it resists being incorporated into the flow of ideology in order to give a *determinate representation* of it. Fiction, not to be confused with illusion, is the substitute for, if not the equivalent of, knowledge. A theory of literary production must show us what the text 'knows', how it 'knows'.

Thus the book substitutes the clear – though not simple – outlines of a fiction for the meanderings of illusion. Fiction is determinate illusion, and the essence of the literary text is to establish these determinations. Thus the *power* of language, settled in the more or less fixed edges of the work, is displaced. To know what a literary text is we must ask: From what new centre is the work of fiction carried out? It is not a question of a real centre, for the book does not replace ideologically decentred illusion with a permanent centre around which the system of language is to be ordered; the book does not endow this system with a subject. Fiction is not *truer* than illusion; indeed, it cannot usurp the place of knowledge. But it can set illusion in motion by penetrating its insufficiency, by transforming our relationship to ideology. (By its nature, ideology is always *elsewhere*, it can never be located; consequently, it cannot be totally subdued, diminished or dispelled.) Fiction deceives us in so far as it is feigned; but this is not a primary act of deception, because it is aimed at one even more profound, exposing it, helping to release us from it.

The text begins from where 'life' reaches its formless conclusions; the two terms, then, form a distinct contract; but they are also inseparable, not because they are simply different forms of the same content, but because they constitute an endless dialectical opposition.

Because the work enfolds this fiction it is an entirely futile critical enterprise to attempt to *reduce* this fiction to some other use of language: internal discourse, ideological discourse or collective discourse. And since the text is fiction rather than illusion it resists interpretation, resists being reduced to non-literary forms of expression. As we shall see, knowledge is not interpretation but explication.

It is therefore important to distinguish the three forms which give three different uses of language: illusion, fiction, theory. These three discourses use more or less the same words, but the relations between these words are so different that there is no bridge, no unbroken path, from one order of discourse to another.

Chapter 11

Creation and Production

The proposition that the writer or artist is a creator belongs to a humanist ideology. In this ideology man is released from his function in an order external to himself, restored to his so-called powers. Circumscribed only by the resources of his own nature, he becomes the maker of his own laws. He creates. What does he create? Man. Humanist thought (everything by man, everything for man) is circular, tautological, dedicated entirely to the repetition of a single image. 'Man makes man' (in this sense Aristotle is the theoretician of humanism): by a continual unbroken investigation he releases from within himself what is already there; creation is self-multiplication. There seems to be a radical difference between theology and anthropology: man can create only in continuity, by making the potential actual; he is excluded, by his nature, from originality and innovation. But this difference is an adaptation.

Anthropology is merely an impoverished and inverted theology: in the place of the god-man is installed Man, god over himself, eternally repeating the destiny he already bears within him. In the terms of this inversion, the opposite of man-as-creator is alienated man: deprived of himself, become other. To become other (alienation), to become oneself (creation): the two ideas are equivalent in so far as they belong to the same problematic. Alienated man is man without man: man without God, without that God who is, for man, man himself.

Formulated thus, the question of 'man' involves unresolvable contradictions: how can man change without becoming other? So he must be protected, allowed to remain as he is: forbidden to transform his condition. The ideology of humanism is spontaneously and profoundly reactionary both in theory and in practice. The only activity allowed to the man-god is the preservation of his identity. The only possible legitimate changes are those which give man what already belongs to him: his property, even if he has never actually owned it. The Declaration of Human Rights, the monument of humanism, is not an institution but a declaration; it abolishes the distance which separates man from his universal, necessary and eternal rights. Man has been changed from what he is (the humanist ideology's explanation of 'religious alienation'): it is enough to change him back, to restore everything to its former place. Alienation is not in itself damaging, but only because of the direction in which it leads; it is enough to change the direction to release the truth which it contains but ignores. Humanism is only a very superficial critique of religious ideology; it does not contest the ideological as such, merely a specific ideology which it wishes to replace.

The purest product of humanism is the religion of art: Roger Garaudy – whose purpose is to give back to man his 'expectations', by starting him on the 'voyage' to the limitless space (if that were all it required!) of himself – is the supreme ideologue of artistic creation. Borrowing a careless phrase from Gorky (careless because it is merely a phrase, unsupported by any argument, and completely mistaken from a theoretical point of view), 'aesthetics is the ethics of the future', he proposes the liberation of man by a return to the religion of art, without seeing that art, exploited thus, is only an impoverished religion. Now, art is not man's creation, it is a product (and the producer is not a subject centred in his creation, he is an element in a situation or a system): different – in being a product – from religion, which has chosen its dwelling among all the spontaneous illusions of spontaneity, which is certainly a kind of creation. Before disposing of these works – which can only be called theirs by an elaborate evasion – men have to *produce* them, not by magic, but by a real labour of production. If man creates man, the artist produces works, *in determinate conditions*; he does not work on himself but on that thing which escapes him in so many ways, and never belongs to him until after the event.

The various 'theories' of creation all ignore the process of making; they omit any account of production. One can create undiminished, so, paradoxically, creation is the release of what is already there; or, one is witness of a sudden apparition, and then creation is an irruption, an epiphany, a mystery. In both instances any possible explanation of the change has been done away with; in the former, nothing has happened; and in the latter what has happened is inexplicable. All speculation over man the creator is intended to eliminate a real knowledge: the 'creative process' is, precisely, not a process, a labour; it is a religious formula to be found on funeral monuments.

For the same reasons, all considerations of genius, of the subjectivity of the artist, of his soul, are *on principle* uninteresting.

You will understand why, in this book, the word 'creation' is suppressed, and systematically replaced by 'production'.

Chapter 12

Pact and Contract

The work is a tissue of fictions: properly speaking it contains nothing that is true. However, in so far as it is not a total deception but a verified falsehood, it asks to be considered as speaking the truth: it is not just any old illusion, it is a determinate illusion. We will be tempted to say, since it must be accepted literally, that it assumes the reader's uninterrupted assent. In so far as the author must rely on his faith and confidence, without which his work would never be read, it is tempting to talk of a pact, a tacit agreement which recognises the self-determining power of fiction.

In introducing this idea of a pact we seem to have given up the study of the conditions of literary production, in order to tackle the question of how the text communicates with its readers. In fact the two problems go together: it is incorrect to begin (by a method which is a mere parody of rigour) by closing off the work in order to break it open again when it is hurled into the world, having thus persuaded ourselves that the problematic interior-exterior corresponds so obviously to a simple chronological distinction (the work is written before it is read). There is no point in pausing over this too mechanical distinction: first, the work in itself, then, the work for others. In fact, the study of literary production inevitably encounters the problem of the transmission of the text. To distinguish and define these problems methodically – as we did with the notion of the writer as his own first reader – is not to claim that they are absolutely and arbitrarily separate.

In fact, the conditions of its communication are produced at the same time as the book, at least the more important conditions; so that these conditions are not absolutely given and they have no temporal priority. Readers are made by what makes the book – though it is a question of two different processes – for otherwise, the book, written from some inscrutable impulse, would be the work of its readers, reduced to the function of an illustration. (This must be taken in *the plainest sense*: the book does not produce its readers by some mysterious power; the conditions that determine the production of the book also determine the forms of its communication. These two modifications are simultaneous and reciprocal. This question would certainly be worth a specific theoretical study, the guiding principle for which is to be found in Marx's statement 'Not only the object of consumption but also the mode of consumption is produced, not only in an objective way but also subjectively.') We must avoid turning all the problems posed by the work into the single question of its diffusion. In a word, we must not replace a mythology of the creator by a mythology of the public.

The literary work is not only the expression of an objective historical situation which assigns it, once and for all, before it is even made, to a determinate public; as we know, it escapes that kind of determination:

> The difficulty does not lie in understanding that Greek art and epos are bound up with certain forms of social development. It rather lies in understanding why they still afford us aesthetic enjoyment and in certain respects prevail as the standard and model beyond attainment. (Marx, Introduction to *A Contribution to the Critique of Political Economy*, Peking, Foreign Languages Press, 1976, p. 44)

The Homeric poems did not make their appearance in the trappings of a false eternity: yet they have not finished being read.

Let us recognise this as an important problem, even if the answer that Marx goes on to suggest (the modern man who surrenders to the charms of Greek art is the father who adores the remnants of childhood in himself: in terms that Gombrovicz might have used, it is the mature seeking out the immature, the incomplete), presented only in an allusion, cannot satisfy us. The ideological nature of this answer is obvious. The work is available beyond the closed circle of its initial intended audience. It is not circumscribed by a spontaneous reading.

Yet it could be tempting to replace the idea of an objective pact, by which the author acknowledges finite external circumstances, with the idea of a subjective pact, according to which a general tacit confidence would be established between the author and his potential readers before even the mediation of the actual work: the author could be taken at his word, the reader could believe and trust. Before the work has even appeared, there is this abstract possibility of a relation between its speech and its audience. In fact, as we have seen, the book does not propose an externally verifiable truth, within fixed limits, limits fixed *with* if not by the text. According to a banal description, which we shall do no more than outline, the reader *enters* the book as though it were another world; the act of reading requires a certain number of implicit or explicit presuppositions – most important, this is a book, nothing other than a book; failing this, we are no longer engaged in reading, but are dreaming, or bored. However, this attitude does not have to be consciously sustained; an implicit acknowledgment can suffice. According to the logic of this analysis, the autonomy and specificity of the text is assured by this prior pact, so large and vague. This pact establishes the imaginary *place* where the book will eventually *happen*. This arrangement makes anything possible, makes the arbitrary true.

This arrangement in fact excludes the possibility of a double compromise: that of the author, who entrusts his work to the public, and that of the reader, who makes a large initial gift of credulity at the moment when he opens the book. This idea of the pact takes us back to familiar critical fallacies: it establishes a false and confusing symmetry between author and reader; it assumes that place, that site which precedes and prepares for the work (thus reintroducing the principles of Aristotelian physics into literary criticism). Finally, it confuses fiction and illusion, sending the reader back to his faith and condemning the author to a gratuitous game.

It must be realised that the 'notion' of a pact is incorrect because it depends on a badly formulated question. The problematic of confidence is a moral problematic; it does not lead to a study of the work as a product of the literary activity, but gives it a different meaning. We are no longer readers; we find a home in the margins of the text. The writer is not called upon to resolve the vague and empty question 'Will I be believed?', but a different and determinate question, 'What must I *do* to be read?' Thus, even if a certain complicity between the text and the reader is possible, it must be seen that this complicity has an obvious purpose: the reader can feel himself being carried along by the author's initiative (or by what he takes for an initiative – we have seen that the act of writing is not simply determined by an individual decision), an initiative to which he is a party, whether he likes it or not. The reverse is not true. The author does not believe what he seems to want others to believe (let us accept this expression temporarily, in spite of its imprecision); he cannot believe it. It is not enough for him to believe in it as he would if, as is sometimes said, he were carried away by the impulse of his 'creation'. The book, a constructed fiction, even if it is variously determined from without by the real conditions of its production (it is autonomous but not independent), is not, however, forestalled or 'prevented': nothing precedes it on its own ground, not even the promise of a future site. If there were a pact, it would be merely between the reader and himself, or between the reader and the author, in so far as he, the author, is his own first and best reader.

We have arrived again at a principle already established: no description of the conventions of reading, however thorough, can replace a theory of literary production; if the author were the reader of his own work it would imply that the work existed, even before it was produced, as an independent model. In a parallel fashion, an attentive criticism of the work, which defines the conditions of its production, is altogether different from a reading; because this criticism is not satisfied with judging the work's false conformity, it reveals its intrinsic difference and its uneven development. (Although the point has not been developed here, the study of the conventions of reading could, however, form the object of a sociology of culture; from such a description could be inferred the real, ideological, 'cultural' conditions of literary communication as a form of recognition. In the absence of these conditions the writer could not produce anything, but this production can in its turn modify the original conditions, without aspiring to determine for itself the path of this transformation. (In a neighbouring domain, *L'Amour de l'art* (The Love of Art) (Bourdieu et Barbel, coll. Le sens Commun, éditions de Minuit) gives a remarkable example of the results that can be obtained on this point.)

Obviously this does not mean that criticism contributes to dismantling the book, to destroying the illusory. The study of literary works presupposes neither a blind faith nor an abstract scepticism: faith and scepticism would be the two extreme forms of the same prejudice. A knowledge of the work is no more determined by the antithesis belief-distrust that it is by that of faith and reason. Because there is no radical ignorance inscribed in its letter, it must be accepted at its word. If the book were merely the arbitrary located in the abstract space promised by the pact, it would constitute an error. But the composition of a fiction is not simply a pretence: the writer is not an imitator, nor even, in Platonist fashion, the artisan of false appearances. He would then indeed be the victim of the tastes and prejudices of the public who would assimilate the work into their own incomprehension.

> Most charming, then, would be the state of mind of the poetical imitator in respect of true wisdom about his creations. . . . Yet still he will nonetheless imitate, though in every case he does not know in what way the thing is bad or good. But, as it seems, the thing he will imitate will be the thing that appears beautiful to the ignorant multitude. (Plato, *The Republic*, X, 602b)

The writer does not pretend to write: he follows the path of a real activity. Though his undertaking may on occasion look frenzied, it is not so, if only because the frenzy is contained within the work: criticism begins where pathology ends. The 'reality' that the book denotes is not arbitrary but conventional, fixed by laws. We could substitute the idea of a contract for the vagueness of a pact; this would demonstrate that the activity of the writer is truly constitutive. (But this idea of a contract only has the value of an image: it denotes the existence of a problem without solving it; it is even misleading in so far as it suggests a spontaneous decision, individual or collective. This voluntarist mythology could only be defeated by an objective study of the conditions which unite or oppose a work to its public.)

Chapter 13

Explanation and Interpretation

Turning away from an old-fashioned *explication de texte*, a criticism with any aspirations to profundity chooses as its purpose the determination of a *meaning*: it describes itself as interpretive, in the broad sense. What is to be gained by replacing explanation (which answers the question, how is the work made?) by interpretation (why is the work made?)? At first it seems that we have enlarged the domain of criticism from a myopic study of means to an exploration of ends, posing the *essential* questions, not only about the form of the literary work, but also about its signification.

The interpreter is one who takes up position at a centre, or rather in an intermediate space, and proceeds to an exchange: for what is offered, he substitutes a term of equal value, at least if he is working scrupulously. What does the interpreter replace when he applies his art to a literary work? The exchange replaces the work by its meaning. In a single gesture two things are revealed – the space of the work and the content which fills this space; it might be said that he installs himself on the site of the work to display the meanings there. In fact, interpretation performs an inverse but equivalent operation: it transposes the work into a commentary, a displacement intended to conjure up the content, unchanged and stripped of the ornament that concealed it. The interpreter realises a copy of the work and, in a miracle of reciprocity, discovers that of which the work is itself a copy.

Interpretation is repetition, but a strange repetition that *says more by saying less:* a purifying repetition, at the end of which a hidden meaning appears in all its naked truth. The work is only the expression of this meaning, an ore which must be smelted to extract its precious content. The interpreter accomplishes this liberating violence: he dismantles the work in order to be able to reconstruct it *in the image* of its meaning, to make it denote directly what it had expressed obliquely. Translation and reduction: focusing the apparent diversity of the work in a single signification. Paradoxically, this reduction ought to be fruitful rather than impoverishing – endowing the text with the brightness and the truth which it lacked. But such an 'investigation' obviously has a critical meaning; the opulence which it brings to light is also a revelation of the poverty of the work: 'That was it, that and nothing more.' Plato said exactly this:

> For if we strip the works of the poets of the colours of poetry and recite them thus diminished to themselves, you know, I think, what they will look like. . . . They can be compared to those faces which, having no other beauty than their freshness cease to attract the eye when the flower of youth has withered. (Plato, *The Republic*, X, 601b)

Reduced to the expression of a meaning, the work may seem rather threadbare: to restore it to elegance, the commentator will have to add the cosmetic of his own style.

Thus we have posited the principles of an immanent criticism: the work encloses a meaning which must be released; the letter of the work is the mask, eloquent and deceptive, which this meaning bears; a knowledge of the work is an ascent to this central unique meaning. Interpretive criticism rests on a certain number of fallacies which have already been exposed: it locates the work in a space which it endows with its own depth; it denounces the spontaneously deceptive character of the work; finally, it presupposes the active presence of a single meaning around which the work is diversely articulated. Above all, it confirms the relationship of interiority between the work and its criticism: commentary establishes itself at the heart of the work and delivers its secret. Between knowledge (critical discourse) and its object (the literary work) the only distance is that between power and action, meaning and its expression. The commentary is contained by the work (or vice versa); in any case they are confused in the fashion typical of the empiricist method.

This essentialist, immanent criticism, repetition, commentary and 'pure' reading, is inadequate: it is not enough to unfold the line of the text to discover the message inscribed there, for this knowledge implies a separation between discourse and its object, not a repetition of what has already been said. Immanent criticism is inevitably confused, because it begins by abolishing that separation. It can, though, seem to be the most rigorous form of criticism in its proclaimed intention to be *faithful to the meaning*, to free it from all the impurities which alter and interrupt it, to ensure an essential adequation between the work and the reader. To recoil from the task of an interpretation is to accept failure or to vanish into the work; it is to privilege the inessential, out of a care for a false objectivity; it is to refuse to listen to a fundamental and haunting image.

Criticism, if it is to be a rational enterprise, must resolve the following problem. On the one hand it can only regard its object as empirically given, otherwise it risks confusing the rules of art with the laws of knowledge. The object of critical knowledge is not spontaneously available; it has first to be construed into a cognitive object – not replaced by an ideal and abstract model, but internally displaced so as to reveal its rationality. On the other hand, this knowledge, if it is to escape the normative fallacy, can only consider the work as it is, and must resist any temptation to alter it. To do otherwise would involve subjecting the work to a new set of rules (no longer technical rules of verisimilitude, but opportunist political or moral rules). Thus we must go beyond the work and explain it, must say what it does not and could not say: just as the triangle remains silent over the sum of its angles. But this manoeuvre must be deliberate: we must not escape from empiricism only to fall into the normative fallacy (judgment and interpretive commentary are the two possible methods of *replacing* the work).

Rejecting the mythology of comprehension, explanation recognises the necessity that determines the work but which does not culminate in a *meaning*. It is not a question of confronting the work with some external truth: rather than passing a normative judgment, we identify the class of truth which constitutes the work and determines its meaning. This truth is not there in the work, like a nut in its shell; paradoxically, it is both interior and absent. If this were not the case, we would have to concede that the work was actually *unknowable*, miraculous and mysterious, and that criticism was futile.

To defeat the interpretive fallacy, we are now led to formulate a methodological hypothesis concerning the nature of the work. The work must be elaborated, *used*, for without this it will never be a theoretical fact, an object of knowledge; but it must also be *left* as it is, if we are to achieve a theoretical judgment and avoid value judgments. It must be constructed and maintained within its proper limits: that is to say, not used for edification. This double requirement will only really make sense if it corresponds to the nature of the work. The writer's work must be open to displacement, otherwise it will remain an object of consumption rather than an object of knowledge; as a pretext for rhetorical compliments it will never be the pillar of a rational investigation.

To step out of the circle of critical fallacies, we must propose a theoretical hypothesis: the work does not contain a meaning which it conceals by giving it its achieved form. The necessity of the work is founded on the multiplicity of its meanings; to explain the work is to recognise and *differentiate* the principle of this diversity. *The postulated unity of the work which, more or less explicitly, has always haunted the enterprise of criticism, must now be denounced:* the work is not *created* by an intention (objective or subjective); it is *produced* under determinate conditions. 'All writing has a meaning, even if this meaning is remote from that which the author had dreamt of putting there' (Sartre, *Présentation des temps modernes* (Presentation of Modern Times)): the work would be *full of meaning*, and it is this plenitude which must be examined. But such an investigation would obviously be fallacious since it would derive its form from a hidden eloquence, arising from within the work, an eloquence which it would complacently express. A proper investigation has nothing to do with these shadowy half-presences: rather than an ideal and illusory plenitude it takes as its object that hollow speech which the work utters so discreetly; it measures the *distance* which separates the *various* meanings.

We must not falter at the prospect of revealing formlessness and imperfection in the work – as long as these words are not taken in a negative and pejorative sense. Rather than that *sufficiency*, that ideal consistency, we must stress that determinate insufficiency, that incompleteness which actually shapes the work. The work must be incomplete *in itself*: not extrinsically, in a fashion that could be completed to 'realise' the work. It must be emphasised that this incompleteness, betokened by the confrontation of separate meanings, is the true *reason* for its composition. The thin line of the discourse is the temporary appearance behind which we recognise the determinate complexity of a text: on condition that this complexity is not that of a 'totality', illusory and mediate.

When we explain the work, instead of ascending to a hidden centre which is the source of life (the interpretive fallacy is organicist and vitalist), we perceive its actual decentred-ness. We refuse the principle of an intrinsic analysis (or an immanent criticism) which would artificially circumscribe the work, and deduce the image of a 'totality' (for images too can be deduced) from the fact that it is *entire*. The structure of the work, which makes it available to knowledge, is this internal displacement, this caesura, by which it corresponds to a reality that is also incomplete, which it shows without reflecting. The literary work gives the measure of a difference, reveals a determinate absence, resorts to an eloquent silence.

As Lenin has demonstrated in relation to Tolstoy, and as we shall try to show in relation to Jules Verne and Balzac, what begs to be explained in the work is not that false simplicity which derives from the apparent unity of its meaning, but the presence of a relation, or an opposition, between elements of the exposition or levels of the composition, those disparities which point to a conflict of meaning. This conflict is not the sign of an imperfection; it reveals the inscription of an *otherness* in the work, through which it maintains a relationship with that which it is not, that which happens at its margins. To explain the work is to show that, contrary to appearances, it is not independent, but bears in its material substance the imprint of a determinate absence which is also the principle of its identity. The book is furrowed by the allusive presence of those other books against which it is elaborated; it circles about the absence of that which it cannot say, haunted by the absence of certain repressed words which make their return. The book is not the extension of a meaning; it is generated from the incompatibility of several meanings, the strongest bond by which it is attached to reality, in a tense and ever-renewed confrontation.

In seeing how the book is made we see also what it is made *from*: this defect which gives it a history and a relation to the historical.

But we must beware of substituting an ideology of explanation for an ideology of interpretation. And for this reason we must eliminate a certain number of assumptions which imply a theoretical misconception of the literary work. Some of these assumptions have already been pointed out: the postulate of beauty (the work conforms to a model), the postulate of innocence (the work is self-sufficient, its discourse abolishes even the memory of that which it is not), the postulate of harmony or totality (the work is perfect, completed, it constitutes a finished entity). To these must be added others, for though they may sometimes contradict those already mentioned, they do not, for all that, produce a theoretical knowledge: the postulate of openness, and the postulate of depth.

Under the pretence of identifying the theoretical incompleteness of the work, we must not fall into an ideology of the 'open text' (cf. Umberto Eco, *L'opera aperta*, Milan, Bompiani, 1962): by the artifice of its composition, the work constitutes the principle of its indefinite variation. It has not one meaning but many: though this possible indefinite multiplicity, a quality or effect accomplished by the reader, has nothing to do with that real complexity, necessarily finite, which is the structure of the book. If the work does not produce or contain the principle of its own closure, it is nevertheless definitively enclosed within its own limits (though they may not be self-appointed limits). The work is finite because it is incomplete.

At the same time, to double the line of the text with the ghostly relief (sculptural) that its incompleteness projects, can be to show another work behind the work, a kind of secret which it masks or translates: and so we fall back into the interpretive fallacy. This last temptation is based on the *postulate of depth*, which has been the principle inspiration of all traditional criticism.

Chapter 14

Implicit and Explicit

> In order to ascertain their real opinions, I ought to take cognisance of what they practised rather than of what they said, not only because, in the corruption of our manners, there are few disposed to speak exactly as they believe, but also because very many are not aware of what it is that they really believe, for as the act of mind by which a thing is believed is different from that by which we know we believe it, the one act is often found without the other. (Descartes, *Discourse on Method*, III)

For there to be a critical discourse which is more than a superficial and futile *reprise* of the work, the speech stored in the book must be incomplete; because it has not said everything, there remains the possibility of saying something else, *after another fashion*. The recognition of the area of shadow in or around the work is the initial moment of criticism. But we must examine the nature of this shadow: does it denote a true absence, or is it the extension of a half-presence? This can be reformulated in terms of a previous question: Will it be the pillar of an explanation or the pretext for an interpretation?

Initially, we will be inclined to say that criticism, in relation to its object, is its *explication*. What, then, is involved in making-explicit? Explicit is to implicit as explication is to implication: these oppositions derive from the distinction between the manifest and the latent, the discovered and the concealed. That which is formally accounted for, expressed, and even concluded, is explicit: the 'explicit' at the end of a book echoes the 'incipit' at the beginning, and indicates that 'all is (has been) said'. To explicate comes from *explicare*: to display and unfold. 'Spread eagle', a heraldic term: one with wings outstretched. And thus the critic, opening the book – whether he intends to find buried treasure there, or whether he wants to see it flying with its own wings – means to give it a different status, or even a different appearance. It might be said that the aim of criticism is to *speak the truth*, a truth not unrelated to the book, but not as the content of its expression. In the book, then, not everything is said, and for everything to be said we must await the critical 'explicit', which may actually be interminable. Nevertheless, although the critical discourse is not spoken by the book, it is in some way the property of the book, constantly alluded to, though never announced openly. What is this silence – an accidental hesitation, or a statutory necessity? Whence the problem: are there books which say what they mean, without being critical books, that is to say, without *depending directly* on other books?

Here we recognise the classic problem of the interpretation of latent meaning. But, in this new instance, the problem tends to take a new form: in fact, the language of the book claims to be a language complete in itself, the source and measure of all 'diction'. The conclusion is inscribed even in its initial moments. Unwinding *within a closed circle*, this language reveals only . . . itself; it has only its *own* content and its *own* limits, and the 'explicit' is imprinted on each of these terms. Yet it is not perfect: under close scrutiny the speech inscribed by the book appears interminable; but it takes this absence of a conclusion as its ending. In the space in which the work unfolds, everything is to be said, and is therefore never said, but this does not suffer being altered by any other discourse, enclosed as it is within the definitive limits which constitute its imperfection. This seems to be the origin of criticism's inability to add anything to the discourse of the work: at most, it might extend the work – either in a reduction or in a pursuit of its discourse.

Yet it remains obvious that although the work is self-sufficient it does not contain or engender its own theory; it does not *know* itself. When the critic speaks he is not repeating, reproducing or remaking it; neither is he illuminating its dark corners, filling its margins with annotation, specifying that which was never specific. When the critical discourse begins from the hypothesis that the work speaks falteringly, it is not with the aim of *completing* it, reducing its deficiencies, as though the book were too small for the space it occupied. We have seen that a knowledge of the work is not elaborated within the work, but supposes a distance between knowledge and its object; to know what the writer is saying, it is not enough to *let him speak*, for his speech is hollow and can never be completed at its own level. Theoretical inquiry rejects the notion of the *space* or *site* of the work. Critical discourse does not attempt to complete the book, for theory begins from that incompleteness which is so radical that it cannot be located.

Thus, the silence of the book is not a lack to be remedied, an inadequacy to be made up for. It is not a temporary silence that could be finally abolished. We must distinguish the necessity of this silence. For example, it can be shown that it is the juxtaposition and conflict of several meanings which produces the radical otherness which shapes the work: this conflict it not resolved or absorbed, but simply *displayed*.

Thus the work cannot speak of the more or less complex opposition which structures it; though it is its expression and embodiment. In its every particle, the work *manifests*, uncovers, what it cannot say. This silence gives it life.

Chapter 15

The Spoken and the Unspoken

The speech of the book comes from a certain silence, a matter which it endows with form, a ground on which it traces a figure. Thus, the book is not self-sufficient; it is necessarily accompanied by a *certain absence*, without which it would not exist. A knowledge of the book must include a consideration of this absence.

This is why it seems useful and legitimate to ask of every production what it tacitly implies, what it does not say. Either all around or in its wake the explicit requires the implicit: for in order to say anything, there are other things *which must not be said*. Freud relegated this *absence of certain words* to a new place which he was the first to explore, and which he paradoxically *named*: the unconscious. To reach utterance, all speech envelops itself in the unspoken. We must ask why it does not speak of this interdict: can it be identified before one might wish to acknowledge it? There is not even the slightest hint of the absence of what it does not, perhaps cannot, say: the disavowal (*dénégation*) extends even to the act that banished the forbidden term; its absence is unacknowledged.

This moment of absence founds the speech of the work. Silences shape all speech. Banality?

Can we say that this silence is hidden? What is it? A condition of existence – point of departure, methodical beginning – essential foundation – ideal culmination – absolute origin which lends meaning to the endeavour? Means or form of connection?

Can we make this silence speak? What is the unspoken saying? What does it mean? To what extent is dissimulation a way of speaking? Can something that has hidden *itself* be recalled to our presence? Silence as the source of expression. Is what I am really saying what I am not saying? Hence the main risk run by those who would say everything. After all, perhaps the work is not hiding what it does not say; this is simply *missing*.

Yet the unspoken has many other resources: it assigns speech to its exact position, designating its domain. By speech, silence becomes the centre and principle of expression, its vanishing point. Speech eventually has nothing more to tell us: we investigate the silence, for it is the silence that is doing the speaking.

Silence reveals speech – unless it is speech that reveals the silence.

These two methods of explanation by recourse to the latent or concealed are not equivalent: it is the second which allows least value to the latent, since there appears an absence of speech through the absent speech, that is to say, a certain presence which it is enough to extricate. There is agreement to relate speech to its contrary, figure and ground. But there is a reluctance to leave these terms in equilibrium, an urge to resolve them: figure or ground? Here, once again, we encounter all the ambiguities of the notions of origin and creation. The unacknowledged co-existence of the visible and the hidden: the visible is merely the hidden in a different guise. The problem is merely to *pass across* from the one to the other.

The first image is the more profound, in so far as it enables us to recuperate the form of the second without becoming trapped in a mechanical problematic of transition: in being a necessary medium of expression, this ground of silence does not lose its significance. It is not the sole meaning, but that which endows meaning with a meaning: it is this silence which tells us – not just anything, since it exists to say nothing – which informs us of the precise conditions for the appearance of an utterance, and thus its limits, giving its real significance, without, for all that, speaking in its place. The latent is an intermediate means: this does not amount to pushing it into the background; it simply means that the latent is not another meaning which ultimately and miraculously *dispels* the first (manifest) meaning. Thus, we can see that meaning is in the *relation* between the implicit and the explicit, not on one or the other side of that fence: for in the latter case, we should be obliged to choose, in other words, as ever, translation or commentary.

What is important in the work is what it does not say. This is not the same as the careless notation 'what it refuses to say', although that would in itself be interesting: a method might be built on it, with the task of *measuring silences*, whether acknowledged or unacknowledged. But rather than this, what the work *cannot say* is important, because there the elaboration of the utterance is acted out, in a sort of journey to silence.

The basic issue, then, is to know whether we can examine that absence of speech which is the prior condition of all speech.

> Insidious Questions: When we are confronted with any manifestation which someone has permitted us to see, we may ask: what is it meant to conceal? What is it meant to draw our attention from? What prejudice does it seek to raise? and again, how far does the subtlety of the dissimulation go? and in what respect is the man mistaken? (*The Dawn of Day*, section 523)

For Nietzsche, these are insidious questions, *Hinterfrage*, questions which come from behind, held in reserve, lying in wait, snares.

'It might be asked': thus Nietzsche inquires, and even before showing how to put questions, he points out the necessity of *asking* questions; for there are several. The object or target of these questions is 'all that a man allows to appear'. Everything: that is to say that the Nietzschean interrogation – which is the precise opposite of an examination, since, as we shall see, it reaches the point of calling itself into question – is of such theoretical generality that we may wonder if it is legitimate to apply it to the specific domain of literary production. What in fact 'becomes visible' is the work, all the works. We shall try to apply this general proposition to a specific domain.

'All that a man allows to appear': obviously the German words say more than the English. *Lassen*: this is both to do, to allow, and to oblige. This word, better than any other, designates the act of literary production. It reveals it – on condition that we do not search there for the shapes of some evocative magic: inspiration, visitation or creation. Production: to show and to reveal. The question 'What does he mean?' proves that it is not a matter of dispossession. Also 'to reveal' is an affirmation rather than a decision: the expression of an active force, which yet does not exclude a certain autonomous actualisation of the visible.

Interrogation penetrates certain actions: 'hiding', 'diverting attention', and, further on, 'cheating'. Obviously, linking all these, there is a single impulse: 'hiding' is to keep from sight; 'diverting attention' is to show without being seen, to prevent what is visible from being seen; which also expresses the image of 'dissimulation': to dissimulate requires action. Therefore everything happens as though the accent had been shifted: the work is revealed to itself and to others on two different levels: it makes visible, and it makes invisible. Not because something has to be hidden in order to show something else; but because attention is diverted from the very thing which is shown. This is the superposition of utterance and statement (*du parler et du dire*): if the author does not always say what he states, he does not necessarily state what he says.

In the text from Nietzsche, then, it is a question of a prejudice, a mystification, a deception. Not by virtue of this or that particular word, but because of speech itself, all speech. A prejudice is that which is not judged in language but before it, but which is nevertheless offered as a judgment. Prejudice, the pseudo-judgment, is the utterance which remains imperceptibly beyond language.

Yet this proposition has two meanings: speech evokes a prejudice as a judgment; but equally, by the *fact of evocation*, it holds it up as a prejudice. It creates an allegory of judgment. And speech exists because it wishes for this allegory whose appearance it prepares for. This is the portion of the visible and the invisible, the revealed and the concealed, of language and silence.

Then we arrive at the meaning of the last questions. '*And yet*': we move to a new level of the systematic order, in what is almost an inversion. It could be said that there is a question directed at the first questions. This question which completes the construction of the trap challenges the first question, setting off the structure of the work and the structure of the criticism of it.

utterance
question 1 } question 2

We can then ask to what extent the first question was based on an error: because this dissimulation applies to everything it must not be thought that it is total and unlimited. Since it is a relative silence which depends on an even more silent margin, it is impossible to dissemble the truth of language.

Naturally it is incorrect to see in this equivocation of speech its division into the spoken and the unspoken; a division which is only possible because it makes speech depend on a fundamental veracity, a plenitude of expression, a reflection of the Hegelian dialectic – that dialectic which Nietzsche (like Marx, an enemy of idols) could only contemplate in its inverted form. If it is insisted that we find references to these questions in poetic form, we would do better to take them from the work of Spinoza. The transition from dissimulation to error, with the essential moment of 'and yet', is also the movement to the third kind of knowledge. In a famous book, Spinoza has posed Nietzsche's questions, posed them concerning Scripture, which could once have seemed to be the model of all books.

So the real trap of language is its tacit positiveness which makes it into a truly active insistence: the error belongs as much with the one who reveals it as it does with the one who asks the first questions, the critic.

The ordinary critic (the one who stops at the first question) and the author are equally remote from a true appreciation of the work: but there is another kind of critic who asks the second question.

The labyrinth of the two questions – a labyrinth in reverse, because it leads to a way out – endlessly proposes a choice between a false and a true subtlety: the one views the author from the critic's point of view, as a critic; the other only judges him when it has taken up position in the expressive veracity of language, and his language. Torn from the false limits of its empirical presence, the work then begins to acquire a significance.

Chapter 16

The Two Questions

Thus the critical task is not simple: it necessarily implies the superposition of two questions. To know the work, we must move outside it. Then, in the second moment, we question the work in its alleged plenitude; not from a different point of view, a different side – by translating it into a different language, or by applying a different standard – but not entirely from within, from what it says and asserts that it says. Conjecturally, the work has its *margins*, an area of incompleteness from which we can observe its birth and its production.

The critical problem will be in the conjunction of the two questions; not in a choice between them, but in the point from which they appear to become differentiated. The complexity of the critical problem will be the articulation between the two questions. To grasp this *articulation* is to accept a discontinuity, to establish a discontinuity: the questions are not spontaneously given in their specificity. Initially, the questions must be asked – asked simultaneously, in a way that amounts to allowing them an equal status.

The recognition of this simultaneity, which precludes any notion of priority, is fundamental because it makes possible – from the beginning – an exorcism of the ghosts of aesthetic legality: by the fact that the question which is supposed to inhabit the mind of the writer is not simple, but divided by its reference to another question, the problem to be explicitly resolved will not be merely the realisation of a project according to the rules of validity (beauty) and conformity (fidelity). Even the question of the formal limits imposed on expression will no longer form part of the problem: it will be completely eliminated as a distinct element of the problematic. In so far as a conscious intention to realise a project of writing begins inevitably by taking the form of an ideological imperative – something *to say* (not the acceptance of rules), in other words something that must not be said – it will have to adopt the conditions of the possibility of such an undertaking: the implements, the actual means of this practice; and the rules will play their part in so far as they are *directly* useful.

The real problem is not that of being restricted by rules – or the absence of such a restriction – but the necessity of inventing forms of expression, or merely finding them: not ideal forms, or forms derived from a principle which transcends the enterprise itself, but forms which can be used immediately as the means of expression for a determinate content; likewise, the question of the value of these forms cannot reach beyond this immediate issue. However, these forms do not exist just in the mode of an immediate presence: they can survive beyond the moment of their usefulness, and it will be seen that this poses a very serious problem; they can be revived, in which case they will have undergone a slight but crucial change in value which must be determined. In fact, these forms do not appear instantaneously but at the end of a long history – a history of the elaboration of ideological themes. The history of forms – which will subsequently be designated as *themes*, in the strict sense of the word – corresponds to the history of ideological themes; indeed, they are exactly parallel, as can easily be demonstrated with the history of any idea: that of Robinson Crusoe, for example. The form takes shape or changes in response to new imperatives of the idea: but it is also capable of independent transformations, or of an inertia, which bends the path of ideological history. But, whatever the mode of its realisation, there is always a correspondence, which could thus be considered automatic: refuting the conception of these two histories as the expression of a superficial question – which is not self-sufficient, because it is based on a parallelism – the question of the work. The level of interpretation determined by this parallelism will only acquire meaning from the elucidation of another level, with which it will have a determining relationship: the question of this question.

The investigation into the conditions of the possibility of the work is accomplished in the answer to an explicit question, but it will not be able to seek the conditions of those conditions, nor will it be able to see that this answer constitutes a question. Nevertheless, the second question will necessarily be posed within the first question, or even through it. It is this second question which, for us, defines the space of history: it reveals the work in so far as it entertains a specific but undisguised (which does not mean innocent) relation with history. We must show, through the study of an effort of expression, how it is possible to render visible the conditions of this effort – conditions of which it has no awareness, though this does not mean that it does not apprehend them: the work encounters the question of questions as an obstacle; it is only aware of the conditions which it adopts or utilises. We could account for this latent knowledge (which necessarily exists, since without it the work would be accomplished no further than if the explicit conditions were not realised) by recourse to *the unconscious of the work* (not of the author). But this unconscious does not perform as an understudy – on the contrary, it arises in the interior of the labour itself: there it is at work – nor as an extension of the explicit purpose, since it derives from a completely different principle. Neither is it a question of another consciousness: the consciousness of another or others, or the other consciousness of the same thing. There is no understudy creative-unconscious to the creative pseudo-consciousness: if there is an unconscious it cannot be creative, in so far as it precedes all production as its condition. It is a question of something other than consciousness: what we are seeking is analogous to that relationship which Marx acknowledges when he insists on seeing material relations as being derived from the social infrastructure behind all ideological phenomena, not in order to explain these phenomena as emanations from the infrastructure, which would amount to saying that the ideological is the economic in another form: whence the possibility of reducing the ideological to the economic.

For Marx and Engels, the study of an ideological phenomenon – that is to say, a conflict at the level of ideology – cannot be isolated from the movement at the economic level: not because it is a different conflict, a different form of the conflict, but because it is the conflict of this conflict. The composition of *an* ideology implies the relation of the ideological to the economic.

The problem of the work, if it exists, is now squarely posed in and by the work, but it is something altogether different from the awareness of a problem. This is why an authentic explanation must attend to several levels at once, though never failing to consider them separately, in their specificity:

1 The first question, properly interior to the work, in the sense of an intimacy, remains diffuse: indeed, it is there and not there, divided between several determinations which give it the status of a quasi-presence. Materially scattered, it must be reconstituted, recalled, recognised. But it would be incorrect to present this task as a deciphering: the secret is not hidden, and in any case *does not conceal itself*, does not resist this census which is a simple classification, changing at most its form; it loses nothing of its nature, its vividness, its mystery.

This first procedure is a question, if you will, of structures. But we have gone far beyond that formulation: to conclude with structures is merely to gather the scattered limbs. It would not be correct to believe that one had thus established a system. What system? In what relation to other systems? In what relation to that which is not part of the system?

2 Once the question has emerged from its half-light, we must find its meaning and its importance. It might be suggested: inscribe it in ideological history, the history which generates the succession of questions and the thread of problematics. But this inscription is not calculated by the simple situation of the question in relation to other questions, or by the presence of history outside this particular work, in so far as it gives it both its domain and its place. This history is not in a simple external relation to the work: it is present in the work, in so far as the emergence of the work required this history, which is its only principle of reality

and also supplies its means of expression. This history, which is not merely the history of works of the same nature, entirely determines the work: gives the work its reality, but also that which it is not, and this is the most important. To anticipate an example which will subsequently be analysed, if Jules Verne chose to be the spokesman of a certain ideological condition, he could not choose to be what he in fact became. He chose to be the spokesman for a certain condition; he expressed that choice. These are two different operations, the conjuncture of which constitutes a specific enterprise: in this case, the production of a certain number of books. These are the two 'choices'; the gap between them measures the absence within the work, but they cannot be judged by the same standards, because they are not of the same nature.

It must then be possible to examine a work from an accurate description which respects the specificity of this work, but which is more than just a new exposition of its content, in the form of a systematisation, for example. For as we quickly come to realise, we can only describe, only remain within the work, if we also decide to go beyond it: to bring out, for example, what the work is *compelled* to say in order to say what it *wants* to say, because not only would the work have wanted not to say it (which is another question), but certainly the work did not want to say it. Thus, it is not a question of introducing a historical explanation which is stuck on to the work from the outside. On the contrary, we must show a sort of splitting within the work: this division is *its* unconscious, in so far as it possesses one – the unconscious which is history, the play of history beyond its edges, encroaching on those edges: this is why it is possible to trace the path which leads from the haunted work to that which haunts it. Once again it is not a question of redoubling the work with an unconscious, but a question of revealing in the very gestures of expression that which it is not. Then, the reverse side of what is written will be history itself.

Moreover, we shall be looking within the work itself for reasons for moving beyond it: from the explicit question, and from the reply which it actually elicits – the form of the question being legible in this answer – we shall certainly be able to put the question of the question, and not the one apart from the other. This endeavour is full of surprises: we realise that in seeking the meaning of the work – not the meaning that it gives itself but the meaning that seizes hold of it – we have at our disposal, in turning to the work itself, material that is already prepared, already invested by the question which we are going to ask. The real resistances are elsewhere, in the reader we might say: but they do not hinder this unforseen inquiry, for the work – it is absurd to repeat this – does not say what it does not say. This is precisely the opposite of an interpretation or a commentary: an interpretation seeks *pretexts*, but the explanation proposed here finds its object wholly prepared and is content to give a true idea of it.

To take a specific example which will later be studied in detail: the 'problem' of Jules Verne breaks down into *two questions*. The important thing is that this dissociation itself remains *within* the problem, that the coherence of the problem should survive: we shall not, for example, be trying to find two Jules Vernes, or to establish a preference for a particular Jules Verne at the expense of all the other possible Jules Vernes. This problem, because it concerns a literary object, is crystallised in what we can call a theme, which is, in its abstract form, the conquest of nature; in the ideological realisation which gives it the form of a *motif*: the voyage, or Robinson Crusoe (a veritable ideological obsession with Verne, and present in all his books, even if only as an allusion). This theme can be studied at two different levels:

1 The utilisation of the theme: initially the adventures of its form, which moreover contain (even though the collocation of the words is casual) the form of the adventure. This raises the question of the writer at work.
2 The meaning of the theme: not a meaning which exists independently of the work, but the meaning that the theme actually acquires within the work.

First question: the work originates in a secret to be *explained.* Second question: the work is realised in the revelation of its secret. The simultaneity of the two questions defines a minute rupture, minutely distinct from a continuity. It is this rupture which must be studied.

Chapter 17

Interior and Exterior

We have until now said a great deal about what was happening *within* the work, and we have also talked about the limits of the work: perhaps we have thus fallen back into the spatial metaphors which were previously denounced.

It must be specified that the limit is not a medium, a place of transitions, of communication between an interior and an exterior, or of a chronological change between a before and an after (the work in itself, and then the work for others): this limit is not a separation, the promontory where an independence is established, but the possibility of an autonomy.

This point is very important because it prevents us from falling into an empiricist ideology of interiority: if the work encloses the warm intimacy of its secrets, composes its elements into a totality which is sufficient, completed and centred, then all criticism is immanent.

We must do away with these images of critical reverie, and realise that the work has no interior, no exterior; or rather, its interior is like an exterior, shattered and on display. Thus it is open to the searching gaze, peeled, disembowelled. It shows what it does not say by a sign which cannot be *heard* but must be *seen*. Allegorically, criticism uses ears and eyes: the inaudible must not escape the gaze. Once again, it seems that the work is addressed to the knowing reader rather than the *ingénu*.

In particular, it must be realised that the work is not like an interior which is wholly congruent with an exterior: such an assumption is responsible for all the errors of casual explanation.

This enables us to resolve very easily the questions of *separable ideological statements* (*énoncés idéologiques séparables*) which are present in the work, although they appear to belong to a different level of statement. (The above expression is borrowed from A. Badiou; on this issue see the study of Balzac in Part III.)

Chapter 18

Depth and Complexity

By means of its stubborn linearity the discourse of the work establishes a certain form of necessity: it advances ineluctably within its appointed limits. The line of the discourse only seems to be fragile: it cannot be interrupted, or changed, or allied with another discourse from which it might receive that *quality* which it seems to lack. The text is established in its systematic thinness. Unless we espouse the normative fallacy, there is nothing to be added, nothing to be corrected in the book as it presents itself.

But it is not a question of approaching the text in an attitude of blind obedience. It must be seen precisely as it is: the conformity of a mechanical fidelity will no longer suffice. It is indeed easy to find it *deep*, like an enigma or mask behind which lurks some haunting presence; this is but one more way of representing the text as a smooth and decorative surface, deceptive in its perfection. If we pose the problem in these terms, a knowledge of the work will involve tearing off the mask, or deducing its necessity: showing that it is the discourse itself which is perverted by the writing – definitively showing and masking, exposing and concealing, itself or another.

Yet this idea of a hidden truth or meaning remains unproductive and misleading: in the proposed exchange between depth and surface there is ultimately just an abstract inversion which disturbs the terms of the problem while leaving the problem unchanged. It appears then that the discourse of the work, in its transparent facticity, says the same thing differently. To consider the work in terms of an opposition between appearance and reality is to invert the normative fallacy, only to fall into the interpretive fallacy: to replace the apparent line of the text by a true line which would find itself placed behind the first. We thus establish an image of the space of the text (this is the space in which that exchange is transacted), of a depth. But this new dimension only repeats the previous one; this depth is the product of a doubling which is ideologically fertile but theoretically sterile, since it places the work *in perspective* but tells us nothing of its determinations.

But the book is not like a form which so simply hides a depth. The book hides nothing, has no secret: it is entirely *readable*, visible, entrusted. But this is not an easy gift, to receive spontaneously. Loquacious with an obstinate silence, the work is not immediately accessible: it cannot say everything at once; its scattered discourse is its only means of uniting and gathering what it has to say. As we have seen, the line of the text can be traversed in more than one direction; its beginning and its end are inextricably mingled. Besides, contrary to first impressions, this line is not simple, but reflects a real diversity. By its very nature the literary work cannot say one thing at a time; for it says at least two things which accompany each other and become entangled, though we must not confuse them. Its form, then, is complex; the line of its discourse is thickened by reminiscences, alterations, revivals and absences; and likewise the object of this discourse is multiple, a thousand separate, hostile and discontinuous realities. This discourse, far from saying or not saying one thing which would be its secret, breaks free from itself, no longer possesses itself, strained as it is between all these opposed determinations.

We must examine the work in its real complexity rather than in its mythical depth. Constrained by its essential diversity, the work, in order to say one thing, has at the same time to say another thing which is not necessarily of the same nature; it unites in a single text several different lines which cannot be apportioned; it is not a question of analysing a necessary sequence but of showing its combination. What the work says is not one or other of these lines, but their difference, their contrast, the hollow which separates and unites them.

This can be seen with an elementary example. Stylistics identifies certain of the problems which a writer must resolve when he is faced with certain particular and decisive choices: between the past definite and the perfect tense, between first- and third-person narration, to mention only the simplest examples. These choices can be explained: but before they can be accounted for they have to be effected. Now the activity of the writer is not solely or directly governed by the laws of stylistics, defined in themselves: on the contrary, it is his activity that determines these laws. The writer is not someone who 'practises stylistics', consciously or unconsciously: his work does not have the status of a strict application. He encounters certain specific problems which he solves as he writes, and these problems, and the solutions which actually constitute them, are never simple, unlike those of stylistics. The writer is constantly obliged to solve several problems at once, at different levels, and each choice affects all the others. Interpretation simply offers a reductive explanation by identifying just one of these choices: this is the simple procedure that Sartre applied to Camus' *L'Etranger* (The Outsider) (see 'Explication de *L'Etranger*,' *Situations I*, Paris, Gallimard, 1947). A true explanation always bears on a composite reality where several determinations converge; it fits together the consequences of laws pertaining to different areas of the reality. This is why we always find gaps and contradictions in the fabric of the work. The movement of the text is systematic, but its system is not simple and complete.

One of the essential reasons for this complexity is that the work never 'arrives unaccompanied'; it is always determined by the existence of other works, which can belong to different areas of production. There is no first book, independent and absolutely innocent: novelty and originality, in literature as in other fields, are always defined by relationships. Thus the book is always the site of an exchange: its autonomy and its coherence are bought at the price of that otherness, which can also be, on occasion, an alteration.

A true reading, one which knows how to read and knows what reading is, ignores none of this multiplicity. Above all it involves

– beyond an enumeration of constitutive elements – an awareness of a harmony or unity, so many deformations and idealisations, the *reason* of its process. It is not a question of perceiving a latent structure of which the manifest work is an index, but of establishing that absence around which a real complexity is knit. Then, perhaps, can be exorcised the fallacies which have bound literary criticism to ideology: the fallacy of the secret, the fallacy of depth, the fallacy of rules, the fallacy of harmony. Decentred, displayed, determinate, complex: recognised as such, the work runs the risk of receiving its theory.

June 1966

II

Some Critics

Chapter 19

Lenin, Critic of Tolstoy

Marx and Engels showed a continuous interest in literary and artistic production, but although there are many allusions and examples in their work, neither of them devoted any extended study to the problems of art. Though they might mention them or study them in passing (Eugène Sue in *The Holy Family*), and even lay the foundations for theoretical thinking (Introduction to *A Contribution to the Critique of Political Economy*), they never developed a method. They showed a constant interest in the subject, without ever dealing with it in its own terms. So that even at the beginning of this century there was still no systematic Marxist aesthetics, apart from the work of Plekhanov, and Lafargue's essays on art and social life.

We do know that there might almost have been such a work, for Marx decided to devote himself to a study of Balzac once *Capital* was completed. Marx and Engels were well informed of new and important literary developments, but they never made anything of this knowledge, because they never had the time. They had to expend all their theoretical energies on the scientific elaboration of the principles of the struggle of the proletariat. The world of literature is related to these preoccupations, but only indirectly; thus it had to be provisionally sacrificed.

This is why Lenin's writings on Tolstoy, which date from the final years of that writer's life, constitute an exceptional work in the history of scientific Marxism. It was that first, rare occasion on which a political leader and a scientific theorist dealt comprehensively with a specific literary problem. Of course, this was not an entire book in which a problem could be thoroughly developed (as in, say, *Materialism and Empirio-Criticism*, which deals with scientific method). They were, rather, a series of occasional articles, written between 1908 and 1911, dealing with different aspects of the same question, under the title *Leo Tolstoy: Mirror of Russian Literature*. They are not an organised sequence dealing with the successive elements of a problem, but their form is both arbitrary and necessary since they constitute the *reprise* of a single theme. Thus all six pieces must be read together.*

I propose to study them as a single text, disregarding their actual chronology. A different approach would certainly reveal a great deal about the development of Lenin's political thought during those three years, but it would ultimately tell us little about Tolstoy himself. We need only observe that the first article (1908) emphasises the contemporary relevance of Tolstoy's work, while the last one (1911) insists on the fact that the Tolstoy era has already passed.

The most obvious characteristic of these texts is that they are the product of a political rather than a literary or a theoretical enterprise. The series reflects Lenin's activities during the period 1908–11, and it is closely associated with his political thinking. During this period of the genesis of Leninist aesthetics (after the 1905 revolution) Lenin was attempting to reshape the Social Democratic Party to the new conditions experienced in the aftermath of 1905. Thus the immediate theoretical task was to define the significance of the events of 1905.

It had been a turning point in the history of the party, the end of an era which had to be retrospectively defined. Between 1905 and 1910 Lenin gave himself to a theoretical meditation on the period of bourgeois democracy, which had begun in 1861 and had ended with the 'peasant' revolution of 1905. This was not, for Lenin, a digression, but a pressing political task on which depended the formulation of new objectives adapted to the new historical period. It was in seeking to demonstrate the positive significance of the defeat of the 'peasant' revolution that Lenin

* Lenin's articles on Tolstoy are reprinted in an Appendix, pp. 299–323 ff.

encountered Tolstoy. He wanted to show the historical and ideological nature of Tolstoy's work in the context of its period, to show in what sense that work deserved the title 'Mirror of the Russian Revolution' (the 1905 revolution, of course). Thus Lenin's contribution to Marxist aesthetics was intimately connected with the elaboration of a scientific socialism. The literary articles were to play their part in this larger enterprise. In certain determinate circumstances, then, Lenin discovered a novel function for literary criticism within a general theoretical activity. To write on Tolstoy's novels was neither a distraction nor a digression. It was not simply a question of paying homage to a great man, but of allotting a true role to literary production at the moment of its potency. Aesthetic and political theory were closely linked, for Lenin's reflections on Tolstoy were to have practical consequences:

> I frequently heard Vladimir Ilich say that we ought to make a careful study of Tolstoy, and in addition to the complete works we should edit many of his stories, articles and extracts in pamphlets and small booklets, distributing hundreds of thousands of copies everywhere among the peasants and workers. (Bontch-Brouévitch, quoted in Lenin, *On Literature and Art*, Moscow, Progress Publishers, 1967)

This project takes on its full significance in relation to the idea of a cultural policy (rather than a cultural administration), which was to become ever more central in Lenin's thinking. Here we have the first real example of a committed criticism, an example which deserves the title 'The Mirror of Criticism'.

The general principle of Lenin's critical method is that the literary work only makes sense if considered in its relation to a determinate historical period. It derives its distinctive characteristics from this period, but it can also be used to illuminate the period (see, in *On Literature and Art*, the note on the populist writer Engelhardt: a scientific study of the economy can draw on the evidence of literary works). Thus there is a necessary relationship between the literary work and history, a relationship which is reciprocal even in its initial moments.

The historical interpretation of literature now takes on a very precise sense: the historical period to which the work corresponds is to be circumscribed, that is to say limited, thus generating two orders of coherence, two unities, the one literary and the other historical. It must not be thought that the problem is resolved by taking that period which coincides with the life of the author, or even the period during which he was actually writing. For even in this case it would remain essential to construe this period, and to show that it comprises a historical unity, determined by specific convergences. However, the content of a literary work does not necessarily correspond to the historical lifetime of its author. Its relationship to historical reality cannot be reduced to the 'spontaneous' or the 'simultaneous'. Some writers are involved with the secondary or anachronistic tendencies of their time. Generally, the writer is behind the times, if only because he invariably speaks after the event. The more he is involved with the materially immediate, the more difficulty he experiences in writing. Thus the question of the writer's historical affinities is far from simple. But it is precisely this issue which scientific criticism must deal with methodically.

A large portion of Lenin's articles are devoted to this problem. The Tolstoy era stretches from the reforms of 1861 to the revolution of 1905:

> Belonging, as he did, primarily to the era of 1861–1904, Tolstoy in his works – both as an artist and as a thinker and preacher – embodied in amazingly bold relief the specific historical features of the entire first Russian revolution. (Ibid., p. 49; see Appendix below, p. 305)

> The epoch to which Leo Tolstoy belongs and which is reflected in such bold relief in his brilliant literary works and in his teachings began after 1861 and lasted until 1905. (Ibid., p. 58; see Appendix below, p. 309)

The qualification 'primarily' is significant. It reminds us that Tolstoy's relationship to 'his' age is in no sense immediate, but must be precisely determined. This age, which corresponds to a great period of Russian history, is complex. Its particular characteristics result from the combination of diverse influences, so that this history can be described on four different levels.

Though the reforms of 1861 marked the formal end of the feudal period, many of the essential features of the feudal economy were to be long preserved. The dominant position of the landowning aristocracy in the rural areas was reinforced – or at least prolonged – by the reforms. They retained control of the state, for its structure was as yet untransformed. With the survival of serfdom and the feudal state, Russia remained, even after 1861, 'rural Russia of the landlord' (ibid., p. 48; see Appendix below, p. 304).

However, this solidity of the economic and political structure was a precarious illusion, already disintegrating. For if we emphasise the passing of the old and the establishment of the new, the period 1861–1905 can also be described as that of the decline of the old patriarchal Russia. The collapse of an entire economic, social and political system, manifested in the much-noticed migration to the towns, corresponds to an accelerating development of capitalism. By means of this revolution bourgeois Russia was establishing itself.

But the most significant feature of political life was peasant protest: a revolt against both the relics of feudalism and the growth of capitalism. This movement, so inadequate and confused achieved temporary successes, but only as it was managed by the bourgeoisie in their own interests, to destroy the remnants of feudalism. Specifically, it borrowed its ideological means from the bourgeoisie: it was to be a populist adventure. The Russian peasant entered history only in an inevitably temporary alliance based on blind compromise. This contradictory ideology, moving constantly between protest and acquiescence, culminated in the abortive revolution of 1905, which, as Lenin observed, was the logical fulfilment of the history of the countryside. This collaboration between the peasants and the interests of capitalism lends the whole epoch its merely transitional character. As early as 1905, in 'Party Organisation and Party Literature', Lenin wrote: 'The revolution is not yet completed. While Tsarism is no longer strong enough to defeat the revolution, the revolution is not yet strong enough to defeat Tsarism' (in ibid., p. 23). This movement from 'not yet' to 'no longer', which could describe the peasant structure of this period, is found everywhere in Lenin's description: 'in the *post*-Reform, but *pre*-revolutionary era' (ibid., p. 50; see Appendix below, p. 307). Or again, 'that multitudinous mass of the Russian people who *already* detest the masters of modern life but have not *yet* advanced to the point of intelligent . . . struggle' (ibid., p. 56; see Appendix below, p. 316).

The revolution of 1905, 'the great Russian revolution', which was to be a peasant revolution, retained this intermediate and provisional quality. It was Lenin's explanation of this fact which demonstrated its positive significance.

However, these explanations are inadequate because they neglect a fourth term which only makes its appearance at the close of this period and dominates the following one: the proletariat. Events between 1861 and 1905, in both feudal, bourgeois and peasant Russia, derive their real meaning from the fact that this is the moment of the emergence of the working class and its party, both consequences of the disruption of the rural areas by the development of capitalism:

> This was fully confirmed by the revolution of 1905: on the one hand, the proletariat came out quite independently at the head of the revolutionary struggle, having founded the Social Democratic Labour Party. (Ibid., p. 66)

> The period of 1862–1904 was just such a period of upheaval in Russia, a period in which before everyone's eyes the old order collapsed, never to be restored, in which the new system was only just taking shape; the social forces shaping the new system first manifested themselves on a broad, nation-wide scale, in mass public action in the most varied fields only in 1905. (Ibid., p. 60; see Appendix below, p. 311)

Though still outwardly feudal, Russia was being transformed into a bourgeois state. The peasant revolution was to culminate in a workers' revolution. The year 1905 marks the moment at which the working class assumes a leading role; this year signifies the end of a historical period, and also the end of the Tolstoy era.

In a scientific analysis of the period we are obliged to take all these elements into account. The first task is to identify them clearly; above all, they must not be confused with one another. If the interests of the various classes are mistakenly identified, any explanation will be falsified, any political action condemned to failure. These four terms which correspond to the interests of four different classes are quite distinct. The difficulty arises because they are all equally important in their respective domains. It is equally true to claim that the leading role in this period is being played by all of them: the landed aristocracy, who still hold political power; the bourgeoisie, who possess the decisive economic strength; the peasant masses, who lead the movement of social protest; the working class, which is just beginning to organise itself. According to the chosen emphasis we can construct very diverse descriptions of the period, and this diversity is apparent in the pictures of life offered by the Russian literature of the time. Schematically, Dostoyevsky gives us the feudal Russia, Chekhov portrays the rise of the bourgeoisie, Tolstoy depicts the peasant, and Gorky describes the beginnings of the urban proletariat. Obviously, any authentically scientific analysis must give equal consideration to all these aspects, establishing between them relationships rather than priorities.

Thus it is only a rhetorical convention to speak of a feudal, a bourgeois or a peasant Russia. To characterise the unity of the period we must demonstrate the relationship and combination of these indissoluble elements, and show them in their interdependence rather than in isolation.

There is an overt conflict between the peasant masses and the landed aristocracy, and also between the working class and the capitalist bourgeoisie. Paradoxically there is a contradiction between these two conflicts, for they cannot be resolved in isolation, but are, on the contrary, obliged to act through intermediaries. The peasants have to borrow the instruments of their struggle from the bourgeoisie, and the proletariat can triumph only in an alliance with the peasantry. The latter are innocently compelled by their historical situation to play a double game: in adopting the bourgeois forms of political protest they are aligned objectively with the bourgeoisie:

> This mass, consisting mainly of the peasantry, showed in the revolution how great was its hatred of the old, how keenly it felt all the inflictions of the modern regime, how great within it was the spontaneous yearning to be rid of them and to find a better life. (Ibid., p. 56; see Appendix below, p. 316)

> This was fully proved by the revolution of 1905. . . . on the other hand, the revolutionary peasants (the Trudoviks and the Peasant Union), who fought for the abolition of every form of landlordism even to 'the abolition of private landownership', fought precisely as proprietors, as small entrepreneurs. (Ibid., p. 66)

Thus the situation of the peasants – as well as their state of mind – is contradictory. At the moment of open conflict they find themselves among the ranks of the bourgeoisie, although their struggle against property is also inevitably a struggle against capitalism. The era is characterised, then, not by real conflicts but by a fundamental collusion which depends on a latent contradiction (economic, political and ideological). The global structure of the period could be articulated around this major contradiction (though it is not the only contradiction, nor is it the most general form of the contradiction).

The culmination of this period, the revolution of 1905, reveals the provisional character of this structure. It also demonstrates that the struggle against feudalism and that against capitalism can only be won if they are waged together under new forms of organisation (i.e. the Social Democratic Party, which only now shows that it is capable of leadership). On a single front – the working class aligning itself with the peasant masses – the political struggle against the feudal state and the economic struggle against capitalist society can be waged together.

This analysis, although merely schematic, enables us to begin a study of Tolstoy and his work in relation to the determinate historical structure.

Obviously the works of Tolstoy do not *themselves* offer such an analysis. What they tell us of their time and what an analysis of that time can tell us are two different things. Tolstoy's relation to history may be obvious, but it is *not* spontaneous (except in terms of some false spontaneity). The relation remains somehow concealed. This does not mean that Tolstoy totally misunderstood his own age. He conveys a certain picture which is incomplete, though it is not *a priori* false. Lenin writes: 'Tolstoy gives us a particular point of view of history' (see ibid., p. 56).

This gives us a first glimpse of the *situation* of the writer. He is involved in the movement of his age, but involved in a way that inhibits him from giving us a complete account. He is unable to, for if he did he would cease to be a writer, he would become identified with a new relation to knowledge and history. The writer is not there to articulate the total structure of an epoch; he gives us, rather, an image, a unique and privileged glimpse. This privilege derives from his social position, as individual and as writer. The role of the writer, you might say, is to dramatise (*faire vivre*) the historical structure by narrating it. Though a point of view may be politically confused, it retains a certain literary value. After the revolution, in a jubilant article ('A Capably Written Little Book', 1921, in ibid., pp. 156–7), Lenin demonstrates, without overt irony, that there can be good reactionary writers. If Tolstoy is a better writer than Gorky, or vice versa, this will depend on purely literary reasons (this rather complex issue will be discussed later), not on the relation of literature to history. All that we can say is that Gorky's work belongs to the post-1905 period, and hence is more relevant to the readers of this period than that of Tolstoy. A writer's appeal depends on his conveying a certain knowledge of his age. (For example, Lenin praises the populist writers for their picture of life in the countryside.) But this knowledge is not necessarily identical with that of the reader, for the writer's position carries certain rights, notably the right to be in error.

This position must now be determined. The total historical structure, as already outlined, really determines Tolstoy's works only in so far as it enables us to take account of his particular point of view. Tolstoy's personal point of view is determined by his social origin: Count Tolstoy spontaneously represents the landed aristocracy. But as a writer, as the producer of a work and an ethic – two aspects which must be distinguished – he enjoys a certain social mobility: he has the status of a traveller. In his work, Tolstoy establishes a novel relationship to the history of his time by drawing on an ideology which is not 'naturally' his own, by looking to the peasant. His notions of Russian society after the Reform are not those of a landed aristocrat. Tolstoy elaborated a philosophy (call it Tolstoyism) which was in fact more appropriate to a different social class. According to Gorky, Lenin said, 'Before this Count there was no authentic *muzhik* in literature' (ibid., p. 246).

This count with the heart of a *muzhik* (the habits of thought of a *muzhik*, what Lenin called 'a peasant orientalism') is psychologically at the centre of the manifest conflict of his age by virtue of the ideas he espoused.

His doctrine, incomplete rather than contradictory, derives from this specific – though not strictly individual – relation to the social structure. Tolstoy incarnates his age, but with a peculiar emphasis, with all the deficiencies inherent in his viewpoint: he grasped that this age was one of turmoil, but he was unable to discern the principle behind all this disorder. Although he was aware of the consequences of the development of capitalism, a development which threatened the existence of count and *muzhik* alike, he was blind to the power of the bourgeoisie, which registers in his writings only as an indistinct threat. Neither did he grasp the establishment of the proletariat, the second development in the latent conflict. Tolstoy is present at history above all by his absences: the material development of power is obscured for him. A point of view is determined rather by what it conceals than by what it reveals. These limitations are as typical of the epoch as they are of the fundamental structure: there would be no point in knowing the relation of forces without also knowing how the specific forces are deployed in this relationship; all these points of contact (*engagements*) contribute to the definition of this relationship. The fragmentation of points of view, which determines the series of partial relations to the historical totality, begets specific ideologies: different in content, but all equally reactionary in form. (Even the ideology of the proletariat is subject to this condition until the moment of its scientific organisation within the programme of the Social

Democratic Party.) In short, a historical period does not spontaneously produce a single, monolithic ideology, but a series of ideologies determined by the total relation of forces; each ideology is shaped by the pressures upon the class which generates it.

By 'a reversal of his entire conception of the world' Tolstoy introduced the 'viewpoint of the naive patriarchal peasant' into literature. Though Tolstoy produced a unique, individual body of work, that work in fact reposes upon a doctrine which belongs to others. It is through them that Tolstoy's work is historically defined:

> an epoch that could give rise to Tolstoy's teachings and in which they were inevitable, not as something individual, not as a caprice or a fad, but as the ideology of the conditions of life under which millions and millions actually found themselves for a certain period of time. (Ibid., p. 60; see Appendix below, p. 312)

Tolstoy's relation to the history of his time is not directly determined by his individual position; this relation is oblique, mediated by a specific ideology, the common term through which the other two are connected. Between Tolstoy's work and the historical process which it 'reflects' (we can retain this term provisionally) there is the ideology of the peasant. It would be a serious mistake to regard 'Tolstoyism' as an original doctrine (which is exactly what the bourgeois critics did in 1910). The writer is only the apparent author of the ideology contained in his work; this ideology is in fact constituted independently of him. It is *encountered* in his work, just as he himself *encountered* it in life. Tolstoy's originality does not inhere in this ideology, for writers are not here to construct ideologies.

The literary work must be studied in a double perspective: in relation to history, and in relation to an ideological version of that history. It cannot be reduced to either one of these two terms. In fact, Tolstoy's work reveals both the contradictions of his age and the deficiencies involved in his partial view of those contradictions. Lenin means just this when he writes that Tolstoy's work reflects some of the conditions of its inception. This is why Lenin called Tolstoy 'the mirror of the Russian revolution'.

But this title only initiates the analysis. Tolstoy's works cannot, as we have seen, be reduced to the ideology which they contain; they are more than that. As well as the doctrine we must discriminate another term without which the work would not exist. And we must not, in the mystifying manner of bourgeois criticism, confuse these two terms. Ideology has no place in the text except as it is confronted by strictly literary means. We must pose the problem of realisation (*mise en forme*), which involves more than a mechanical translation (besides, translation requires an initial command of two languages, otherwise they could not be superimposed). To make novels, for example, out of ideological materials would imply a non-ideological definition of the novel. (Bourgeois criticism, particularly when it concerns itself with pure literature, with art for art's sake, uses what are actually ideological norms; and when it deals with partisan literature it performs a similar reduction to ideology.) If, as we have just seen, an ideology is always in some respect incomplete, perhaps literary forms can – in their way – complete it. The literary work can only be detached artificially from its ideological content – this is the first point of Lenin's demonstration; but this implies that it can in some manner be distinguished from this content. Lenin offers an idea of this distinction when he writes on Gleb Ouspensky: 'With his perfect knowledge of the peasantry (let us say, of peasant problems and of the peasant spirit) and his great artistic gift which reached the very heart of things'. It is this notion of the 'great artistic gift' which must now be elucidated.

But the distinction remains imprecise, even though the necessity for it has been demonstrated. The work contains its ideological content, not just in the propagation of a specific ideology but in the elaboration of a specific form. This form, the artist's 'gift', the criterion of artistic excellence, is embodied in a specific 'perception' of the historical process and of ideological motives. We might say that the great writer is one who offers a clear 'perception' of reality. But this idea of perception raises all kinds of problems. It is obviously not the same as a theoretical knowledge; the writer's version of reality cannot be confused with the scientific analysis which the Marxist party would give, simply because the writer uses his own special methods. His knowledge is implicit, blind to its own scope and origin. But if it can only be reconstituted from its remains, it can no longer be called a knowledge. Neither could it be termed an ideological knowledge (grasped and conveyed by means of an ideology) if we once define literature as the critique of ideologies. And even if the literary perception were to be considered as the analogy of a knowledge, as a certain *way* of knowing, the object of this knowledge would still remain to be established. Would it be the ideological perception of reality, or the reality itself? In the first case, literature would be merely the vehicle of information and of ideological materials; and in the second case, it could be no more than the receptacle of certain material data. For example, when he was seeking to define the uses to which the work of the populist writer Engelhardt ('the painter of rural life') might be put, Lenin insisted on the distinction between doctrine and data, between the angle of vision and the elements of the real as they might be rendered by a scrupulous observer. It is precisely because the doctrine is inadequate to the data that the structure of the work is contradictory. Once it had been stripped of all the elements borrowed from ideology, might not the intrinsic function of literature be to furnish perceptions distinct from the doctrine, perceptions upon which an authentic knowledge might be grounded?

> Not only would it be interesting and instructive to use the data and observations supplied by Engelhardt as the basis for a judgement of the rural situation, but it would also be a legitimate procedure for an economic investigator. If the scholars trust the evidence of the surveys which are often partial and inadequate, which lack a sound theoretical basis, why should we not have faith in those observations gathered over eleven years by a man with a remarkable gift and an absolute sincerity, one who is intimate with his subject. (Ibid., p. 78)

In making this suggestion, which inaugurates the scientific use of literary texts, Lenin goes beyond the writer to the scientific observer who is latent within the great artist. The text is rendered transparent, and its specifically literary realisation becomes 'a striking real meaning', 'a simple and direct means of depicting reality', and, he later says, 'a pitiless exposure'. But this is a strange notion, for precise observation is not necessarily pitiless; it is difficult to see how such observation could, in itself, become the object of a theoretical knowledge, how indeed it could be conveyed in a book.

If the text did furnish the components of a scientific knowledge, this would be because it disclosed certain spontaneous data which correspond immediately to the real. This would be an easy solution to the problem posed in the letter to Gorky of 1908: how can a literary work be 'correct' if it is based on incorrect doctrine? Because the ideological censor lets through a few memories of the real, against which it struggles. In this sense there could exist a reactionary realism (cf. ibid., pp. 156–7 on Averchenko); the ideological dream is infiltrated by the reality it seeks to repress. But this notion of the mechanical reproduction of reality contradicts the theory of knowledge that Lenin himself had expounded. This phantom of the real that supposedly haunts the text is itself a fantasy.

The text is not directly rooted in historical reality, but only through a complex sequence of mediations. We have seen that ideology, *an* ideology, comprises the first of these mediations; we have also seen that the relationship between text and ideology is not spontaneous. Thus it would be an absurd tautology to conceive of this relationship as being grounded in the presence of elements of the real. The text is not a direct reflection of the real, nor is there any spontaneous signification (a point to be developed later). We are actually dealing with a two-fold dialectical series:

1 Historical process
2 Ideology } (1)

3 Ideology
4 ? } (2)

It is this fourth term that we are now seeking to identify, in asking what is specifically literary in the text; there is obviously little point in trying to resolve our problem by identifying it with the first term.

That is to say that the analysis of a literary work will use neither the scientific concepts used to describe the historical process, nor ideological concepts. It will require new concepts which can register the literariness of the text. It is at just this point that Lenin seems most poorly equipped, ignorant of precisely these concepts. But never mind: bourgeois criticism is even less well equipped than he, for it can deploy only ideological concepts. When he defines the specific and pitiless gaze with which the writer confronts the real, the historical and the ideological, Lenin writes: he is a very gifted artist, a great painter, he has portrayed in bold relief. Of John Reed's book he wrote: 'He paints a precise and extraordinarily vivid portrait'. It is because 'Tolstoy is a great writer' that he has surpassed others. This is in the same vein as Engels, when he wrote:

> A novel of the socialist tendency perfectly fulfils its function when, by a faithful picture of real relations, it destroys the conventional illusions about these relations, when it shakes the optimism of the bourgeois world, when it casts doubt on the eternal nature of existing society, even if the author does not propose answers, even though he might not openly take sides.

The writer *embodies*, *expresses*, *translates*, *reflects*, *renders*; all of these terms, of equal inadequacy, constitute our problem. Perhaps this problem is the same as the former one.

The image in the mirror

We have to re-analyse these critical texts from a new point of view; for the moment, we have an account of the work of Tolstoy which is complete in its own fashion, within the limits of its insufficiency. *Within* the work of Tolstoy we know that we are looking for its relation to history; but we do not know how such a study might be pursued, nor do we know *what* materials we shall be practically concerned with. In the interpretation which has just been offered it is as thought the text itself had been abolished for the sake of its content. We have accounted for everything except the works of Tolstoy in their specificity.

Obviously a knowledge of these works is not the same as a knowledge of what they were made from.

From Lenin's account we must isolate what will define the work of the writer. For tactical reasons this new description must be kept separate from the earlier one, though in fact they are inextricable. The articles on Tolstoy elaborate some important concepts – concepts which could form the basis of a scientific criticism if they were clarified and justified. The problem arises because although Lenin uses these concepts he never considers their theoretical coherence; very deftly, he makes use of them, but never grounds them in a theory of literature (as he was, in *Materialism and Empirio-Criticism*, to do for the concepts of scientific criticism). Though these ideas have their origin in the domain of political theory, they can be considered out of that context, as concepts of literary criticism. But if we want to use them beyond that justifying context, they must travel through the detour of theory. Our itinerary is just this detour.

Mirror, *reflection*, *expression* – these are the key notions of the Lenin articles. Lenin gives us his definition of literature in the proposition that the work is a mirror (recalling that mirror on the highway which serves as the ritual emblem of a realist literature). But Lenin uses the mirror to refer to a concept rather than an image. It must, then, be limited by a definition at least. In fact, it is qualified immediately by the statement that the 'thing' is not there for its own sake: 'We can hardly call "mirror" that which does not give a precise reflection of the world.' Thus the mirror is only superficially a mirror, or at least it reflects in its own special way. We are not concerned with just any reflecting surface which would give a direct reproduction of any object. And rather than the facile notion of a distorting mirror, Lenin suggests a fragmented image. Could it be a broken mirror?

In effect, the relationship between the mirror and what it reflects (the historical reality) is *partial*: the mirror selects, it does not reflect everything. The selection itself is not fortuitous, it is symptomatic; it can tell us about the nature of the mirror. We already know the reasons for this selectivity; Tolstoy's version of his age is incomplete because of his personal and ideological relation to it. In particular, we know that he could not grasp its revolutionary characteristics; thus it is not because he reflected the revolution that he earned the title of mirror of the revolution. If the work is a mirror it is certainly not by virtue of any manifest relation with the period 'reflected'. Tolstoy 'did not manifestly understand' his age, he 'manifestly turned away from it'. What is seen in the mirror of the work is not quite what Tolstoy saw, both in himself and as an ideological spokesman. Thus the image of history in the mirror will not be a reflection in the precise sense of a reproduction or facsimile. Indeed, we know that such a reproduction is impossible. The fact that we can recognise Tolstoy's era in his work does not prove that he truly knew that era. Tolstoy's relationship to his mirror is analogous to that of certain workers to the revolution of their own period: they participated spontaneously – and perhaps effectively – in that revolution, without understanding either its scope or its origins.

Initially this can be explained by the complexity of the revolution – the fact that it is not a single conflict but a struggle articulated by a multiplicity of determinations (as in the above analysis); the historical process unfolds at several levels simultaneously and is intricately knotted. It is thus possible to participate at a single level, in ignorance of all the others (although this ignorance is vulnerable). Even in the 'great revolution' there is an important peasant element, by which Tolstoy and his work are situated in history: 'Tolstoy had to reflect at least *some* of the essential aspects of the revolution'. But it is not simply a case of one element; this immediate relation is necessarily incomplete, not only by its content but in its very form. All those who played a part in this revolution – and who did not? – were involved in an immediate relation with at least one element of the total situation; but this relation was only superficially immediate, for it was actually determined by the totality. So these ideas – 'element of a situation', 'part played in an event' – would indeed be deceptive if they were to tempt us into a *mechanical* analysis. The reflected element, with its apparent spontaneity, is actually determined by both short- and long-term factors, by its place in the complex structure. Its positive presence is less important than the fact that it is, as it were, inscribed from the outside (*creusé de l'extérieur*), inserted obliquely by all the conditions that have generated it. The work is perhaps a mirror precisely because it registers the partiality of its own reflections, the incomplete reality of simple elements. It is privileged because it does not have to elaborate the totality in order to display it; it can reveal just the necessity of that totality – a necessity which can be deciphered from the work. It is the task of scientific criticism to achieve such a reading. The mirror can reveal in this way because it is not a mechanical reproducer of images (blind images which would merit only condemnation) nor an instrument of knowledge – though knowledge has its own appropriate instruments. It is an indispensable *revelation*, a revealer, and it is criticism that helps us to decipher these images in the mirror.

The secret of the mirror is to be sought in the form of its reflections; how does it show historical reality, by what paradox does it make visible its own blindness without actually seeing itself?

The notion of the mirror takes on a new meaning once it is supplemented by the idea of the analysis which defines the partiality of its reflections. But this analysis is itself deceptive, since it tends to suggest that the real is the mechanical product of a *montage*. It must be interpreted in a way that does not sacrifice its real complexity. In actual fact, it is not enough to say that the mirror catches a fragmented reality; the very image in the mirror is itself fragmented. The image renders real discontinuities by means of its own complexities. Thus the work of Tolstoy is not homogeneous; it has not the limpid continuity of the reflected image; it is not all of a piece. To think that it is would be an idealisation, a refusal to understand such as liberal-bourgeois criticism might attempt. We return to the notion that the mirror is not a simple reflecting surface: the work of Tolstoy is itself an assemblage. And, just as Freud has established that a dream has to be deconstructed into its constitutive elements before it can be interpreted, Lenin states that the literary text must be studied in the same way – not in the pursuit of a factitious totality, but according to its real and necessary discontinuity.

The revolutionary, if he is to see himself mirrored in the work of Tolstoy, must be aware of the deceptions of reactionary *and* liberal criticism. Instead of trying to assimilate the whole of

Tolstoy he must be able to identify the mirror within his work. Otherwise the literary work is merely being used as the pretext for a declaration of political or ideological faith. Just as it is not a complete reflection, neither is Tolstoy's work a primary reflection, simple and complete in itself. Confronted with the complexity of the historical process, we must be able to articulate the complexity of the text. 'The great Tolstoyan image was not cast in metal, a single unalloyed block. And all his bourgeois admirers rise to honour his memory not because he was all of a piece but precisely because he was not' (Lenin, *On Literature and Art*).

The bourgeois judgment of Tolstoy was not just incomprehension or ignorance. It was a significant misreading. The bourgeois reading of Tolstoy is implicit in Tolstoy's own works; it is an index of their imbalance.

The first task is to distinguish carefully the two aspects of Tolstoy's work, that which must be rejected and that which is to be preserved, with no third category: 'when Tolstoy expresses his prejudices rather than his wisdom, that in him which belongs to the past rather than with the future' (ibid.), and 'this heritage which the Russian proletariat appropriate and study' (ibid.). This in itself is revealing. It would appear that Tolstoy left, in 1910, a double 'estate', one bourgeois and the other proletarian; yet from what we already know, Tolstoy was a peasant writer rather than a bourgeois or a proletarian. In all the variety of its possible uses his work would seem de-centred, stripped of its intrinsic qualities, condemned to a stealthy or oblique relationship to itself. This split within the work is the symptom of the presence of ideology, as though in an enclosure or cavity:

> It was this rapid, painful, drastic demolition of all the old 'pillars' of old Russia that was reflected in the works of Tolstoy the artist, and in the views of Tolstoy the thinker. (Ibid., p. 54; see Appendix below, p. 314)
>
> By studying the literary works of Leo Tolstoy the Russian working class will learn to know its enemies better, but in examining the *doctrine* of Tolstoy, the whole Russian people will have to understand where their own weakness lies, the

> weakness which did not allow them to carry the cause of their emancipation to its conclusion. (Ibid., pp. 56–7; see Appendix below, p. 317)

We have already established that Tolstoy's literary works must not be confused with the Tolstoyan ideology, that foreign body in their midst. But this distinction acquires a new significance: there is a conflict within the text between the text and its ideological content, conflict rather than contiguity. Thus, beyond the fact that it is addressed simultaneously to several different audiences (as we have just seen, the literary work belongs to the working class while the doctrine is a means of understanding for the entire Russian people), we always find the same theme: the literary work is profoundly dissymmetrical. There is more than one mirror, and the images that they offer are not simply complementary. The text, from its many facets, gives out more than a simple light.

The problem is, not to interpret this multiplicity as equivocation. Let us look immediately at the central example: in his first article, of 1908, Lenin writes:

> the contradictions in Tolstoy's views must be appraised not from the standpoint of the present-day working-class movement and present-day socialism (such an appraisal is, of course, needed, but it is not enough), but from the standpoint of protest against advancing capitalism, against the ruining of the masses, who are being dispossessed of their land – a protest which had to arise from the patriarchal Russian countryside. (Ibid., p. 30; see Appendix below, p. 301)

Two years later, in his second article, he writes:

> That is why a correct appraisal of Tolstoy can be made only from the viewpoint of the class which has proved, by its political role and its struggle during the first denouement of these contradictions, at a time of revolution, that it is destined to be the leader in the struggle for the people's liberty and for the emancipation of the masses

> from exploitation – the class which has proved its selfless devotion to the cause of democracy and its ability to fight against the limitations and inconsistency of bourgeois (including peasant) democracy; such a viewpoint is only possible from the viewpoint of the Social-Democratic proletariat. (Ibid., pp. 50–1; see Appendix below, p. 307)

At first sight, the contrast seems embarrassingly obvious: in fact, Lenin is proposing to pass 'two exact judgments' on Tolstoy. The first bears on the very point of view by which Tolstoy's gaze is defined; the second, denying the false interiority of the work, reveals the work by the expedient of a decisive confrontation. Nothing enables us to choose between these two undertakings, which are finally opposed only through their equivalence, their necessary relation. Tolstoy proclaims himself a writer precisely by the work's power to effect within itself a precise variation – precise because it cannot be accused of ambiguity. The sliding of points of view within the work of Tolstoy is not an 'either . . . or . . .' but a '*both at once*', exactly situated within their conflict. Once again we encounter the notion of a double reading, though this time in a stronger sense, since it is a question of two *exact* readings. In that case, perhaps the exactitude results from their conjunction.

It is for this reason that the truth of Tolstoy's work – and there must surely be some truth in it, something from which one could know the truth – should be sought in the presence of a conflict: more precisely, it might be said that the content of Tolstoy's work has something to do with contradiction. Lenin in fact states that: Tolstoy's work is great because it reflects the contradictions of the epoch. Does this mean that it reflects, term for term, the elements of the contradiction, producing or reproducing an image of the contradiction? Such a notion is a denial of Tolstoy's work as such, an appropriation for the sake of a too directly satisfying explanation. It is obvious that the contradictions of the epoch are (and must remain) external to the work, because they are of a different nature. If there is a contradiction in the work it must thus be a different kind of contradiction, obeying the laws of a more subtle transposition.

The critical question, as formulated by Lenin, is expressed thus: What do we see in the mirror? The answer: the object in the mirror has something to do with contradiction. This is because, once again, the mirror does not reflect *things* (in which case the relationship between the reflection and the object would be one of mechanical correspondence). The image in the mirror is deceptive: the mirror enables us to grasp only *relationships* of contradiction. By means of contradictory images the mirror represents and evokes the historical contradictions of the period, what Lenin calls 'the faults and weaknesses of our revolution'. The mechanism of the mirror functions thus:

contradictions in the book	←————	historical deficiencies
	reflection in the mirror	

We must now identify these terms and find out which contradictions are involved. The determination of the real contradictions of a historical period poses problems which we do not have to deal with here. But what can the contradictions in Tolstoy's work be? And what is their relation to the real contradictions? Lenin devotes the whole of the third paragraph of his first article to an enumeration of the contradictions in Tolstoy's work ('work' being taken in the widest possible sense to include all that Tolstoy had *done*, that is to say the books as well as the doctrine and the influence):

1	great artist protest	}	landlord obsessed with Christ quietism (in all its forms)
2	criticism realism	}	non-violence preaching

The first contradiction relates Tolstoy's work, in so far as it is defined by aesthetic criteria, to Tolstoy's real situation, in so far as it defines the subject of his narratives (who is speaking?). But this second term of the contradiction is itself contradictory, since it implies the conflict between Tolstoy's natural situation (his relationship *by birth* to history) and his ideological situation (which allows him to *displace* his relation to history). The production of the books depends on this conflict, since Tolstoy has no other reason to change his relation to history except that of becoming a writer, and since his preaching remains essentially a preaching by means of books. Therefore, the first contradiction is between the book itself and the (contradictory) conditions of its production. The second contradiction, which remains the same, stated in three different forms, defines the very *content* of the work. The contradiction attacks the book from the interior and the exterior.

These contradictions are 'glaring': that is to say, they are obvious enough not to constitute a secret in the work. They are not manifest, however: Tolstoy's work communicates them to us without announcing them. They are *in* the work, but not as its explicit content; in this role we find only *some* of the real contradictions (for example, the contradiction between political violence and the comedy of justice denounced by Tolstoy). The contradictions structure the whole of the work; they shape its fundamental disparity. (For the image in the mirror we could perhaps here substitute the 'figure in the carpet' exemplified by a famous short story by Henry James.)

These contradictions define Tolstoy's work since they give it both its limits and its meaning – a meaning which is only intelligible when reckoned from those limits. The limits: Tolstoy could not have a complete knowledge of the historical process (and because his knowledge is incomplete it is not, precisely, a knowledge). The meaning: these limits are necessary if it is the case that 'the contradictions . . . are not accidental' (ibid., p. 30; see Appendix below, p. 301). This meaning defined by limits, this content determined from without, enables us to say that the work of Tolstoy is *expressive*, that it is defined by its relation to something other than itself. We rediscover, in an inverted form, something we already know: we have seen that the work cannot include an ideology – which by itself does not belong to it – unless it establishes that ideology in a relation of difference with itself; we now see that the work can only exist if it introduces into itself this alien term which precipitates an internal contradiction.

'The expression of contradictory conditions', the work must therefore 'reflect', independently of its fragmented reality (it is dispersed in the multiplicity of its terms – terms which are distinct, or at least analysable), the ensemble of the contradictions which define the historical situation as an insufficiency. This ensemble is not confused with this or that specific contradiction (for example, with one of the contradictions which Tolstoy describes directly) or with a simple general contradiction which is the product of all the others. The work is privileged in that it gives, in its own fashion, *a complete view* of the historical complexity: its point of view is completely significant. We have already seen that the work is defined by its lack, its incompleteness. We are now stating that the work is complete, that is to say, adequate to its meaning. These two propositions do not annul each other. On the contrary, they are an extension of each other: the work is not at fault in relation to another work in which the absences would be made good, the insufficiencies remedied; these absences make it exist, make it irreplaceable. The mirror is expressive in what it does not reflect as much as in what it does reflect. The absence of certain reflections, expressions – these are the true object of criticism. The mirror, in certain areas, is a blind mirror: but it is still a mirror for all its blindness.

Because of the contradictory conditions in which it is produced, the literary work is *simultaneously* (and it is this conjunction which concerns us) a reflection and the absence of a reflection: this is why it is itself contradictory. It would therefore be incorrect to say that the contradictions of the work are the *reflection* of historical contradictions: rather they are the consequences of the absence of this reflection. Once again we see that there can be no mechanical correspondence between the object and its 'image'. Expression does not mean a direct reproduction (or even knowledge), but an indirect figuration which arises from the deficiencies of the reproduction. Thus the work has a self-sufficient meaning which does not require to be completed; this meaning results from the disposition of partial reflections within the work and from a certain impossibility of reflecting. The function of criticism is to bring this to light.

The concept of expression is therefore much less ambiguous

than that of reflection, since it enables us to define the overall structure of the work: a contrast which is based on an absence. The contradiction or deficiency *fills* the work of Tolstoy; it delineates its general architecture. The dialectic *in* the book (we recall Brecht's notion of a dialectic of the theatre) arises from the dialectical relation between the book and the real dialectic of the historical process. The conflict or contradiction, as it appears in the book, is itself one of the terms of the real conflict. This is why the contradictions in the book cannot be those of reality; they are the product of that reality, the culmination of a process of dialectical elaboration, which involves the intervening mediation of the means peculiar to literature. The interpreter is at the centre of a relationship of exchange; through his work Tolstoy gives us access to history itself, but to accomplish this he places himself (or he *is* placed – it is the same thing) within the historical conflict. Placed thus at the centre of an exchange, he explores the paths of a new economy.

We have yet to grasp the workings of this interpretation, that is to say, to know the terms of the dialectic in the book. What are the terms of the contradiction which Tolstoy exposes? Several answers are given to this question: between ideology (as enclave) and the work (defined by its relation to literature); between the questions (ideally posed) and the answers (ideally given); between the data and the observation which restores them. But all these answers paradoxically converge in one answer: when Lenin speaks of the contradiction in Tolstoy's work it is the ideological contradiction which he always has in mind:

> the contradictions in Tolstoy's views are indeed a mirror of those contradictory conditions in which the peasantry had to play their historical part in our revolution. (Ibid., p. 30; see Appendix below, p. 301)

At the same time as it establishes an ideological content the book presents the contradiction of that content: this content only exists enveloped in the form of a contestation. Thus we perceive that there can be both a contradiction in 'the ideas' and a contradiction between the ideas and the book which presents them.

It is hardly necessary to insist on the contradictions in the ideas, an elementary formation. Essentially, it is a question of the conjunction and the contrast between the vehement protest and practical quietism; Tolstoyism, torn between accusation and forgetfulness. We know that this duplicity is not peculiar to Tolstoy but that initially it is the deed of 'millions and millions of people', of the peasant masses:

> Tolstoy's point of view was that of the patriarchal, naive peasant, whose psychology Tolstoy introduced into his criticism and his doctrine. Tolstoy's criticism is marked by such emotional power, such passion, convincingness, freshness, sincerity and fearlessness in striving to 'go to the roots', to find the real cause of the afflictions of the masses, just because this criticism really expresses a sharp change in the ideas of millions of peasants, who had only just emerged from feudalism into freedom, and saw that this freedom meant new horrors of ruin, death by starvation, a homeless life among the lower strata of the city population, and so on and so forth. Tolstoy mirrored their sentiments so faithfully that he imported their naiveté into his own doctrine, their alienation from political life, their mysticism, their desire to keep aloof from the world, 'non-resistance to evil', their impotent imprecations against capitalism and the 'power of money'. The protest of millions of peasants and their desperation – these were combined in Tolstoy's doctrine. (Ibid., p. 55; see Appendix below, p. 315)

The mirror therefore reflects term for term the elements of the peasant outlook. By means of this image these terms appear to be contradictory. We must now establish what it means to talk of ideological contradictions, and in what conditions we are justified in so doing.

If we examine the nature of ideology in general (see Louis Althusser's 'Marxism and Humanism' in *For Marx*) it is soon obvious that there can be no ideological contradiction, except if we put ideology in contradiction with itself, if we induce contradiction within the framework of a dialogue (which is also ideological). By definition, an ideology can sustain a contradictory debate, for ideology exists precisely in order to efface all trace of contradiction. Thus, an ideology, as such, breaks down only in the face of the real questions: but for that to come about, ideology must not be able to hear these questions; that is to say, ideology must not be able to translate them into its own language. In so far as ideology is the false resolution of a real debate, it is always adequate to itself *as a reply*. Obviously the great thing is that it can never answer the question. In that it succeeds in endlessly prolonging its imperfection, it is complete; thus it is always equally in error, pursued by the risk that it cannot envisage – *the loss of reality*. An ideology is loyal to itself only in so far as it remains inadequate to the question which is both its foundation and its pretext. Ideology's essential weakness is that it can never recognise for itself its own real limits: at best it can learn of these limits from elsewhere, in the action of a radical criticism, not by a superficial denunciation of its content; the criticism of ideology is then replaced by a *critique of the ideological.*

It is therefore correct to say that ideology, rather than being alienated or contradictory, is captive. But captured by what? If we reply that it is captive of itself, we lapse into fallacies, false contradiction. Ideology is, in fact, a captive of its own limits (which is not the same thing). Ideology is enclosed, finite, but it mistakenly proclaims itself to be unlimited (having an answer for everything) within its limits. It is for this reason that ideology cannot create a system, which would be the condition for contradiction. (There can only be contradiction within a structured system; otherwise, there is merely opposition.) Ideology is a false totality because it has not appointed its own limits, because it is unable to reflect the limitation of its limits. Ideology has received these limits, but it exists solely in order to forget that moment of origin. These abiding limits, which are both permanent and permanently latent, are the source of that dissonance which structures all ideology: the dissonance between its explicit openness and its implicit closure.

Thus the ideological background, which constitutes the real support of all forms of expression and all ideological manifestations, is fundamentally silent – one might say unconscious. But it must be emphasised that this unconscious is not a silent knowledge, but a total misrecognition of itself. If it is silent, it is silent on that about which it has nothing to say. We should therefore preserve the expression in all its ambiguity: it refers to that ideological horizon which conceals only because it is interminable, because there is always something more, but it refers also to that abyss over which ideology is built. Like a planet revolving round an absent sun, an ideology is made of what it does not mention; it exists because there are things which must not be spoken of. This is the sense in which Lenin can say that 'Tolstoy's silences are eloquent'.

Ultimately, by interrogating an ideology, one can establish the existence of its limits because they are encountered as an impassable obstacle; they are there, but they cannot be made to speak. To know what an ideology means, to express this meaning, we must therefore go beyond and outside ideology; we must attack it from the outside in an effort to give form to that which is formless. This is not an enterprise of description: the symptomatic weaknesses are not to be located in the answers, which can always contrive a display of impeccable logical coherence; they are to be located in the questions which are left unanswered.

Thus when Lenin tells us that 'the ideas of Tolstoy reflect weaknesses and inadequacies' (op. cit., p. 30; see Appendix below), this means that the status of the image in the mirror is not

purely ideological. Between the ideology and the book which expresses it, something has happened; the distance between them is not the product of some abstract decorum. Even though ideology itself always sounds solid, copious, it begins to speak of its *own absences* because of its presence in the novel, its visible and determinate form. By means of the text it becomes possible to escape from the domain of spontaneous ideology, to escape from the false consciousness of self, of history, and of time. The text constructs a determinate image of the ideological, revealing it as an object rather than living it from within as though it were an inner conscience; the text explores ideology (just as Balzac explores the Paris of the *Comédie humaine*, for instance), puts it to the test of the written word, the test of that watchful gaze in which all subjectivity is *captured*, crystallised in objective form. The spontaneous ideology in which men live (it is not produced

spontaneously, although men believe that they acquire it spontaneously) is not simply reflected by the mirror of the book; ideology is broken, and turned inside out in so far as it is transformed in the text from being a state of consciousness. Art, or at least literature, because it naturally scorns the credulous view of the world, establishes myth and illusion as *visible objects*.

Tolstoy's work is engaged in a sterile social critique; but behind that futile generosity there figures a historical question which is placed within our grasp. Thus the work is certainly determined by its relation to ideology, but this relation is not one of analogy (as would be a reproduction): it is always more or less contradictory. A work is established against an ideology as much as it is from an ideology. Implicitly, the work contributes to an exposure of ideology, or at least to a definition of it; thus the absurdity of all attempts to 'demystify' literary works, which are defined precisely by their enterprise of demystification.

But it would not be correct to say that the book initiates a dialogue with ideology (which would be the worst possible way of becoming caught up in its game). On the contrary, its function is to present ideology in a non-ideological form. To take up the classical distinction between form and content – although the use of this distinction could not be generalised – it could be said that the work has an ideological content, but that it endows this content with a specific form. Even if this form is itself ideological there is an internal displacement of ideology by virtue of this *redoubling*; this is not ideology contemplating itself, but the mirror-effect which exposes its insufficiency, revealing differences and discordances, or a significant incongruity.

Thus we can gauge the distance which separates the work of art from true knowledge (a scientific knowledge) but which also unites them in their common distance from ideology. Science does away with ideology, obliterates it; literature challenges ideology by using it. If ideology is thought of as a non-systematic ensemble of significations, the work proposes a *reading* of these significations, by combining them as signs. Criticism teaches us to read these signs.

We seem thus to have exhausted the meanings of the concept of the mirror: it is the meeting place of reflections which are shaped on the ground of a blind surface, just as colours, at the right moment, constitute a picture on the canvas. Lenin teaches us that it is not so simple to look in the mirror: he has undertaken a rigorous scrutiny of mirrors.

In the margin of his *Lettre sur les aveugles* (Letter on the Blind), Diderot tells the story of a young lady of Salignac: 'Sometimes for a joke she would stand in front of a mirror to dress herself up and imitate the looks of a coquette preparing for the fray. Her mimicry was so accurate that it caused great laughter.' It is better to close our eyes to this laughter. If it is a game we might ask who is being tricked, the mirror which replies, or the one who thinks he sees the blind person because he contemplates his reflection. But in this performance the one who does not see is confident: near to her image, she controls it. Of the same person, Diderot tells us: 'When she listened to singing she could distinguish brown and blonde voices.' When night blinded the eye she found a more certain vision. 'As night approached, she used to say that our reign was ending and hers was about to begin.' We do not know whether night, that 'queen', triumphing over images, preserves images or makes them disappear; does she only know of them? Thus the *Lettre sur les aveugles*, with this time the famous Saunderson, necessarily introduces us to a *science of reflections*. 'I asked him what he meant by a mirror: a machine, he said, which throws things into relief far from themselves, if they are properly positioned in relation to it. It is like my hand which does not have to touch an object in order to feel it.'

'A machine which throws things into relief far from themselves': the mirror endows an object with new proportions, studies objects through other objects which are not quite the same. The mirror extends the world: but it also seizes, inflates and tears that world. In the mirror, the object is both completed and broken: *disjecta membra*. If the mirror constructs, it is in an inversion of the movement of genesis: rather than spreading, it breaks. The images emerge from this laceration. Elucidated by these images, the world and its powers appear and disappear, disfigured at the very moment when they begin to take shape. Hence the childish fear of the mirror which is the fear of seeing *something else*, when it is always the same thing.

In this sense literature can be called a mirror: in displacing objects it retains their reflection. It projects its thin surface on to the world and history. It passes through them and breaks them. In its train arise the images.

December 1964

Chapter 20

Literary Analysis: The Tomb of Structures

The objects of literary criticism are works of literature, works that are equally works of language. Literary criticism is thus quite distinct from the other forms of art criticism: 'musical language' and 'pictorial language' are obviously metaphorical expressions; even though these works may sustain some relationship to language in general, it ought to be remembered that a relationship in the strict sense, supposes a difference, an initial distance between the terms of the relation. Neither music nor painting is a language; the media they employ have nothing to do with language as scientifically defined by linguistics: among all the forms of artistic expression, literature alone is related to language, even though it is not itself a language. Language itself is certainly the material of the writer's work, and literary criticism in its efforts to elaborate a certain knowledge of these works of language (not works of language – products of language) has the duty and the right to draw upon the science of language which depends upon linguistics. Literary criticism will not only want to know the hypothetical rules of language: more important, it will want an answer to the question: What is language? Only then will criticism be able to answer its own question: How is a work (this work) made? We will have to ask ourselves why the critical question breaks formally from the linguistic question, and does not ask: What is literature?

But the terms of this obligation ought to be properly fixed. We must identify and isolate them. Literature is a work, and thus it belongs to the realm of art. It is the product of a labour, which implies a material to work on and a means of doing that work, autonomous terms. The material and the product of the labour are necessarily distinct: the knowledge of the work and the science of the material are not simply extensions of each other, whether by logical deduction or empirical descent. They cannot help or teach each other anything until the moment of their separation. So any assimilation, however furtive, of literature to language, or of literary criticism to linguistics, is doomed from the beginning. For knowledge to be transferred from one discipline to another, the autonomy of both inquiries must be recognised: autonomy of the object and of the method – the reciprocal aspects of a single obligation. That is to say that the discoveries of linguistics cannot be spontaneously appropriated by literary criticism: scientific borrowing is not a colonisation, a new world founded from a fragment of the mother country. Thus we already know that the concept of structure, *according to its scientific definition in linguistics*, may suggest new directions to literary criticism, but it cannot resolve all critical problems at a stroke; and even if it did resolve them, it would not itself have been able to formulate them. Contact between two different disciplines is for the sake of clarification, not for confusion.

However, this distinction between language and literature is still very inadequate: 'literature' is not the only use of language. Specific linguistic practices produce ideologies, mythologies, literary works, scientific knowledges, and explicit systems of social representation (which we shall call *codes*). These terms are all distinct, and should be individually defined, though they can be grouped into a general class. They belong to the same universe since, in their various ways, they all derive from the existence of language, though they do not belong to or depend on it directly. The literary work is the encounter of two determinations: on the one hand a work of language, on the other hand a 'work of art'. (This is a strange pleonasm: isn't every work the product of an art? With a similar redoubling of meaning we talk of a scientific knowledge; this redundancy could start us on a separate inquiry into the nature of knowledge.) Literature is precisely located where two different activities intersect. We must ask whether the two terms have an equal force in the encounter.

Having postulated these terms, it remains obvious that literary criticism is concerned with language, especially in so far as it brings a new discourse to bear on authentic discourses (produced from language). So that in its form, as much as in its object, it sends us back to the essential question: What is language? It moves from a written text to a reading, but this reading only has any critical authority if it begets a new text. Reading begets a writing; and, vice versa, a writing emerges from reading; and writing is perhaps already a form of reading. Here is the idea to which the literary structuralists attach such a great importance:

> Unlike the art critic or the musicologist, the literary critic uses the same medium as those he is criticising, a source of formidable confusion – primarily for the critic himself. Thus criticism is simultaneously outside the space of literature, because it speaks of writing, and inside this space because its speech is writing. (G. Genette, 'Reply to an Inquiry into Criticism', *Tel Quel*, 14)

In some way, the work is read before it is written, or, conceivably, read while it is being written; such would be the lesson of the work of Borges (see Genette's article in the Borges number of *L'Herne*).

Henry James's famous short story 'The Figure in the Carpet' is built around this same idea, though James uses it to mystify rather than to clarify. This narrative, not to be taken seriously except in its demonstration of the corrosive effects of scorn, presents in anecdotal form the problem of the relation between an author and his critics: every work hides 'buried treasure' which it is the critic's task and justification to unearth. The work's only value to the author is as a temporary repository; he waits in vain to be read, to see others reading what he himself has read in his work. We know how this story ends: incited by certain devious confidences from the author which merely hint at the existence of the secret, the tenacious critic manages to unearth it, and to make the author admit that this is the very same secret which he had previously concealed. But for all that, the secret is not yet divulged; it disappears completely along with the person to whom it has been entrusted. The interested party – the narrator of the story, who is also a critic, but an unfortunate one – is as wise at the end as he was at the beginning. This paradoxical ending naturally suggests that perhaps there was no secret. This is an exemplary mystification, less for the idea that it offers than for the constantly implied disparagement of the idea. Obviously someone is being made fun of in every line of the narrative, and we, the readers, are probably the victim as we try to find *a* meaning. In the familiar reflexive tradition, Henry James writes a work in which the activity of reading, our reading, is the theme. But it is a splendid 'structuralist' adventure as well.

Let us return to the theme of reading:

> There was nevertheless something else I had absolutely to learn. 'Should you be able, pen in hand, to state it clearly yourself – to name it, phrase it, formulate it?'
>
> 'Oh,' he almost passionately sighed, 'if I were only, pen in hand, one of *you* chaps!'
>
> 'That would be a great chance for you of course. But why should you despise us chaps for not doing what you can't do yourself?'
>
> 'Can't do?' He opened his eyes. 'Haven't I done it in twenty volumes? I do it in my way,' he continued. 'You don't do it in yours.'
>
> 'Ours is so devilish difficult,' I weakly observed.
>
> 'So is mine. We each choose our own. There's no compulsion.' (Henry James, 'The Figure in the Carpet')

Each in their way, the author and the critic are talking about the same thing. Or rather, they speak the same language, which does not mean that they are saying the same thing. This could have two meanings: the author is already a critic, and the critic is simply repeating in his own words what has already been said (the apparent meaning). But also: if the author is already a critic, this is because the critic is a kind of author. Criticism is writing, because fundamentally writing is reading. It can be shown how this formulation is mistaken, for example in a study of the work of Borges, where the *myth of reading* has to be interpreted rather than taken literally, and where the problem of writing is posed independently, well before the problem of reading. (See the study of Borges in Part III.)

This confusion between literary writing and critical writing is especially significant because it exactly defines – and we will have to ask why – structuralist criticism. Roland Barthes opens his *Essais critiques* with a very 'written' preface in which he demonstrates how the activity of the critic is a prolongation of that of the writer. Or rather – but what can it matter since the terms are reciprocal? – it paradoxically precedes it: the critic is a 'reprieved writer', one who endlessly postpones the act of writing. From this fact, criticism derives its privilege: the act of writing (reading) is found here in its nascent state, secretly proclaiming its true nature. The critic, almost a writer, is no longer an understudy: he is a prototype, a guide, a prophet of new signs. We read in him the exemplary vocation of the writer. A revealer of structures, criticism is itself the structure of the book.

Notice, briefly, that this idea of criticism applies electively to certain privileged objects. Whether or not he is acknowledged (Genette is always invoking him; Barthes hardly mentions him, though this silence does not signify a real absence), Valéry is the model of the writer-critic or critic-writer, one who announced his desire for a *hollow writing*, writing for the sake of reading, writing that very reading, in other words, nothing. We know that he wanted to found a style on commentary, in the form of variations, bestowing on others what he desired to bestow on himself, listening in every work for that formal rigour which must be reflected back, articulated by an echo, before it can be set down. In this sense, Valéry is the first structuralist in literature, and it is no surprise that the structural method applies precisely to his work. Naturally we must still ask whether his is the work of a writer or a forger; Valéry's repeated desire to imitate himself and to be no more than this imitation, suggests the second possibility. Notice that the structural method which works so well on Valéry's illusory work seems to have no relevance to what is still the major event of our literary history: surrealism. (Yet Roland Barthes assimilates 'the structuralist activity' to the surrealist activity. The one would have supplanted the other. It would be interesting to know what Breton would have thought of this. On page 214 of *Essais critiques* we find this mysterious announcement: 'Perhaps surrealism produced the first experience of structural literature, one day we must come back to this.' This enigmatic 'perhaps' hides several notions: Have we yet reached 'this'? When? And when will we come back to it?) If surrealism still escapes the structuralists this is because it is not as near to death as some would prefer. Let us take this weakness as an established fact and look for its causes.

The idea of structure, which seems to come from linguistics, where it is justifiably applied to literary objects, is actually used in literary analysis in a sense remote from its original one. It goes back to the entirely unscientific hypothesis that the work has an intrinsic meaning (though this does not imply that this meaning is explicit); paradoxically, this enables it to be read before it has even been written. So that, and here we return to Henry James, to extricate a structure is to decipher an enigma, to dig up a buried meaning: the critical reading performs the same operation on the work that the writing had to perform on the signs (or on the themes) that it combined. Criticism produces merely a pre-established truth; but that might be called an innovation, because ideally it precedes the work.

It is significant that this 'process' is called an analysis: the critic is an analyst; he performs structural analyses, just like Lacan, Lévi-Strauss and Martinet in their fields. But the analogy is obviously deceptive. The analysis that retrieves a previously hidden meaning is, as we shall see, the exact opposite of a scientific analysis.

Nevertheless, this analysis, which does employ a specific method, does not approach literature as empirically given: before analysis, it does 'reconstitute' literature as an *object of analysis*. The literary work is constituted as a message, and its function is to transmit a certain message; critical analysis consists of isolating the message. (In spite of all the noisy protestations, it seems that the opposition between the structural method and the

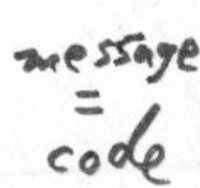

traditional method is little more than a formality. Both, with their different methods, seek a means of interpretation in the letter of the work. The dispute is fierce, but it is not over fundamentals.) The work has no absolutely autonomous value; at most it is an intermediary, that which leads towards a secret. Between the message and the code from which it is generated, there is little more than a compound which analysis will break down into its elements. The code itself is the very material of communication; it embodies that complicity which makes literature possible. It is hidden in the depths of the work, sustaining it; but it pleads to be translated. The code makes possible the work of both the writer and the critic.

Criticism, then, proposes to restore for us that initial object without which there would be no reading, and certainly no writing. Understanding is reductive – a return to the structure that reposes within the work, and from which the literary only *seems* to have strayed, having disguised it only to cling to it more securely. This myth of interiority belongs with the myth of anticipation that we have already encountered. Thus, structuralist criticism proposes a *return* to the work as it is in itself; it ranks itself among the 'criticisms of signification', denounces the crude methods of explanation, particularly historical explanation. (In his *Sur Racine* (On Racine) Barthes tries to revive claims for the transhistorical value of literature.) Valéry is a precursor on this issue as well. This odyssey of speculation ends when it meets the essence of the work 'which composes every line, chooses every word, dots all the i's, puts in all the commas' (Henry James, op. cit.).

Analysis is the discovery of the rationality, the secret coherence of an object. This was precisely how Hegel described the reign of the animal spirit.

> The goal of all structuralist activity, whether it be reflexive or poetic, is to reconstitute an 'object', in a way that demonstrates the rules of the functioning (the 'functions') of this object. Thus the structure is in fact a *simulacrum* of the object, but a controlled, interested simulacrum, since the copy of the object brings out something previously

> invisible, or, if you prefer, incomprehensible in the natural object. The structural man takes the real, decomposes it and then recomposes it; this is apparently a trifling matter (which sometimes provokes the verdict that the structuralist enterprise is 'insignificant, uninteresting, useless'). However, from another point of view, this trifle is crucial; for between the two objects, or the two moments of the structuralist activity, something new is generated, and this novelty is nothing less than the general form of the intelligible itself: the simulacrum is the object added to the object, and this addition has an anthropological value in that it represents man himself, his history, his situation, his liberty and the very resistance which nature offers to his mind. (Roland Barthes, *Essais critiques*, p. 215)

This passage is especially typical of the 'structural thinker', down to the pathos of the concluding sentence, where confused thinking ('the intellect added to the object'?) is the price paid for that rousing finale. Thus – Saint-Exupéry could have written it, and Roger Garaudy, if he has not already done so, will inevitably write it tomorrow – the structure is the man. But this is also the precondition of a very general activity, indifferently 'reflexive or poetic': we always find the same sliding between literary production and literary criticism. Nevertheless, we have a new determination: structure is a simulacrum. Analysis is a repetition, another way of saying what has already been said; reading complements writing. This repetition ensures a certain fidelity: structural criticism will not say anything that has not already been said in the work itself. We are told that this repetition is not entirely futile because it produces a new meaning: this is obviously a contradiction: meanings can only be elucidated ('revealing that which was inevitable') because they are already there. Yet this contradiction is worth interpreting: it indicates a certain *inverted* representation of structure. We have only to stand the terms on their feet in order to identify the procedures of structural analysis as they are imagined by Roland Barthes.

It is, in fact, easy to see in this text a very indistinct reminiscence of Plato: when Barthes says that analysis elaborates a copy of the work it must be understood that the work is itself a copy. The object analysed is considered as the simulacrum of a structure: to rediscover the structure is to construct a simulacrum of the simulacrum. This method of analysis which allows for a confusion between reading and writing actually derives from the very traditional theory of the *model*. Thus the structure is postulated on the basis of a certain conception of the literary activity.

This is why structural criticism considers literature to be an imitative activity: from these methodological premises it constructs an inevitably illusory object. We are being offered a very thorough version of a familiar notion: the writer does not write, he merely appears to be writing; his production is merely an appearance because the object of this production is located *behind* it. Literary criticism, consequently, can be subsumed as an aspect of the theory of communication: its autonomy is illusory: its object exceeds absolutely the limited domain of literature: it is the art of transmitting and interpreting messages.

A consequence of this attitude is the notion of literature as de-realisation: and this is why Barthes, in spite of everything, places great emphasis on the theme of writing. The writer (and it is pointless to dwell on the skeleton-key distinction between *écrivain* and *écrivant*) is defined not by his representation of the real but by the hold on language that his particular code furnishes. Writing is not the expression of anything in particular; it is, on the contrary, inexpressive. It is the communication of a message in a *style* which is both original and conventional (because it refers to an intelligible code). An author's writing is obviously the primary object of literary criticism (if by writing we mean that the writer uses a formal language, though this posits merely a generality). But this must not hinder the recognition that this language which is reached by means of writing is not an illusory object (an artifice, a means), a mirror for the structural man, but a complete universe (a reality, probably reality itself). Literary production derives value and dignity from the fact that it gives us a measure of words which is *simultaneously* a measure of things: not one *or* the other, as proposed by the structuralists.

(Yet this abstract dissociation of two mutual terms provides an easy means of distinguishing between good and bad literature:

the former is a reified message whereas the latter claims to represent the real. It is significant that structuralist *criticism* is abetted by a structuralist literature: in this instance literary production derives from a prior criticism. But this so-called proof does not prove the scientific value of the method it aspires to exemplify: if there is a structuralist literature this is because not all literature is structuralist and therefore amenable to the method. The method thus seems to be artificial and arbitrary, in so far as it is unable to account for the totality of its domain:

> Socrates: Let us just think it out thus: there is an art of painting as a whole?
> Ion: Yes.
> Socrates: And there are and have been many painters, good and bad?
> Ion: Certainly.
> Socrates: Now have you ever found anybody who is skilled in pointing out the successes and failures among the works of Polygnotus son of Aglaophon, but unable to do so with the works of the other painters; and who, when the works of the other painters are exhibited, drops into a doze, and is at a loss, and has no remark to offer; but when he has to pronounce upon Polygnotus or any other painter you please, and on that one only, wakes up and attends and has plenty to say? (Plato, *Ion* 532e)

Only a specific work can interrupt the critic's slumbers. Far from being a general method, structuralism tends to turn the critic into a specialist. Each structure, a monolithic unity, is closed upon itself: structuralist criticism would like to be able, in the manner of Leibniz's God, to pass from one structure to the next, declaring the reasons for their universal harmony, though lacking the means for this task. For these reasons, we might eventually prefer those obsessional critics who project their private enthusiasms on to all literature. This, with uneven success, is the method of Sartre, Starobinski and Butor; in their case, the ideology, instead of functioning as a formal system, appears as an explicit content. The explanation is confused, but it can possess an authentically literary value.

In so far as each work can be traced to its principle it is good in itself; in its fashion it is incomparable and unequalled; the structuralist can only study it in itself, in its individuality. Unless, through and beyond specific works, he relates it to a general definition of literature (literature as message, for example). Thus, the only possible generality is an abstract generality. In this indefinite continuum of distinct originalities, all works are good, and all critics are also good (thus we arrive at the gratuitous nature of criticism, which is linked to its abstract character). The critic will never concern himself with the real labour of the writer, but with writing in general: what is *one* doing when one is writing? (Where does Barthes mention the specific problems that Racine had to solve? The means he possessed? The real conditions in which he found himself, without necessarily being aware of them?) The work is never related to the real conditions of its production, but to its principle, its ideal possibility (which is its simulacrum). The relation between the work and its production is precisely that which Hegel describes as corresponding to the Reign of the Animal Spirit. Indeed, this constitutive moment is characterised by the fusion of theory and creation; the author is his own critic (that is the only way to preserve his originality). Let us reverse the proposition, since creation also depends on its theory: the critic is his own author; thus the notion of a *structuralist literature*. Hegel – though not with Barthes in mind, but the Schlegel brothers, who had given him the model of the intellectual animal – had already identified the structural ideology and put it into its proper place.)

On the contrary, literature as pure message is subsumed into mythology. Its characteristic function is like that of the imaginary in general: literary analysis is just one form of semiology. The work seems to tell us something, but in fact it says nothing: this appearance is what must be elucidated. But the general principle behind this illusion infinitely exceeds the particular conditions which determine any actual writing. The writer is the priest of some general mystery. Interpretation tackles this mystery directly, and only then descends to particular instances; the critic, like the writer, writes, but he has the advantage over his rival of being able to ask: What is literature? – the question that the writer is constantly evading by means of his style. Interpretation is the analysis of an enigma, an unravelling which shows us the trap into which we so nearly fell. Criticism is thus a denunciation: the mystery is revealed as factitious. One demystifies, as it were, without realising that this operation implies a more profound mystification. The literary work, a temporary artifice, like the heroine in Poe's story 'The Oval Portrait', loses all its reality, that reality which has been absorbed by the simulacrum.

Such a notion of criticism has an undeniable *polemical* value. Literary production is conceived of as the secondary elaboration of a pre-existing system, something already shared between author and reader which alone makes communication possible. The product, the work, occurs as a device which can be explained by reference to the structure which inhabits it. It is not a *creation*, the product of a moment or an intention. Literary structuralism enables one to grasp the economy of this mythology: by studying or announcing a study of literary composition all the false uncertainties of 'the lived' are excluded (this illusory life which lacks only life itself). But this programme, in its positive aspects, is not very new: Plato had already replaced the useless myth of creation by the critical myth of inspiration, according to which the individual author is dispossessed of his work from the very beginning. It is worth noting a further aspect of the kinship between structuralism and Platonism: that this analysis applies to both the author and his interpreter, to Homer as to the *Ion*. It will also be remembered that this definition of the poet implies an artistic process in which only appearances count: 'the artist drapes the veil of uncertainty over things', as Nietzsche wrote in an astonishingly Platonic text (*The Wanderer and his Shadow*, No. 32); the illusory art of illusion.

The activity of the rhapsodist is twofold: he recites and he comments; he presents the work only in order to transpose it immediately. For the Greeks these two operations must have formed a whole: to present the work is also to present its double. The idea of commentary is worth exploring: this simple repetition opens up within the work a possibility of indefinite proliferation. The critical process thus manages to expose a play of mirrors in the text: the book is shattered, dispersed amongst its reflections.

There is then a general structure (literature) of which each particular structure is an image. Enveloped by the gaze of the critic, the work is merely the elaboration of a mirage. Entangled, folded into one another, the analysis and its object become strictly interchangeable, a sign that the analysis is unscientific.

On the fate of commentary, we must quote the pages which Foucault allots to it in the preface to his finest book, *The Birth of the Clinic*:

> But is it inevitable that we should know of no other function for speech (*parole*) than that of commentary? *Commentary* questions discourse as to what it says and intended to say; it tries to uncover that deeper meaning of speech that enables it to achieve an identity with itself, supposedly nearer to its essential truth; in other words, in stating what has been said, one has to re-state what has never been said. In this activity known as commentary which tries to transmit an old, unyielding discourse seemingly silent to itself, into another, more prolix discourse that is both more archaic and more contemporary – is concealed a strange attitude towards language: to comment is to admit by definition an excess of the signified over the signifier; a necessary unformulated remainder of thought that language has left in the shade – a remainder that is the very essence of that thought, driven outside its secret – but to comment also presupposes that this unspoken element slumbers within speech (*parole*), and that, by a superabundance proper to the signifier, one may, in questioning it, give voice to a content that was not explicitly signified. By opening up the possibility of commentary, this double plethora dooms us to an endless task that nothing can limit: there is always a certain amount of signified remaining that must be allowed to speak, while the signifier is always offered to us in an abundance that questions us, in spite of ourselves, as to what it 'means' (*veut dire*). Signifier and signified thus assume a substantial autonomy that accords the treasure of a virtual signification to each of them separately; one may even exist

without the other, and begin to speak of itself: commentary resides in that supposed space. But at the same time, it invents a complex link between them, a whole tangled web that concerns the poetic values of expression: the signifier is not supposed to 'translate' without concealing, without leaving the signified with an inexhaustible reserve; the signified is revealed only in the visible, heavy world of a signifier that is itself burdened with a meaning that it cannot control. Commentary rests on the postulate that speech (*parole*) is an act of 'translation', that it has the dangerous privilege images have of showing while concealing, and that it can be substituted for itself indefinitely in the open series of discursive repetitions; in short, it rests on a psychologistic interpretation of language that shows the stigmatas of its historical origin. This is an exegesis, which listens, through the prohibitions, the symbols, the concrete images, through the whole apparatus of Revelation, to the Word of God, ever secret, ever beyond itself. For years we have been commenting on the language of our culture from the very point where for centuries we had awaited in vain for the decision of the Word. (Trans. A. M. Sheridan, London, Tavistock, 1973)

Foucault has undertaken to rescue the history of ideas from this fate (although he does sometimes lapse into commentary on literary works: witness the ambiguity of his book on Roussel, and to some extent *The Order of Things*). We ought to ask whether this is not possible and essential in the domain of literary criticism.

Can there be a criticism which would not be commentary, which would be a scientific analysis adding an authentic knowledge to the speech of the work without, meanwhile, denying its presence? Instead of an *art of reading* could there be a *positive criticism* which would speak of the conditions for making a book? A science is not an interpretation of its objects; it is a transformation, an attribution of significations which the objects themselves did not initially possess. There is nothing in the movement of 'falling' bodies which acknowledges or 'obeys' the laws of gravity (nature is not a kingdom with a king who brings his realm under the law); these bodies fell and will always fall without announcing the law of their falling. But it was knowledge that was dedicated to the *production* of this law: in other words, the law is not *in* the falling bodies, it is elsewhere, by their side, on a different level which is the domain of scientific knowledge; this explains the failure of empiricism, which claims to set out the lessons of experience, to hear and to transcribe the silent story of the world. The transformation effected by theoretical knowledge leaves the object-reality intact; it does not de-realise it, probe its origins or its depths, it endows it with a new dimension. Thus the knowledge of a literary work is not a demystification or an undoing; it is the production of a new knowledge; the enunciation of its silent significance.

In fact, a true analysis does not remain within its object, paraphrasing what has already been said; analysis confronts the silences, the denials and the resistance in the object – not that compliant implied discourse which offers itself to discovery, but that condition which makes the work possible, which precedes the work so absolutely that it cannot be found in the work.

The analysis and constitution of a structure, or more plainly a structuration, are two names for the same operation, because through an arrangement of elements we are not pursuing a presence or an interiority. The goal of knowledge is not the discovery of a reason or a secret: through an indispensable sequence knowledge alludes to that radical otherness from which the object acquires an identity, that initial difference which limits and produces all reality, that constitutive absence which is behind the work. If the notion of structure has any meaning it is in so far as it designates this absence, this difference, this determinate otherness.

Freud, in spite of his ambiguous project for a 'depth' analysis, was not seeking for a latent meaning beneath the conscious discourse: he initiated a new rationality in so far as he located this meaning *elsewhere* – in that other place, the place of structures, which he called the unconscious. The unconscious, which is not, properly speaking, a reality but a concept (hence the dangers of a realist interpretation of the doctrine of the unconscious), a peculiar speechless language from which nothing will ever emerge but structures, the images of the discourse and the words of the dream. To analyse an utterance is not to trace its genesis but to illuminate that other thing from which it is produced; in this sense structure is radically distinct from genesis. The verb 'to structure' is obviously transitive: the structure appropriates its objects from without; it transforms by constructing them, rather than treating them as empirical data. In the scientific discourse of Martinet, for example, if we have properly grasped the essential role played by the theory of double articulation, 'structure of the signifier' does not mean structure *in* the signifier, but the ensemble of the segments of the utterance, defined independently of all utterance, which constitutes language, without which there would be neither signifier nor signified nor utterance. The linguistic system thus construed does not exist, as Saussure had already realised. Structure is thus of a different nature from its objects; it is not a copy. Analysis is not a repetition but the production of a new knowledge.

If this representation of structure is correct, we must ask where the structures of literary utterance are located. If there is a structure, it is not in the book, concealed in its depths: it inhabits the book but is not its content. Thus, the fact that the book can be related to a structure does not imply that it is of a homogeneous substance; the structure sustains the work in so far as the work is diverse, scattered and irregular. Indeed, the traditional conception of the work of art turns upon the central concept of *harmony*. Whether this harmony is natural (reproducing the harmony of a place or of a feeling: Lamartine) or artificial (the work is the effect of applied rules which in themselves guarantee consistency), in both cases the judgment of the work is a judgment of order. The work exists only in so far as it realises a totality; it is the product of an arrangement. (It is significant that any genetic analysis culminates in this kind of ordered immutable object. Structure is the only concept that can account for an authentic temporality, because it can *think irregularity*.) It does not matter whether this order, this organisation, is intuitive or discursive: the work presents itself (and it is not anything more than this presence) as a consistent entity.

It is easy to criticise the idea of consistency by analysing the antinomies of aesthetic judgment. But the idea of totality is the most tenacious because it derives from a deeper prejudice and thus survives the critique of classical aesthetics (briefly, a theology of 'creation').

A totality: a certain relation links the parts and thus *makes* them into a whole. The work succeeds in so far as it realises this convergence: otherwise it is merely the shadow of a work, a failure. This is how the privileges of form are represented: the form is that which gives body, which endows the work with its organic existence. The work is held together by the internal necessity of these relations: it owes it to itself to exist. It is full of itself: those elements which are the object of analysis only enter into its composition in so far as they find *their* place in the work. This representation of literary space is entirely borrowed from Aristotelian physics, an aesthetic physics in which objects are identified by their qualities. The diversity of elements is relative, a prior material, necessary to the realisation of order but with no existence independent of it. Thus literature is easily reinserted in the series of the arts: on condition that these arts are defined as *the activity of producing imaginary organisms.* This organic unity which constructs the work from a formal exigency also endows it with a meaning, a content. Criticism is consequently *interpretative*: it elucidates the principle of this unity, the rationality of this whole.

This is exactly Lévi-Strauss's procedure when he interprets or analyses (for him the two operations go together) the story of Asdiwal, which is successively divided and reassembled. First he defines the different levels in relation to a '*subjacent* structure, common to all the levels'. The myth is constructed like a 'musical score': its apparent diversity supposedly conceals a unity. Elements of the myth, horizontal sequences and vertical schemes are combined to form the text of a *message*:

> All the paradoxes conceived by the native mind, on the most diverse planes – geographical, economic, sociological, and even cosmological – are, when all is said and done, assimilated to that less obvious yet so real paradox, the

dilemma which marriage with the matrilateral cousin attempts but fails to resolve. But the failure is *admitted* in our myths, and there precisely lies their function. (Lévi-Strauss, *Structural Anthropology*, vol. 2, trans. M. Layton, London, Allen Lane, 1977, p. 170)

The myth only lends itself to analysis in so far as analysis can identify an intention in the myth; inversely, we ascertain what the myth has to say by constituting its 'structure'. The myth resolves the contradictions of the real which are necessarily diverse and scattered; in this sense it belongs to the domain of the imaginary. The myth presents reality by means of a number of deformations; but the whole constituted by these deformations is structured: it is thus significant.

We are dealing with an exemplary positive analysis: Lévi-Strauss articulates what is *in* the myth. But, at least in this specific case, he does not see what is not in the myth, without which the myth might not perhaps exist. The structure is construed in relation to an intention (whether the intention produces the myth or vice versa), and the intention is thus the object of a *psychology* but not of a true *logic*. Logic precisely enables us to grasp how a relation between two such terms can establish itself on the basis of their difference: if unity is postulated from the beginning (in the *intention*, for example) there is no further problem. In reality, the structure is the very space of difference: in principle, then, it is absent from the relation which it helps to explain. In this text of Lévi-Strauss, the structure is ineluctably *present*: even though it is temporarily silent. In so far as it contributes to the imaginary resolution of a contradiction, it affirms the permanence of that contradiction. Such a contradiction could only be imaginary: it is impossible to think the real presence of a contradiction; it can only be conceived as an absence. It will then be claimed that the myth exists to give *form* (rather than body) to this absence.

Even if the conception of structure proposed by Lévi-Strauss (the presence of an absence, not a true absence) is an appropriate solution to the problem of analysing myths, the question must still be asked whether it can be used as it stands in literary analysis.

The concepts of order and totality produce satisfying *descriptions* of literary works; they pose the problem of the interpretation of their object; above all, they establish a certain peculiar rigour in the work, a certain tenacity and solidity; it produces itself rather than being produced. Thus, as we have seen, is eliminated the problematic of creation. But this rigour is necessary only because it is also totally imaginary: thus described, the work differs from all others in that it might not have existed. (This distinction is also a certain form of resemblance. In relation to the question, What is literature? all works are similar.) This necessity is thus gratuitous, precarious. The entire description is based on a logical fallacy: the work is all of a piece, like a solid body in a literary space; the analysis strives to establish precisely this self-presence of the work.

A different hypothesis, more fruitful though hardly ever used, might be offered: the work exists above all by its determinate absences, by what it does not say, in its relation to what it is not. Not that it can conceal anything: this meaning is not buried in its depths, masked or disguised; it is not a question of hunting it down with interpretations. It is not in the work but by its side: on its margins, at that limit where it ceases to be what it claims to be because it has reached back to the very conditions of its possibility. It is then no longer constituted by a factitious necessity, the product of a conscious or unconscious intention.

To take up a vocabulary well known to novices of philosophy, structural criticism or metaphysical criticism is only a variant of theological aesthetics. In both cases the aim is a causal explanation: a personal intention in the case of the aesthetics of creation; an abstract intention, presented in the form of an entity, in the case of structural analysis. Perhaps the time has come to elaborate a positive criticism which would deal with laws rather than causes. The critical question would then be: *In what relation to that which is other than itself is the work produced*? Positive is, as we know, also opposed to negative: and Comte opposes the 'demystification' of metaphysics to that positive knowledge which is uniquely equipped to define real relations. We also know that metaphysical ideologies and positive science are not just different answers to the same question: positive science requires a different question.

Indeed, the structural method is content to give a new answer to the old question of aesthetics, just as the writers themselves have asked it. The real critical question is not: What is literature? (What does *one* do when *one* writes, or reads?) The question is: What kind of necessity determines the work? What is it really made from? The critical question should concern the material being used and the implements so employed.

From without, then, structure is that which dispossesses the work of its false interiority, its secret cause, revealing that basic defect without which it would not exist. At this point the treaty with linguistics and psychoanalysis takes on its full significance. The literary work is also doubly articulated: at the initial level of sequences (the fable) and themes (the forms) which establish an illusory order; this is the level of organicist aesthetic theories. At another level, the work is articulated in relation to the reality from the ground of which it emerges: not a 'natural' empirical reality, but that intricate reality in which men – both writers and readers – live, that reality which is *their ideology*. The work is made on the ground of this ideology, that tacit and original language: not to speak, reveal, translate or make explicit this language, but to make possible that absence of words without which there would be nothing to say.

We should question the work as to what it does not and cannot say, in those silences for which it has been made. The concealed order of the work is thus less significant than its real *determinate* disorder (its disarray). The order which it professes is merely an imagined order, projected on to disorder, the fictive resolution of ideological conflicts, a resolution so precarious that it is obvious in the very letter of the text where incoherence and incompleteness burst forth. It is no longer a question of defects but of indispensable informers. This distance which separates the work from the ideology which it transforms is rediscovered in the very letter of the work: it is fissured, unmade even in its making. A new kind of necessity can be defined: by an absence, by a lack. The disorder that permeates the work is related to the disorder of ideology (which cannot be organised as a system). The work derives its form from this incompleteness which enables us to identify the active presence of a conflict at its borders. In the defect of the work is articulated a new truth: for those who seek to know this truth it establishes an original relation to the real, it establishes the revealing form of a knowledge.

November 1965

III

Some Works

Chapter 21

Jules Verne: The Faulty Narrative

I The problem posed by the work

The works of Jules Verne possess for us an immediate historical significance, if only as a consequence of the audiences they have attracted. These audiences have been of at least two sorts, both of them eminently representative of our historical era: the French bourgeoisie of the Third Republic which 'commissioned' and had Verne's work acclaimed by the Académie française; and also the people of the Soviet Union, who have become the guardian of his reputation by keeping his work in print. At least two publics have found themselves in Verne's work and tied that work indissolubly to their own historical moment: to the conquest of France's colonial empire and the exploration of the cosmos, to the construction of the Suez Canal as to the cultivation of virgin lands. Obviously it is not a question of identifying these two readings as the expression of a formal continuity within a single project: history demonstrates that the transition from one project to another is not smoothly continuous but discontinuous. Thus the work of Jules Verne, far from deriving a vague coherence from these projects, will on the contrary appear as the expression of a *complex ideological phenomenon* (not necessarily 'contradictory') which, by its very duration, acquires a variety of meanings. It is this variety which demands to be explained. A first question is posed: it is not a matter of reducing the work to *a* meaning, whether manifest or latent; it is that strange power of *internal variation* which solicits our attention – that diversity which gives it *a priori*, its coherence.

But what will an explanation involve in this case? Will it be sufficient, in order to dismantle the work, simply to relate it to the history in which it is embedded? Or rather to demonstrate its secret relationship with history? And thus to reveal its meaning. We should find ourselves writing the history of an ideological theme – (We shall see that the real themes of the work are not the same as these *general* – and generous – ideological themes which constitute a *subject*, a descriptive project, but do not contribute to its realisation. The real themes are indistinguishable from the actual elaboration of the work. Thus we already know that the secret of the work is not contained in the ideological themes, which merely indicate a general intention. The work is revealed rather in the instruments of its production; it is these, its real means, that we may legitimately call themes) – the conquest of nature, the expression of a historical phenomenon which revealed what had previously remained a secret of history: the exploitation of natural energy. The history of this conquest and exploitation deserves to be recorded (although this opportunity has been almost entirely neglected), and it may be thought that it contains the work of Jules Verne as one of its specific manifestations. But the work surpasses this history entirely: the general history of a theme implies the priority of history itself; without such a priority the theme remains insubstantial, in an isolation that is the very essence of the ideological. In that case, the (interpretative) explanation succeeds because it snatches at its object from too great a distance, and sweeps it off its feet. This procedure is not, as has so often been suggested, a betrayal of the object, but rather perhaps an extravagance. By being too enthusiastically situated the work is *simplified*: it becomes merely the site of a meaning; its real complexity has been abolished.

As against the excesses of interpretation it is usual to posit the systematic description, which does not alter the work, because it proposes only to *disengage* a structure, a specific coherence, to establish a principle of closure which constitutes the work, that *sufficiency* evident in the internal relations of its various parts.

This structuring, which is a relatively simple operation (especially in the case of an author like Verne, who wanted to make his work as transparent as possible by emphasising the obviousness of its articulations), which involves an analysis (the isolation of particular themes, the definition of mythical symbols) and a re-assembly (the establishment of a hierarchy among its elements), is the exact opposite of a historical analysis: the logic of the work is the logic of its composition, a logic which is immediate and immanent, even if the study of composition goes beyond a mere problematic of forms. We are satisfied with a singular totality – the work reduced to a coherent whole – from which we have stripped away all that is factitious or contingent. Indeed, this singular totality is precisely the opposite of an individual essence: the work is situated there, and, *independently of the fact that it is situated*, it is simply this situation, this arrangement, which is to be accounted for. Such an individualisation, such an isolation, is a pure abstraction, a de-realisation. But it is also, as in the previous instance, a simplification, a reduction to the single dimension of a *reason* (*raison*).

It thus appears that the choice is to be between two radically opposed methods: that of interpretation, which moves towards the work, seizing upon it from a distance, or that of description, which moves away from the work in order to estrange it from itself. Perhaps it is possible, from the outset, to escape from this contradiction by placing ourselves in that very gap which separates interpretation and description: we should speak of the work by moving it beyond itself, by establishing it in the knowledge of its limits. The question is then no longer one of commentary or reconstitution or unification, but one of explanation – explanation which dislodges the work internally, just as it was obliged to deviate from its intentions in order to realise them. Neither is it a question of rediscovering its very nature in the movement of the history in which it is involved; it is a question of compelling it to speak its true purposes: those purposes which it could itself have known before being written. Thus we are proposing a very different question: What is the principle of the work's *disparity*? In this instance it is conceded that – to borrow a well-known metaphor – the work unfolds in more than one plane.

Interpretation nominates the work as situation; description makes of it a simple disposition. We must ensure that the one does not exclude or obscure the other, measuring the work by that real distance between its disposition and its situation. The opposition is not to be abolished, but exploited, regarded as the *crux of the problem*. There is no question of mistaking the one for the other, of confusing them: deriving the situation from the disposition (an epiphany), or deriving the disposition from the situation (deduction). There is a qualitative difference between these two points of view, a difference which makes them irreducible, although, as we shall see, they define between them a single question which is totally new. It is this differential relation which will define the area of the problematic: and it is this which will enable us to present the work simultaneously in its reality and in its limits, taking into account the conditions of possibility and impossibility which make it visible.

The only point of departure for the specific study of a work – by no means that upon which it actually depends, but its real beginning – is the validity of an ideological project. In the present case it is the general theme of the conquest of nature: it will be seen that it is immediately elaborated by means of specific themes (different in nature? how organised?) which are the real themes of the work. Verne begins by asking himself this question: Is it this conquest of nature which defines the content of the history of the contemporary world? Aware of the topicality of this question he also asks himself: How can this be expressed? The answer will be: By means of fiction.

> We live in an age in which anything can happen, we are almost entitled to say: in which everything has happened. If our story does not seem probable today, it may well do so tomorrow, thanks to the scientific knowledge of the future, and it will not enter anyone's head to regard the story as a legend. Moreover, nobody would invent legends at the close of this practical and positive nineteenth century. (*Carpathian Castle*, ch. 1)

The future is hidden in the present: *mobilis in mobili*. We shall again encounter this image (which is not an image) at a later stage. Above all, this era has produced a new kind of narrative – one which gives the imaginary its function as reality: this is why fiction is the privileged form of expression during this historical transition. In this manner, the literary work *immediately* becomes reality. This intersection of the ordinary and the extraordinary, which is the literary form of the *sensation*, is related to a specific aspect of the narrative – the voyage; and it is this voyage which gives the work its title. The plan thus sketched out can be ordered by a bookseller in this 'historic' contract:

> Jules Verne's latest work will be progressively added to this edition which will be kept carefully up to date. The titles already published, as well as those planned, will in their entirety encompass the scheme that the author devised when he adopted for his work the subtitle: *Voyages to Worlds Known and Unknown*. He actually intends to summarise all the knowledge – geographical, geological, physical, astronomical – accumulated by modern science, and to recast in an appropriate and attractive form, the history of the universe . . .
>
> Among contemporary productions there is no other which answers more fully the noble impulse of modern society to know at last the marvels of this universe in which its destiny is enacted. (Hetzel, Preface to vol. 1 of his edition of *The Complete Works: The Adventures of Captain Hatteras*)

'To know' also implies, as we shall see, to act, to transform. 'To know at last' – it is that 'at last' which defines the modern. And the object of the narrative will be both 'the marvels' and those voyages in the area which separates the known *and* the unknown – an area which is also a certain form of conjunction.

Thus we appear to have grasped both the general project and the meaning of the work. However, this initial question is not the inevitable one: within this question the problem of the work itself remains untouched, external to the project, or at least not directly dependent on the project. So many people would like to write, but actually write nothing, that we are not justified in only considering the writer's intentions when we seek to understand his work. We are obliged to examine not only the conditions of the possibility of the project, but also the validity of the means employed in its realisation. And if, refraining from opposing the meaning of the project to its effective formulation, we display the conjunction (though not, of course, the confusion) of these elements, we can propose a different question: What did Verne *actually* find that he had done? What is the relation between the initial project and the work for which it was simply a pretext or condition? It is a question of studying the work from the conditions of its possibility – conditions which produced something quite different even while they made the work possible. Thus a second question, superimposed on the first, enables us to confront the work with itself, without recourse to interpretation, to commentary that merely translates the work into another language. This will be the question which makes *explanation* possible.

II Analysis of the work

Note that I shall be dealing with only a limited number of novels: those written in the first period (1863–78), which are in fact the best known, and which coincide, for Verne, with the task of inventing a new literary genre. *The Mysterious Island* was published in 1875. The field has thus been deliberately limited because it seemed pointless to accumulate and duplicate references, whereas it is simple to pick out what is characteristic. It also seemed pointless to contest certain statements with references drawn from Verne's later work. Obviously he developed, and once he had devised themes he would put them to various different uses. See in particular the pessimism of the later works: *Robur*, *The Begum's Fortune*, *The Barsac Mission*, *The Last Adam*. They amount to an attempt to close off the future by means of that which had been devised to portray its opening out. This issue is studied by Michel Butor in *Répertoire I*. It is interesting that Verne's work has a history, but it is not this aspect of his work which has been historically important, and the study of this development belongs in another domain. The disparagement of science is a new ideological theme, not a denial of the earlier work but a new questioning of the means of its realisation. Thus this description of the work of Jules Verne is not complete, but it is sufficient to its purpose.

A THE POINT OF DEPARTURE: THE IDEOLOGICAL PROJECT

It seems not only possible but necessary to begin from the work itself, rather than at a distance or simply by moving through it. It is even inevitable that we must begin where the work itself begins: at the point of departure which it has chosen, its project, or even its intentions, which are able to be read all through it like a programme. This is also what is called its *title*.

Firstly, then, a general and explicit theme against which the work is continuously defined: the internal transformation of the social order by a process which is history itself, but which has now (and here arises the theme of modernity) come to predominate: the conquest of nature by industry. This is an easily identifiable ideological theme:

> Verne belongs to the progressive line of the bourgeoisie: his work proclaims that man is capable of everything, that even the most distant world is an object within his reach, and that property is only after all a dialectical moment in the general subjection of nature. (Barthes, *Mythologies*, trans. Annette Lavers, London, Cape, 1972)

The idea of an industry takes on a very general meaning which brings together individual and social conditions, both ingenuity and labour. (One must, however, mention that individual and social conditions could only be rather artificially distinguished within Verne's work: society is represented entirely by typical individuals – the expert or the adventurer, who are actually identical. This is to say that everything in Verne which seems to derive from individual psychology is merely allusive, and that all his descriptions of character only seem to be irritating failures because there is neither psychology nor character.) To resume, this unity of the individual and the social, of ingenuity and labour, is visible in the privileged object of the machine.

This theme is immediately made more specific – and the problem will then be to know if these themes are similar or different, independent or in a hierarchy. It must be pointed out that the general theme is only the appearance of a theme: it only indicates a certain movement at the level of society or its ideology – a movement which is of the greatest importance for the emergence of the work, but *on its own level*, not in so far as it is translated into a general idea which deforms and simplifies that movement.

Man's domination of nature, the *subject* of all Verne's work, though sometimes in a disguised form, is presented as a conquest, as a movement – the propagation of the presence of man in the whole of nature, which is also a transformation of nature itself. Nature is invested by man: this is Verne's *elementary* obsession (elementary because it is conscious and deliberate). A total conquest is possible; man penetrates nature only because he is in total harmony with it. The great novelty is that this movement, like a voyage, has an ending, and that this ending can be seen and described: the future bathes in the present, the future is completely contained in the present. See the opening of *Carpathian Castle*, already quoted. Butor has covered this definitively in his *Répertoire I*. Science, the supreme work of man, enjoys a close intimacy with nature: science will eventually know and transform nature entirely. (Note that for Gramsci this intimacy is only the result of an equilibrium: it implies a voluntary limitation, the decision not to press too far ahead in fiction (in contrast to Poe or H. G. Wells). This would explain the obsolescence of Verne's work: this equilibrium condemns it because it is dated and ought to be revised. But is Verne's work obsolete?)

> 'It will be done,' answered Captain Hood, 'just as some day voyages will be made to both the North and South Pole!'
>
> 'Evidently!'
>
> 'Or an exploring party to the lowest depths of old Ocean.'
>
> 'Doubtless.'
>
> 'Or a journey to the centre of the earth?'
>
> 'Bravo, Hood!'
>
> 'As everything will be done!' I added.
>
> 'Even an aerial voyage to each of the planets of the solar

> system!' rejoined Hood, whom nothing daunted.
>
> 'No, captain,' I replied. 'Man, a mere inhabitant of the earth, cannot overstep its boundaries! But though he is confined to its crust, he may penetrate into all its secrets.'
>
> 'He can, he must!' cried Banks. 'All that is within the limits of possibility may and shall be accomplished. Then when man has nothing more to discover in the globe which he inhabits – '
>
> 'He will disappear with the spheroid which has no longer any mysteries concealed from him,' put in Captain Hood.
>
> 'Not so!' returned Banks. 'He will enjoy it as a master, and will derive far greater advantages from it.' (*The Steam House*)

'He can penetrate all secrets': Nemo will reach the Pole (which, as will be seen, is the most pointed representation of totality). The site of this movement, the place which both tolerates and encourages it, is not the world as infinity but the earth as habitation. Barthes speaks correctly of the 'enclosing' gesture of Verne:

> Verne was a maniac for plenitude: he never stopped putting the finishing touches to the world, stocking it, making it as complete as an egg; he repeats precisely the gesture of the eighteenth-century Encyclopaedist or the Dutch painter: the world is complete, the world is full of determinate continuous matter. (Barthes, *Mythologies*)

(This notion of enclosure is obviously interesting as it relates to the representation of the cosmos as interiority, as the space of an intimacy, the very notion against which science was obliged to struggle at the beginnings of its modern period (see the work of Koyré and Francastel on this issue). Here we come up against the first theoretical regression in Verne's work, a regression which immediately announces the ideological character of that work.)

The movement amounts to an exploration, contained within the limits of its imaginary-real perfection. It is possible to see in this adequation of man to his adventure, of science to nature, a first example of the aphorism which defines the work: *mobilis in mobili*.

Rather than the quotations chosen by Michel Butor to illustrate this natural faculty of dreaming, I would offer the following, taken from chapter 14 of *Journey to the Centre of the Earth*:

> It is generally known that basalt is a brown rock of igneous origin; it takes forms which are surprising in their regularity. Here Nature proceeds geometrically, working in human fashion, as if she were furnished with set square, compasses, and plumb-line. If elsewhere she uses with artistic effect masses flung in disorder, the beginnings of cones, imperfect pyramids, here, wishing to give an example of regularity, and anticipating our early architects, she has created severe order, unsurpassed by the splendours of Babylon or the marvels of Greece.
>
> I had indeed heard tell of the Giant's Causeway in Ireland, and of Fingal's Cave in Staffa, but I had never yet beheld the spectacle of basaltic structure; now at Stapi this phenomenon appeared in all its beauty.
>
> The sides of the fjord, and the whole coast of the peninsula, were composed of a succession of vertical columns, thirty feet high. These straight and well-proportioned pillars supported others laid horizontally and projecting beyond them so as to overhang the sea. At certain intervals, under this natural roof, one had a vision of beautiful arched gateways, through which the waves from the open sea rushed, breaking themselves in foam. Some fragments of basalt columns, broken off by the fury of the ocean, lay along the beach like the ruins of an antique temple, ruins eternally young, over which the centuries pass without effect.

It would be difficult to find, even amongst that other, 'great' literature, descriptions finer than this, which is unsurpassed in its richness and simplicity. This description, even more conceptualised than thematised, offers us an explicit example of the debate between regularity and irregularity, a debate which is ultimately only a dialogue. Nature is represented in terms of art, but a certain ambiguity in the vocabulary of stumps and columns blurs the boundary between the two categories. The description is indirect; it presents an unexpected inversion: 'ruins eternally young'. Nature as architecture: not simply a cliché but the revelation of a profound secret. What begins as a description, in fact reflects on the rudimentary dialectic of nature (that found in novels).

In the transparent forms of its own past, nature dreams the future of man. Thus the movement which paradoxically involves the future in the present can be represented only in the form of an imaginary variation of the real – a variation which signifies a certain optimism, the hope that the imaginary is the real. Verne's speculations, and our speculations based on his work, concerning the probability of the invention, the precision of the detail, the truthfulness of the fiction – all derive from this initial identification of the imaginary and the real. Obviously this identification depends on a certain conception of science, a conception which is not entirely mythological but is given *a priori*, as a representation. Science is the 'equal sign' between the real and the imaginary. Its power is thus essentially poetic.

It will be recalled that in the speech which Barbican makes to the Gun Club (see *From the Earth to the Moon*, ch. 2) it is the reminder of the fiction of the past, from Cyrano de Bergerac to Edgar Allan Poe, which precedes the announcement of the real project. ' "And now," said Barbican, "that we have allowed a large share to poetry, let us tackle the issue directly" ' (ch. 7). Thus is reverie built on a plan like that which Leibniz attributes to the Palace of the Fates: the possible precedes, announces and affirms a better reality. The real is the fulfilment of a fiction. (This is why science fiction is also poetic. Technology, as the illustrators had grasped, can be ornamental, can be decorated, can be made fashionable in a way that surprises us today, but for those first readers it was thus rendered more familiar – almost, indeed, commonplace.) As Michael Arden says when faced with the vehicle which will convey him to the moon:

> 'I am only sorry that the shape is not more streamlined, the nose-cone more stylish; it should have been finished

off with a cluster of metal ornaments, with a chimera for instance, a gargoyle, a salamander coming out of the fire with his wings spread and his mouth open . . .'

'What's the use of that,' said Barbican, whose practical mind did not appreciate artistic beauty.

'The use, Barbican? Well, if you have to ask me that, I am afraid you will never understand!'

'Tell me anyway.'

'Right. In my view, its always best to put a little art into what you do. . . .'

Ultimately, the transformation of nature is accomplished by nature itself, and there is nothing to differentiate the work of nature from the work of man (science and art). Nature itself creates machines and cities: it not only produces energy but transforms it as well (a special example: the volcano which as though by chance adorns the edge of the world); at any rate nature creates energy which can be transformed and tamed. The works of man are always fundamentally natural:

A savage, wandering somewhere beyond the limits of the horizon, might have believed that some new crater was forming in the bosom of Florida, although there was neither any eruption, nor typhoon, nor storm, nor struggle of the elements, nor any of those terrible phenomena which Nature can produce. No, it was man alone who had produced these reddish vapours, these gigantic flames worthy of a volcano, these tremendous vibrations resembling the shock of an earthquake, these reverberations rivalling those of hurricanes and storms; and it was his hand which precipitated into an abyss, dug by himself, a whole Niagara of molten metal! (*From the Earth to the Moon*, ch. 15)

Inversely:

But, unlike the European Switzerland, it is not given up to the peaceful industries of the shepherd, the guide, and the hotelkeeper. It has Alpine decorations only, just a crust of rocks, and earth and venerable pines spread over a mass of iron and coal.

> Should the traveller through these solitudes stay on his way to listen awhile to the voice of nature, he would not, as on the slopes of the Oberland, hear the gentle murmurs of insect life, or the herd-boy's call, enhancing the silence of the mountain. On his ear in this wild spot would fall the heavy sound of the steam hammer, and under his feet would echo the muffled explosions of powder.
>
> He would feel as if the ground was as full of trap-doors as the stage of a theatre, and that at any moment even the huge rocks might sink and disappear into unknown depths. (*The Begum's Fortune*, ch. 5)

The works of man have thus a somewhat ambiguous quality: that energy which is tameable and tamed has about it something monstrous because it can produce and be produced. Electricity has a double power: it is nature unchained, but it is also man unchained (see *Carpathian Castle*, and *The Mysterious Island*). In this it acquires a dubious power; it begets a number of enigmatic objects which disturb by their very presence. To this we shall return.

The imaginary is the real, just as the future is the present. There is at this level a perfect unity between the content of the work and the form which it receives. This coherent and harmonious creation takes the pure form of an identification. But what is the source of this harmony? Does the work contain from the beginning the secret of its own substantiality? On the contrary, this harmony can only seem very fragile indeed, determining as it does only one very specific level of production: this level merely derived from an internal doubling. For this reason it does not manifest all the conditions for the realisation of the work.

This general *intention* draws its forms of representation from a very specific mode of expression: the imaginary narrative, the fiction. Butor has demonstrated excellently how Verne's representation of the world directly dictated a style:

> If the dreams of Jules Verne are so 'natural', this is because they are for him the very dreams which he hears or sees in nature, nature in the strictest sense of the word. There is for him no significant difference between human artefacts and natural phenomena. The real is merely a kind

> of Assumption of the imaginary. The transition from the real to the imaginary is accomplished imperceptibly, because Nature is herself a dreamer and man eventually realises those same dreams, on a smaller and less noble scale perhaps, but more perfectly in this: he completes these dreams, he realises their true purposes. He fulfils those promises which are inscribed within things. It is indeed remarkable, this copious storehouse of arches and pillars and vaults, these would-be castles, these natural cathedrals. (*Répertoire I*, pp. 133–4)

At this primary level, at the level of the project, elaborated as far as the general means of its realisation (a literary *genre*: the imaginary narrative) but not the real implements of its fabrication (it is at this moment of generality, of totality, that criticism usually concludes), at this level then we have: (1) *a subject*, one that implies a total vision of the world, an ideology (seemingly complete), a subject which even depends on the vision and the ideology in so far as it is a summary of both; (2) the general shape of a representation: the book will be a narrative, it will belong to the literature of fantasy.

We now need more detail of the subject; we need to identify *spontaneously* and provisionally its essential thematic objects. This specificity is located entirely within the kind of coherence that has already been described; it does not involve any movement beyond the generality and totality of the established project.

Conquest, movement and transformation will be expressed in three major themes: the voyage, scientific invention, and colonisation. The three are actually equivalent: the scientist is in fact a traveller and a coloniser; all combinations are obviously possible. The most general title of the work is 'the voyage'; the protagonist is the scientist, not necessarily the inventor but perhaps simply the practitioner, the one who brings the objects of science to life (for Verne science has its reality only in the material objects that it produces); it might be the engineer, or even the patron (as in *Carpathian Castle* and *Twenty Thousand Leagues Under the Sea*). Verne acknowledges no gap between the theory and the practice of science; there is simply a constant flow from the one into the other. The theme of colonisation is less explicit, less frequently emphasised, as though it had to be kept out of sight; but the scientist is a conqueror, an appropriator, one who moves into the unknown as the expression of his power. This theme becomes important in *The Mysterious Island* and *The Children of Captain Grant*, where the enterprise is openly described.

These concrete representations, these individualised subjects, also determine the form of the narrative: conquest – the convergence of the real and the imaginary – is lived as an adventure, and the narrative will be an adventure story with a typically episodic structure. The opening of *The Adventures of Captain Hatteras* reveals the secret of this fictional voyage by showing how there is an immediate continuity between the natural theme of movement and the operations of the 'fantastic'. In fact, the form of the novel is not so much a deduction from its content as the one sliding into the other; the voyage functions as a point of departure, as the nexus of the fiction:

> For a thinker, a dreamer, a philosopher, after all, nothing more moving than a ship about to sail; the imagination eagerly follows it in its battle with sea and wind, on that bold course which does not always end in the harbour, and if only something unusual happens the ship takes on an eerie form for even the most common-sense minds.

Reciprocally, the traveller-scholar-colonist will also be an adventurer, and thus he acquires a real form, a character, a social specificity: Nemo appals him. Nemo, Fogg, Glenarvan, Cyrus Smith, Paganel, Hatteras: disturbing, familiar, or even merely comic, the adventurer has a distinct countenance. Consider the 'originality' of Verne's characters: it is not only a question of a psychological or literary motif but also of a way of designating, of pointing towards the basic role of the character: the privileged subject of an extraordinary adventure. This is how Phileas Fogg, for instance, is both an absurdity and a fantastic hero.

Thus we have seen established a subject specified in individualised representations, the determination of a certain form of writing with its specific episodes, its psychological types, and even its ethics – all of which is both borrowed and bound together in the coherence of a genre: a total narrative *form*. But here deduction has its ending: we must move to a different level of analysis in order to find new *means*.

But, it must be emphasised once again, this remains at a level of generality: the project has crystallised in a typical intention, but also, most significantly, in other concrete forms: a publisher's contract, an audience, a plan of publication, collaborators, publicity, illustrations. This level is the practical, the conscious point of departure of the enterprise: it will suffice for the beginnings of a description of the work. But it is not self-sufficient.

In fact:

1 It is a question of an ideological representation, linked to the general conditions for an ideology. This ideology expresses equally the state of society as a form of social consciousness (whence the subject-programme); a state of literature or of writing – the form of the narrative, the typical characters; and even the situation of the writer, in so far as this representation reflects the ideology of the profession: an audience, a publisher, amongst others. This representation is *imported* into Verne's specific project: the ideological programme (the conquest of nature, the social position of science) enters literature and it will express itself there, but it does not have the freedom of the city, because it is not, initially, constituted as a fiction. As it is, it certainly cannot become literature; it must first undergo a few alterations, submit to a secondary elaboration which will transform it into a literary object. Verne's contract with the firm of Hetzel commits him to producing regularly novels 'of a new type'; in a letter to his father Verne specified that this means 'the science novel'. Verne is clearly aware of what he is doing: joining a new form and a new content in a new work. For this purpose, the project must create and employ new means (other than a programme), means which meet the requirements of the real *practice* of literary production. These means will not necessarily be borrowed from the same areas of ideology; they will probably need to be sought elsewhere.

2 The transition from the ideological project to the written work can only be accomplished within a practice which begins

from determinate conditions. At this moment of the analysis it would be tempting to say that Verne has *everything necessary* for the writing of his books; but in fact he has nothing at all and must seek out other means: those true *themes* of his work – in their individuality, in the specificity of the writing of a page – which, unlike the ideological subject, cannot be immediately representative of a generality. For us these themes define another level of description, corresponding to the time of production, which can be called *figuration*. Naturally it remains to be seen whether this second level sustains and continues the first level, or whether it puts it into question; and then whether, at this new level, it is self-sufficient.

B THE REALISATION OF THIS PROJECT: ITS FIGURATION, AND THE SYMBOLOGY OF THIS FIGURATION

The signs

The journey through science and through nature, which is the historical process of the future within the present, by means of the language of the fiction, has to *figure* man's total mastery over nature. Figuration is something rather more than representation, since it is a question of devising, or at least collecting, the visible signs in which this important adventure can be read: the reading of these signs will give a certain representation of the project but it is necessary first to discover the signs. We can find in Michel Butor's *Répertoire I* the index of these signs (before they are incorporated into the movement of the work they in fact have no other unity than that of their presence within a catalogue) – an index which is adequate as a beginning. We will not take up all these signs here, but will simply extricate the most important examples, and locate them in relation to each other. A sign denotes itself as such by its obsessional character: its efficacy derives from its various repetitions. The signs thus form a veritable series, a series inevitably limited. Most frequently and conspicuously we find the following: the centre (of the earth), the straight line, the document in code, the volcano, the sea, the trail (of a previous voyage – this is another form of code); and we even find 'psychological' signs: haste, the fixed idea. (Obviously there is only an apparent psychology, in so far as we are dealing with signs necessarily symbolic and allusive: the psychology is there for other reasons; if it can seem schematic, it should also not be taken seriously.)

The achievement of this mastery, the possession of the figures, can be shown, narrated, at two levels of feeling:

Time

The eighty days that Phileas Fogg gives himself to enclose the earth within the narrow limits of a temporal rectitude. Accordingly, it is the case that the earth can be circled in a predetermined time. The venture is regulated by reference to a static rule which must be observed, that is to say, imposed upon the obstacles which present themselves. It is significant that the success of this enterprise is embodied in a *circuit*, that is to say, in the movement of closure which reduces divefsity to a fixed form: this circuit is the mobile equivalent of the fixed point of the pole. Analogously *From the Earth to the Moon* is also a 'direct journey in ninety-seven hours twenty minutes'.

Space

The thirty-seventh parallel of *The Children of Captain Grant* is an exact replica of Fogg's eighty days. Over and above all the possible accidents which may arise from man's encounter with nature (but these obstacles are actually identical since they determine the adventure equally) the surface of the earth can be crossed in a straight line. Even *Tribulations of a Chinaman in China*, in spite of their absolute disorder, displays a certain regularity:

> 'But where are you going?'
> 'Straight ahead.'
> 'Where will you stop?'
> 'Nowhere!'
> 'And when will you return?'
> 'Never'! (ch. 11)

In the same way, Michael Strogoff will go directly to Irkutsk; he will overcome the obstacles men place in his path as though they were natural obstacles; the myth of science is in this case replaced by a purely novelistic myth. But, at the centre of the novel, there is always a real *journey*. The voyage is a conquest because it manages to draw a straight line over the world (and for *The Children of Captain Grant*, the witness to this conquest is Paganel, the geographer). The theme of the line is accordingly linked to that of the cipher: the secret of regularity is buried in a mutilated disguised document which must be interpreted, and the reason for movement depends on the multiplicity of possible interpretations (which each correspond to a region of the world). The cipher with its secret is a dynamic motif (it has the same meaning in *Journey to the Centre of the Earth*); but behind all these various interpretations, there remains a constant, the thirty-seventh parallel. (It is motifs such as these which elucidate the relationship between Verne and Rousseau.) The adventure is finished when the line is completely traced: the cipher only delivers its last secret at the moment when the world is contained entirely within the limits of a dominant principle – limits which are like the pole of all interpretations, and which are also enclosed within a circuit. The success of the adventure – the father rediscovered by the son, who had already found another father anyway – is confirmed in the perfection and purity of a voyage:

> And so the crossing of South America, following an absolutely straight path, had been finished. Neither mountains nor floods could turn the travellers aside from their imperturbable route, and, if they did not have to combat with the malice of men, the elements unleashed against them put their generous courage roughly to the test. (*The Children of Captain Grant*, end of part I)

In the same way, Captain Hatteras 'marched invariably towards the North', the visible sign of his madness. Once again the psychological themes are merely forms derived from the symbolic image of the conquest: the straight line, the pole, the centre of the earth. When Grant's children arrive at the end of the journey, the author says that they are demoralised, about to give up, a sign that they are at the end, that they are going to finish. Paradoxically – but this paradox is the very logic of the image – the straight line is exact: thus the parallel is the equivalent of the pole. A pure trajectory, it gathers into a single point, because in overcoming obstacles it abolishes distance. This is one of the basic themes of the speech given by Michael Arden to the people of Tampa-Town:

> 'Yes, gentlemen,' continued the orator, 'in spite of the opinions of certain narrow-minded people, who would shut up the human race upôn this globe, as within some magic circle which it must never outstep, we shall one day travel to the moon, the planets, and the stars, with the same facility, rapidity, and certainty as we now make the voyage from Liverpool to New York! Distance is but a relative expression, and must end by being reduced to zero.
>
> . . . 'And then you talk of the distance which separates the planets from the sun! And there are people who affirm that such a thing as distance exists. Absurdity, folly, idiotic nonsense! Would you like to know what I think of our own solar universe? Shall I tell you my theory? It is very simple! In my opinion the solar system is a solid, homogeneous body; the planets which compose it are in actual contact with each other; and whatever space exists between them is nothing more than the space which separates the molecules of the densest metal, such as silver, iron, or platinum! I have the right, therefore, to affirm, and I repeat, with the conviction which must penetrate all your minds, "Distance is but an empty name; distance does not really exist!" ' (*From the Earth to the Moon*, ch. 19)

Enclosed in the straight lines of the adventure, the universe manifests its *plenitude*.

NOTE ON THE VOYAGE, NATURE AND THE MACHINE

The traveller draws his inevitably straight line across the irregularity of nature in order to reform it: in this his enterprise is an allegory of scientific work. Dedicated entirely to this rigour, the traveller is himself metamorphosed into the instrument of its production: in several instances Phileas Fogg is compared to a machine; elsewhere he is represented as an object perfectly obedient to mechanical laws of movement – a star:

> He was not travelling, he was describing a path around the earth; he was a solid body following an orbit round the terrestrial globe in accordance with the laws of mechanics. (*Around the World in Eighty Days*, ch. 11)

> Fogg soared in majestic indifference. He was sweeping quite rationally in his orbit around the world, without worrying about the minor planets that gravitated about him. (Ibid., ch. 18)

Similarly, Hatteras finishes as no more than a magnetic needle. Similarly, too, the astronauts who undertake the journey from the earth to the moon finally become an artificial star.

If the voyage succeeds, the explorer is no more than this trajectory. If the voyage fails the man does not for all that rediscover an individuality or a subjectivity; he returns to the inertia of an arrested object. *The Begum's Fortune* gives a fine example of this when we see the unhappy and evil scholar (the two inevitably go together) caught like an insect in the lense of an enormous magnifying glass, the prisoner of his failure, returned to earth as a natural curiosity:

> It would have been in complete darkness but for a dazzling white light which streamed through the thick glass of a bull's-eye, fixed in the centre of the oak floor. For purity and brilliancy it might be compared to the moon when she is in her full beauty.
>
> Perfect silence reigned within these mute and eyeless walls. The two young men fancied themselves in the antechamber of a tomb.
>
> But before bending over the glass, Max hesitated for a moment. He had attained his object! The secret which he had come to Stahlstadt to learn, was about to be revealed to him!
>
> This feeling, however, soon passed off. Together he and

Otto knelt beside the disc and looked down into the chamber beneath.

A horrible and unexpected sight met their astonished gaze.

The glass disc, being convex on both sides, formed a lens, which immensely magnified everything visible through it.

Here was the secret laboratory of Herr Schultz. The intense glare which shone through the disc, as if from the lantern of a lighthouse, came from a double electric lamp, still burning in its airless globe and still incessantly fed by a powerful voltaic pile.

In the middle of the room, motionless as marble, and enormously magnified by the refraction of the lens was seated a human form.

Fragments and splinters of shells were strewn on the ground around this spectre.

There was no doubt about it; it was Herr Schultz himself, recognisable by his horrid grinning mouth and his gleaming teeth; but a gigantic Herr Schultz, suffocated and frozen by the action of a terrible cold produced by the explosion of one of his frightful munitions of war.

The King of Steel was seated at his table, holding an enormous pen like a lance in his hand as if he were writing. Had it not been for the stony glare of his dilated eyeballs, and his set mouth, he would still have seemed alive. Here this awful corpse had been for a month, hidden from all eyes, and now discovered like a mammoth concealed for ages in the glaciers of the Polar regions. Everything around him was frozen, the re-agents in their jars, the water in its receivers, and the mercury in its containers! (Ch. 18, 'The Kernel of the Nut')

The individuals who participate in the great symbolic progression of the adventure lose all their individuality:

Next day, Thursday, August 27th, was a great date in the subterranean journey. I cannot even now think of it without feeling my heart beat with fear. From that time on, our reason, our judgment, our ingenuity, went for

> nothing, and we became merely the playthings of the forces of the earth. (*Journey to the Centre of the Earth*, ch. 41)

Also important in this same book is Axel's dream (at the end of chapter 32): 'All life on earth is summed up in me, and my heart beats alone in this desolate world.'

The heroes of this journey to the centre of the earth are brought home backwards. The return is achieved in spite of them, almost without them, for they have not succeeded in completely identifying with their function, exploration, in the pure curve of this exploit. Access to the centre is denied to them; the line cannot be closed and thus it is not entirely straight. When nature cannot be conquered – that is to say, completely inhabited – men integrate themselves into that which is most finite in it, its diversity; they become an element in this diversity, they transform themselves into objects, and thus their place upon a broken line is a potent image of this state.

For these men, then, one choice is possible: to become things of perfect movement, machines, in the strong, exact sense which Verne gives to this word (and, once again, it is the linear trajectory which for him best describes the form of the machine), or abandoned objects, as though interrupted, left to the detour of a broken movement. Man's adaptation to the machine is not only a programme: it determines in detail the destiny of the characters, what might be called their *figure*. Far from nature being fashioned in the image of man, it is man who models himself upon natural objects. Man is in things: *mobilis in mobili*.

Accordingly Verne's work is not to be presented as inspired by a kind of heroic Manicheism: the posture of man confronting the chaos of nature. On the contrary, nature is *prepared* for the adventure of its transformation, and man only lives this adventure on condition that he too must lend himself to this movement which he imposes in so far as he accepts and receives it at the same time.

Between the terms 'man', 'the machine', 'nature' there is thus established a series of identities. The relations between man and the machine only seem complex because of their simplicity: there is no true relation, but an equivalence, or even a sort of mimicry. Man produces the machine because he is assimilated to the machine, and he may even seem to be a reflection of the machine. Thus the technical object receives a privileged form, specifically destined to describe this act of envelopment, of dressing: it is inhabited by man himself; it is man's true home. The best example of this is obviously *The Steam House*. The machine is not in front of man, separate from him, but around him, attached to him by all the links of similarity and contiguity. Thus, man and the machine are definitively complementary: the machine cannot exist without him nor he without it. Nemo stops with the *Nautilus*; like her he wedges himself in a point of that nature which he has for so long circumscribed; but he also involves it in his own death, for the machine, now unoccupied, has no further *raison d'être*. It would be interesting to compare this with a novel on the same subject which is exactly contemporary: the relations between man and the technical object in *Les Travailleurs de la mer* (The Toilers of the Sea).

Verne's work is simply a long reverie or meditation on the theme of the straight line – which represents the articulation of nature on industry, and industry upon nature, which is *narrated* as a narrative of exploration. Title: 'The Adventures of a Straight Line'. Adventures all the more rigorous in that they are uncertain, in that one never knows what point of the journey one is at, whether the cipher will render its secret, whether rectitude can be preserved to the end. In fact it is not a question of an abstract linearity: on the contrary, it is concretely animated, produced from one end to the other, threatened at each moment. Rectitude is won from a radical diversity, places and events, the description of which is important; but it must be repeated that this opposition, for it to be lived, is not dominant and does not depend on a fundamentally dualistic representation. This is precisely where one could situate Verne's entire poetic enterprise: his desire to account for an abundance, an original irregularity (which is typical of the exemplary setting, the sea), against the background of which the human effort to organise stands out the more clearly, which in the extreme cases seems to have been applied to its object (see in *The Children of Captain Grant* the consideration of the geometrical division of Australia).

This is the moment to examine the importance for Verne of the geographical map, which is a real object, but is also poetic in so far as it entirely retrieves nature. By means of a map the journey is a conquest of the same sort as a scientific adventure. It recreates nature, in so far as it imposes its own norms upon it. The inventory is a form of organisation, and thus of invention. This is the meaning of the geographical novel:

> Is there any truer pleasure, any satisfaction more real than that of the mariner who checks off his discoveries on the ship's chart? He sees the shores gradually take shape beneath his gaze, island by island, promontory by promontory, as though they were emerging from the waves. At first the boundary lines are vague, broken and interrupted! Here a single camp, there an isolated bay, further off a gulf surrounded by blankness. Then the discoveries fill up, the lines join, the dots on the map form features; the bays impinge upon the completed coastlines, the capes extend from positive shores; finally the new continent, with its lakes, streams and rivers, its mountains, valleys and plains, its villages, towns and cities unfurls in all its magnificent splendour across the globe! Ah, my friends, a discoverer of countries is a true inventor! He has the same feelings and surprises! But now this mine is exhausted! Everything has been seen and identified, everything in the way of continents and new worlds has been invented, and the rest of us, latecomers to the science of geography, have nothing more to do.
>
> 'But my dear Paganel, of course we have,' said Glenarvan.
>
> 'But what then?'
>
> 'What we are doing now!' (*The Children of Captain Grant*, part I, ch. 9)

The chaotic richness of nature is only a temporary obstacle, for it denotes the presence of an immense *reserve* which man will be able to exploit. Moreover, the straightness of the line can only be appreciated, acknowledged, at the moment when the line is completely drawn: meanwhile it seems very fragile: 'We are progressing from indiscretion to indiscretion' (*The Adventures of*

Captain Hatteras, ch. 18). This could be compared to the characteristic progress of science, which we may find surprising: 'Here is a fact unsuspected by science. – Science, my boy, is made from mistakes, mistakes which it is well to know, for they lead gradually to the truth' (*Journey to the Centre of the Earth*, ch. 31). It is precisely for this reason that one moves forward: without the permanent presence of this danger, without the threat of this rupture, there would be no movement: 'Captain Hatteras sought to profit from all opportunities of moving forward, whatever the consequences might have been' (*The Adventures of Captain Hatteras*, ch. 15).

All the other symbolic images which are the true heroes of the adventure – the Pole, the Centre – are merely the diverse representations of this line in its conclusive rectitude, of this central point which will render the world to itself, definitively:

> He always dreamt of walking where no man had walked before.
>
> . . . And it was in fact his wish to go to the end of the world. (*The Adventures of Captain Hatteras*, part I, ch. 12)

> Hatteras, stationed at the front, stared at that mysterious point towards which he felt himself drawn by an irresistible force, like the magnetic needle which points to the pole. (Ibid, part II, ch. 21)

However, one of these objects, the train, harbours a specific power, and thus deserves to be studied separately. It cleaves nature, leaps obstacles (as in an episode in *Around the World in Eighty Days*), and is at the same time an image of the form of the journey – this furrow – and the perfect realisation of human industry. Moreover, the machine in this case possesses the advantage of not being isolated in some special artificial place – the factory, for example; it remains in permanent and visible contact with the diversity of nature:

> 'We are in a civilised country, though this is not obvious, and our route, before the end of this day, will cross the railway between Murray and the sea. Well, my friends, must it be said, a railway in Australia, that seems really astonishing.'

'And why is that, Paganel?' asked Glenarvan.

'Why! Because that clashes! I know very well that you others, accustomed to colonising distant lands, who have electric telegraphs and universal exhibitions in New Zealand, you find that all very straightforward! But that baffles the mind of a Frenchman like me, and overturns all his ideas about Australia.'

'Because you consider the past and not the present,' replied John Mangles.

'Of course,' replied Paganel, 'but trains snort across the desert, the columns of smoke envelop the branches of the mimosa and the eucalyptus, the echidnas, the platypuses, and the cassowaries, fleeing before the express trains, savages taking the 3.30 to Melbourne, to Kyneton, to Castlemann, to Sandhurst or to Echua, that is what would astonish anyone other than an Englishman or an American. Your railways drive out the poetry of the desert.'

'What does that matter if progress penetrates!' replied the major. (*The Children of Captain Grant*, part II, ch. 12)

Passepartout awoke and stared out of the window. He could hardly believe that he was actually crossing India by train. It seemed so unlikely, yet nothing could be more real! The engine, controlled by the hand of an English driver and stoked with English coal, puffed its smoke across plantations of cotton-trees, coffee trees, clove trees and red-pepper trees, and its steam whirled in spirals among the palm-trees through which he could catch a glimpse of picturesque bungalows, abandoned monasteries, and richly ornamented temples. Then appeared vast plains extending far out of sight; jungles which lacked neither snakes nor tigers scared at the whistling of the engine; and, at last, forests cleft by the railwayline but still haunted by elephants which stared pensively at the train. (*Around the World in Eighty Days*, ch. 2)

In the wake of the train we always find the same images: the smoke unfurls across rare trees, the train takes possession of the forest and the desert, peopling it, decorating it as much as a temple or flights of birds; Verne pushes the contrast to its limit, to the point of mingling with the multiple universe which it possesses by imposing its trajectories. In allusion to the 'natural impluvium' (see the description of the fjord of Stapi), the train 'whinnies': the image is facile, perhaps not particularly striking, but it obeys exactly the rules of Verne's imagery; it is intelligible. It must be emphasised that Verne's favourite effect, and one which the illustrators of Hetzel stressed especially, is this encounter between nature in its primitive state and the machine in its most elaborate state (the steam house in the jungle, the Albatross above the familiar landscapes, the submarine in the natural cave).

One can thus show – and the preceding analyses were merely examples, not a complete inventory – that the general themes crystallise in specific images, objects, natural places, or even psychological attitudes. (Two of these attitudes, typical, figurative, and not simply anecdotal, are especially important: the *fixed idea* (Lindenbrock, Hatteras, Fogg . . .), which functions as the equivalent of the central image (the centre, the volcano, straightness); and *speed* (Lindenbrock), an important theme which will be taken up later: it is obviously significant that the adventurer is in such a hurry.) These are individual themes which are symbolic images. This is the level at which we find the true *work* (*oeuvre*) of Jules Verne, the product of his creation, at least in the literalness of its content; this is what he has *made*, this is what distinguishes his work from all other written works, and which establishes the final object of all the possible readings: these are the themes which have sustained the curiosity of many generations of readers, given substance to their imagination of the great programme of the conquest of nature. We would ask how far these images have been produced by Verne himself – but if he has not made them, at least he has brought them together and organised them into a system – how far he has taken them from the fund of images which the long history of the narrative of the fantastic placed at his disposal, that reserve from which the language of fiction has been progressively elaborated: that general history which has never been written, except perhaps at certain points, that is to say, frequently on its reverse side. The general project had to be embodied in images which were not original, which were sought in another domain, a domain which is not that of ideological projects but that of language in its reality. This was the only way to have established the continuity of a narrative, which groups the images in the logic of a series, and even into a totality of narratives. This can be called the stage of *figuration*, to distinguish it from that of *representation* (statement of the ideological project, transposition of this project into a general narrative form).

However, the identification of striking images is not enough to explain the *inscription* of the subject. At this moment of the analysis, one could think that the work in its real diversity had been produced by a simple deduction from the initial project, and that accordingly it could be studied at this level as an independent reality: independently of the works themselves, and of that 'beyond' through which they exist. The reservoir of images seems to establish a closed and self-sufficient totality. But it is not enough to bring the images together, to group them in an analytic unity, which as a pure disorder would be unreadable, and which would also inevitably be incomplete.

We must give the narrative a formal unity corresponding to the content which it has discovered, which directs and organises it. Once again we encounter the problem of the coherence between the form of the narrative and its thematic content, though this time at the level of the unfolding of the narrative. We shall see that this form is systematic, in the same way that the special images were enclosed within the limits of a determinate inventory. We must now study the movement of the fable.

The fable

The problem will be the same, displaced from the objects to the form which organises and animates them: given an ideological programme (to describe in advance man's total mastery of nature), how to find the means of expression, that is to say, the form of the narrative which will make it possible to translate it? It must be said immediately that this form will only be artificially separate from the content which surrounds it, initially because we are concerned with an adventure story; that is to say, one in which the episodes, the encounters, give (or try to give) impetus to the narrative; accordingly we must not hesitate to talk once again about thematic objects which, strangely, will give the exposition its *angles*, if not its outline.

One of these thematic objects, which has been little discussed until now, and which is only an element of the image of straightness, will become important: the image of the trace or landmark. The journey goes forward because it is the progressive deciphering of a familiar-distant totality; the succession of possible ciphers is the occasion of so many repetitions; it is the reason for its progress. One after the other, Hatteras overtakes the ruins of the expeditions which have gone before him to the Pole, and the identification of these traces is an important moment in his progress, which stage by stage impels him to the final goal which he alone will attain: the open sea at the Pole, the northern Arcadia, the central volcano.

In the same way (and this example will be decisive) Lindenbrock and his nephew Axel move towards the centre only because they possess a coded message, and because they are able to recognise its reflection all along their route: for them it is the visible safe sign of *the closure of the line*. The two examples are analogous and yet inverse: Hatteras progresses through the failures of others, and also, for those who go with him, 'from indiscretion to indiscretion'; Lindenbrock, on the other hand, walks in the footsteps of a previous hero, *who has arrived*, who has even returned, and who, like Hatteras and Nemo, was himself marked out for success, among those who reach the goal, who close the line: Arne Saknussen. The journey through the crust of the earth is a new figuration of *mobilis in mobili* (right down to the identification of the explorer with the natural setting: Axel's dream). But here the guide is no longer a living presence, as was Nemo: he must be discovered and followed. Saknussen is the Nemo of another time: he is equally an outlaw, an alchemist burnt at the stake, rejected by his contemporaries, and thus projected towards the future, the only one able to attain the centre. The conqueror is always an exceptional being. Hatteras goes mad, Nemo is a political rebel, Saknussen is a convict, and Robur is definitively hounded from *our* world. Humanity can only follow the same road if it discovers their traces, if it is loyal to their absent presence which is disguised in the form of a cipher to be translated. After them, or even with them, there cannot be an exploration in the strict sense of the word, but only discovery, retrieval of a knowledge already complete, and which can also be definitively lost (Robur).

The journey, in all its progressive stages, is disclosed as having ineluctably happened before. This explains the theme of haste – a theme which is emphatically not a rigmarole of imitative psychology: with Verne the picturesque is always there for some other reason. Lindenbrock is the man who, in his garden, pulls the leaves to make them grow more quickly: beyond the comic portrait of an eccentric scholar there is that destiny of the explorer, always in a hurry because he is always late.

Finally, someone has gone more quickly than he, has *anticipated* him. And this 'someone' is in the last analysis not even the wretched hero (who would thus be marked for success), but is nature itself, which is always in advance, and which must simply be caught up with; this, for Verne, is the significance of the activity of the scholar. One must hurry, one must violate time: as with Phileas Fogg's eighty days. To explore is to follow, that is to say, to cover once again, under new conditions, a road already actually travelled. To explore, through this systematic form of the narrative of exploration, is to retrace time, to anticipate: to recover a little of lost time.

For the first time we encounter this aberrant and important phenomenon in the work of Jules Verne: anticipation is expressed only in the form of a regression or a retrospection. The relation between the past and the present is reflected in the real relation between the present and the past. The conquest is only possible because it has already been accomplished: the fiction of progress is only the attenuated reflection of a past adventure which is almost effaced. The advance, in its literal form, is like a return. And this is why it does not matter greatly that it is interrupted by a failure: Lindenbrock will only reach the antechambers of the centre; the mere sight of the first corridors (which have already been thoroughly explored) suffices to deny him access; at the end, the eruption of the central volcano completely closes the gateway to adventure, cuts the line at its beginning. In the same way, Nemo, in his death, effaces all the signs of his adventure by returning with all the products of his work to the chaos of nature. In the same way, Robur is finally lost in the sky. In the same way, Hatteras forgets how to even communicate his secret to others. Finally, anticipation does not follow a process of acquisition which shows in a flash what *will be lost*, obliterates all trace of what has been.

Accordingly, something absolutely extraordinary has happened; the succession of thematic images, in the systematic form of a narrative of exploration, produces an avant-garde meaning (the project, which is to write the future) with its real formation: a return, a regression. The future can only be told in images in the shape of yesterday. And we can, without hesitation, adopt the results of More's *Le Très curieux Jules Verne* (The Very Curious Jules Verne) (Gallimard). Nemo is the image of the father (there is no point in reproducing all the evidence; the main link is the character of Hetzel). Anticipation, the object of which is finally a deduction from origins (which is at once nature, the wretched hero and the father; this is the first time that we have come across the importance in Verne of all the images of the father) will, after all, only be the search for first pathways. We see that in this sense the future resembles that which has already been seen.

Anticipation will be this search for origins. Thus, the structure of the fable is always related to a very simple model: a journey in the footsteps of the other, and in fact it is the history of a return.

Various conclusions can be drawn from this analysis:

1 The fable which shapes the narrative does not correspond to the initial project until that project has been subjected to a reversal: the future projects itself in the form of the-past-definitively-surpassed (the symbolic death of the father). Verne wants to represent a forward movement, but in fact figures a movement backwards.

2 However, this form is filled by the special thematic figures (without any discord appearing between them) to the extent that

it could seem artificial to study them separately. So that the level of figuration is as coherent as that of the general representation: the actual discord between the subject and its elaboration is no more reflected in this second level than in the first. The moment of figuration, in so far as it is an autonomous moment, is as homogeneous as the moment of representation.

The analytical description leads us to a paradoxical result: it enables us to make the distinction between two levels – *representation* and *figuration*; the discord which has appeared between these two levels shows that the distinction was not artificial. However, such an analysis is inadequate, because it leaves these two levels – which might be called elements, aspects, points of view or elements of the exposition – side by side, like stable elements, or at least apparently so, each measurable in relation to its own legality. Two coherent and *incompatible* realities are thus revealed: the method employed thus far gives us no insight into their coexistence, or even their simultaneity, within a single work, which yet exists (this is the least that one could say). This discord does not denote a failure but a *success*: this is why it demands explanation.

Rather than a contradiction between terms at the same level, we perceive a real incompatibility between the representation of the project and its figuration. Does this incompatibility signal a weakness in the work of Jules Verne? Must we say that Verne has not found the words through which he could have said what he had to say? (Which, *a priori*, is not the same as what he wanted to say: the fact that such a discontinuity should be possible gives the problem its meaning.) One could even go further, and say, for example, that the actual coherence between the thematic images and the structure of the fable is illusory, and that it conceals an antagonism: that is to say, that the 'form' betrays the content; the plot imposes on the themes a mistaken meaning which the themes do not necessarily display; in this case, some other organisation of the signs was possible which would have guaranteed both a new coherence and loyalty to the initial project. Did the crystallisation of the given project into an image necessarily produce an inversion of the intended ideological line? We can see the answer which is hiding behind this question: a reactionary distortion of the work was inevitable; it corresponds to the actual movement of Verne's project, and it serves finally to characterise the ideological situation which was the ultimate condition of its realisation. This contradiction between the form and the content in Verne's work would be the reflection, term for term, of the contradiction in the ideological project. Accordingly, it will be said that the composition of the work was not only inevitable but also fatal.

But it is too tempting to decompose Verne's work in this way, and to show that his great project is distorted: this is how one reaches the point of showing that the persistent themes of the narrative are organised according to a rigorous system which perfectly describes the closure, an example of the contradictory character of the bourgeois project of liberation.

This is the short cut taken by Barthes when he insists on the flagrant contradiction between Verne's project and the imagery which he offers: this is an easy definition of bourgeois reverie, out of breath and looking for a place to rest, which must be distinguished from poetic reverie which constructs a pure movement and which arises from the Drunken Boat rather than directing it. This is the kind of criticism which the preceding description seems to lead to: a criticism which, to be coherent, has to base itself on a series of identifications which are naturally implicit. The falsely polemical enterprise of a *mythology* is always based upon a reduction of the general to the particular: the world is like a house, and the house is like a ship, and thus the work of Jules Verne. This progression can be followed, in either direction according to need; Verne's work embodies the bourgeois ideal of progress, but it is also a real picture of confinement, whence its failure, or at least the contradictory aspects of the enterprise. The explanation is grounded in the most mechanistic of materialisms: in order to affirm a contradiction it postulates a systematic coherence of all the levels and decrees their rigorous connection. These distinctions are made the better to confuse us; he complains of no longer finding the coincidences he had initially posited. The rationalism of equivalences is only a methodological instrument which serves to flush out, like game birds, failures and contradictions; and this chasing after witches is called demystification.

It must be stated precisely that the point of greatest resistance of this method, which is also its charm, is that nothing which is said by this means is false; but the analysis is always incomplete; this is in fact its basic condition, since the incompleteness will be given as the solution to the problem posed by the work. Accordingly, there is failure and contradiction: and it is not enough to produce them, they must be explained, and this is what Barthes does, by appealing to the historical situation of the writer. This situation not only endows him with a dated programme, but at the same time it gives him all the contradictions of an epoch and its dominant ideology, which are then transposed into the work as they are.

(At the very least this is surprising, since Barthes elsewhere criticises all historical interpretations of the literary work. (See the last section of *Sur Racine* on the transhistorical essence of literature.) Must it be said that his thinking has developed? It is more probable that he believes historical interpretations to be justified when he is dealing with a work which is not a classic, cannot be perfect, and is therefore not truly literary. Verne is not Racine (and who would complain?), and for what does not deserve to be called a work, everything is permitted, as it would not be for others. However, Verne's work exists as much as, and even more than, that of Racine, and if it deserves an appropriate explanation it does not admit of the skeleton-key interpretations which have too often devolved upon it. It even deserves this explanation all the more in that it is closer to the centre of its age: we have seen that it is perfectly *representative* – there is no doubt of this. This kind of study will perhaps disclose the secret of a work completely involved in history, which makes no pretence of escaping history – the desire to write a novel of a new type in order to narrate a new object should not be considered such a pretence – a work which does not seek any of the disguises of eternity, and this is not necessarily a weakness.)

Also it seems useless and even very dangerous to speak of *contradiction*: at the point which the description has reached, the contradiction could not be located. There can only be discovered a contradiction at the level of representation through a projection of the contradiction of the figures. In fact there is no such thing as an ideological contradiction: the inexact character of an ideology *excludes* contradiction (see the final section of Chapter 19, 'Lenin, Critic of Tolstoy'). At the source of ideology we find an attempt at *reconciliation*: also, by definition, ideology is in its way coherent, a coherence which is indefinite if not imprecise, which is not sustained by any real deduction. In this case, the discord is not *in* ideology but in its relation with that which limits it. An ideology can be *put into contradiction*: it is futile to denounce the presence of a contradiction in ideology. Also, the ideological project given to Jules Verne constitutes a level of representation which is relatively homogeneous and consistent, linked internally by a kind of analogical rigour: the *flaw* is not to be sought in the project. Similarly, the inventory of images and their insertion into the chosen fable is in itself perfectly consistent. Verne begins with an ideology of science which he makes into a mythology of science: both the ideology and the mythology are irreproachable in their authority. It is the path which leads from the one to the other which must be questioned: it is in this *in between*, which, as we shall see, has its marked place in the work, that a decisive encounter occurs. In the passage from the level of representation to that of figuration, ideology undergoes a complete *modification*– as though, in a critical reversal of the gaze, it were no longer seen from within but from the outside: not from its illusory and absent centre (an ideology is centred at all its points, that is to say, perfectly *credible* because its centre is excluded), not from its centre then, but from the limits which hold it in check and impose upon it a certain shape by preventing it from being a different ideology or something other than ideology.

What is particularly interesting in the work of Verne is that in one moment at least it encounters this obstacle, which is ultimately the condition of the *reality* of the ideological project, and that it manages to treat it as such, as an obstacle. It is obviously unable to overcome the obstacle by its own means: as soon as this limitation is grasped, as though by an unconscious movement of resolution, the book begins to walk alone, to move in an unforeseen direction. It is not a question of a true resolution: the conflict remains intact, at the end of an almost autonomous development which only enlarges the gap which separates the work in its true production from the conditions of its appearance.

In fact, between the contradictory situation of bourgeois ideology at the beginning of the Third Republic and the difficulties experienced in an analysis of the work of Jules Verne there is a large difference, which could not have escaped Verne himself, otherwise he would not perhaps have deserved the title of 'author'. Certain of the contradictions which characterise his epoch, he knew, not thoroughly, of course, but better perhaps than Barthes: he has reflected them, he is even aware of having made them the true subject of his work, which is thus not as unified as one would like to think, nor as naive. If Verne has *felt* the contradictions of his time – and we shall see that this is in fact the case – and if he nevertheless wanted to give an uncritical picture of this time (and this is not true, at least for political criticism) and the picture is actually defective, this is because there is a dislocation (*décalage*) between the ensemble of the historical contradictions and the defect proper to his work, a dislocation which must be considered as the true centre of his work. In this case, it is not enough to say that Jules Verne is a bourgeois of the early Third Republic with all that this implies (business, scientism, as well as all that makes a bourgeois revolution). We know that a writer never reflects mechanically or rigorously the ideology which he represents, even if his sole intention is to represent it: perhaps because no ideology is sufficiently consistent to survive the test of figuration. And otherwise, his work would not be read. The writer always reveals or writes from a certain *position* (which is not simply a subjective viewpoint) in relation to this ideological climate: he constructs a specific image of ideology which is not exactly identical with ideology as it is given, whether it betrays it, whether it puts it in question, or whether it modifies it. This is what must finally be taken into account in order to know what the work is made of. And the author does not always need to say what he is making.

(This is the general problem of all interpretation: how to understand, how to grasp, in the elaboration of a new work, the interference of the old and the new, a debate never resolved, a duplicity which finally gives the work its consistency: thus, how can we describe Bosch's attempts to establish a new painting, in the margins of the modern, by working on archaic forms (cf. the study of J. Combes, Tisne, ed.). Or again, in Althusser's analysis of Montesquieu, the first scientific theorist of societies appears at the same time as the implicit defender of the most reactionary theories (because he draws inspiration from the political ideology of 'feudalism'). Here again it is pointless to search for a contradiction; this ambiguity is only apparent; behind it we see the historical conditions for the appearance of any slightly revolutionary work, which must inevitably rely upon the object of its criticism – initially because it finds there an important part of its conceptual armature.)

Indeed, in his work Verne systematically elaborated this conflict proper to a new situation which elaborates the future in forms already outdated. Thus he attempts to resolve the question of the relation of the bourgeoisie to its own past, to its history, and manages to clarify at least certain *limits* of a historical situation (by testing its dominant ideology). For in his work there exists a privileged thematic object in which one could read the ultimate conditions of a problematic of production. This motif is privileged because it joins exactingly, in its real presence, form and content (sign and fable): it is both a particular theme and the origin of a plot, in so far as it *shows* on a 'unique object' the links in an ideological series, which will take the form of a narrative, which will shape the fable. Let us say, in anticipation, that it is in this unfolding of the narrative that we will discover the discord which had until now appeared between the two different levels of the account. This apparently simple narrative is in fact the confrontation, the encounter of two opposed and even irreconcilable narratives: the narrative no longer progresses by following the episodes of an adventure, except on the surface; its movement is that which impels an ideological problematic. This theme is that of the island. Rather than an image it is now a matter of a *revealing theme*, which sustains in its materiality a complete ideological series. We cannot confidently say that all the images which have been studied thus far are expressive in this manner for the simple reason that they are not in themselves expressive; the recurring question is whether these images could show *something else* within some other organisation of the work.

But this question is meaningless in relation to Verne's favourite theme. This theme is complete – not an image for a meaning which transcends it. That is to say, it is absolutely *objective*: it presents in one moment the totality of its possibilities. When it is put to work, as it will be in the experimental novel *The Mysterious Island*, it undergoes a variation which returns it to its point of departure, but not a mutation. It could thus be said that at this third level of the formulation we arrive at the junction of the symbolic and the real (that reality which the work defines, obviously), in so far as the vehicle of the meaning alludes solely to this meaning, and is accordingly not open to any *commentary*. One could study thoroughly the regression or the discord which is the token of the narrative through this revealing and profoundly expressive theme: completely, that is to say, at a stroke; one could then answer the question of whether the inversion of the fable, the return to origins, has not definitively contaminated the object of the narrative. Now we can see clearly what could be called, though without its usual pejorative implications, that defect which is not a lack but which constitutes the work itself. Note that the term 'defect' is preferable to that of 'contradiction': it acknowledges that what is not said could not be said.

It is fruitless to be wondering what role is played by creation in the production of a literary work: this mythological representation, the residue of all the possible theologies, is contradicted by the fact that the work is preceded by an ideological project, a project which is always excessive, which engulfs (*dépasse*) the conscious intentions of the individual author; there is also all that 'material variety', the repertoire of images and fables, without which nothing could be done, and which would not exist if it had to be invented afresh each time. The way in which the conditions of its possibility *precede* the work (a fact which is so obvious but which centuries of criticism have ignored) systematically censures in advance any psychology of inspiration, even if this psychology is expressed in a theory of an intellectual will, to produce novel beauty. Against these metaphysical and supernatural representations must be advanced a coherent conception of the business of the writer, which is not the same as the business of writing. (It is absolutely not a question of describing a literary or artistic work as pure technique.) This work is possible only because it answers a historical requirement, a certain necessity of working at a given moment under particular conditions.

Accordingly the work is inevitably limited by the conditions of its appearance, limited in a way that has surprising consequences. But this idea cannot be formulated in such a simple way. It suggests a certain ambiguity: does the work arrive to fill up a frame which is already there, is it *not* really produced, but summoned from without?

Thus this criticism of the idea of creation, in the absolute sense of the word, seems to deprive the work of both originality and specificity (spontaneity is not in question, for this critical concept is without interest). Between the conditions of the appearance of the work and this actual appearance there will be an identity or repetition. Verne's work is so important because it enables us to demonstrate that there is a dislocation between these two moments. The work exists only because it is not exactly what it could have been, what it ought to have been: it arises not from the simple linkages of a mechanical production which would lead progressively from the outside to the internal reality; on the contrary, it is born of the obscure realisation which is certainly not conscious from the beginning – of *the impossibility of the work's filling the ideological frame for which it should have been made.* This is where we can locate the personal intervention of the author in the work of literary production, a work which begins collectively (in so far as it invokes a society or a tradition, though if we stop at this determination we are merely dealing with a problem of communication), but which ends as an individual stand in the immense debate of real works and ideological imperatives; this is when the problematic of expression or of revelation intervenes. Verne pursued this process to its very end, since, as we can see in at least one of his novels, he took this incompatibility which defines a historical situation as his very subject. Interestingly, he does not attempt a resolution of the difficulty, a conclusion to the debate, an obliteration of the incompatibility; in fact, he poses the problem, but does not offer a solution; the discord forms the very structure of the novel which concludes with the statement of discord. And thus the fundamental question of the situation of the writer, although objectively treated, since it gives the narrative its true plot, remains so objective that one could never know if the author had really perceived it, or whether it intruded without his knowledge as a fundamental theme, a theme so unworkable that it escaped from his direct grasp: an irreducible, unchangeable image which cannot be conjured away by being given a 'history'. Paradoxically, it is in this that Verne is a true *author*: because perhaps without having needed to intervene, he knew how to acquiesce in this decisive interrogation, which placed in question the very work in which it appeared. Obviously the critic has no need to *unmake* Verne's work: it furnishes the principle of its own decomposition·

C THE REVEALING THEME

The island: image for a fable or fable for an image? *The Mysterious Island*

1 *The theme as an ideological instrument*

When Verne chose to write the history of an island – and though he does not take it from its moment of origin he follows it to its end, the moment when it crumbles into the sea – he did not only decide to make it the *subject* of the novel, in the anecdotal sense of the word. Since the eighteenth century, life on an island has been a *model* of the fable or reverie: Defoe, Marivaux, Rousseau . . . and Verne's real project is to work out a variation on this model, precisely to confront one form with another. Also, even before it is the story of a lived experience, the mysterious island is the contestation of a symbolic character: Robinson Crusoe; so that it is indeed a novel about a novel. The other Robinson Crusoe, that of Defoe, appears between the lines of Verne's book, overwhelmed, denied, to a degree that remains to be defined. The novel in fact begins with an evaluation of the theme of Robinson Crusoe: not as a true or thrilling history, but as a complete theme, the description of an experience, which furnishes all its own means and implements.

In fact, in *Robinson Crusoe*, the fable and its image (the island) are the pretexts for a *lesson*: that history of the formation of a man, or rather his reformation (since it is a question of a second life, which takes shape against the distant ground of the first). This is obviously an educative book. Rousseau even saw it as a means of education so complete that he wanted to put no other book into Emile's hands:

> Is there no way of correlating so many lessons scattered through so many books, no way of focussing them on some common object, easy to see, interesting to follow, and stimulating even to a child? Could we but discover a state in which all man's needs appear in such a way as to appeal to the child's mind, a state in which the ways of providing for those needs are as easily developed, the simple and stirring portrayal of this state should form the earliest training of the child's imagination.
>
> Eager philosopher, I see your own imagination at work. Spare yourself the trouble; this state is already known, it is described, with due respect to you, far better than you could describe it, at least with greater truth and simplicity. Since we must have books, there is one book which, to my thinking, supplies the best treatise on an education according to nature. This is the first book Emile will read; for a long time it will form his whole library, and it will always retain an honoured place. It will be the text to which all our talks about natural science are but the commentary. It will serve to test our progress towards a right judgment, and it will always be read with delight, so long as our taste is unspoilt. What is this wonderful book? Is it Aristotle? Pliny? Buffon? No; it is *Robinson Crusoe.*
>
> Robinson Crusoe on his island, deprived of the help of his fellow men, without the means of carrying on the various arts, yet finding food, preserving his life, and procuring a certain amount of comfort; this is the thing to interest people of all ages, and it can be made attractive to children in all sorts of ways. We shall thus make a reality of that desert island which formerly served as an

> illustration. The condition is not, I confess, that of a social being, nor is it in all probability Emile's own condition, but he should use it as a standard of comparison for all other conditions. The surest way to raise him above prejudice and to base his judgements on the true relations of things, is to put him in the place of a solitary man, and to judge all things as they would be judged by such a man in relation to their own utility.
>
> This novel, stripped of irrelevant matter, begins with Robinson's shipwreck on his island, and ends with the coming of the ship which bears him from it, and it will furnish Emile with material, both for work and play, during the whole period we are considering. His head should be full of it, he should always be busy with his castle, his goats, his plantations. Let him learn in detail, not from books but from things, all that is necessary in such a case. Let him think he is Robinson himself; let him see himself clad in skins wearing a tall cap, a great cutlass, all the grotesque get-up of Robinson Crusoe, even to the umbrella which he will scarcely need. He should anxiously consider what steps to take; will this or that be wanting. He should examine his hero's conduct; has he omitted nothing; is there nothing he could have done better? He should carefully note his mistakes, so as not to fall into them himself in similar circumstances, for you may be sure he will plan out just such a settlement for himself. This is the genuine castle in the air of this happy age, when the child knows no other happiness but food and freedom.
> (Rousseau, *Emile*, Book III, trans. B. Foxley, London, Dent, Everyman, 1911)

Here we notice the appearance of the idea that the concrete individual is also a genetic being: a collusion of the most abstract and the most concrete.

Robinson Crusoe is a true fiction, in the Platonic sense. At the moment when Verne is writing, Emile has not grown up, but, historically, he has grown old: he needs a new *Robinson Crusoe*.

There is thus nothing episodic or futile in the choice of the subject: this choice involves work upon an already constituted theme, a variation, the repeat of an initial motif, in the double sense of a decomposition and a restitution. From the beginning the adventure is defined as a theoretical or a thematic debate.

In other words, *Robinson Crusoe*, the old as much as the new, is grasped as a *representative and didactic* form: it is not only the frame for a history, but also the manifestation of a lesson or an idea. On Verne's island, whose contours are drawn with such careful irregularity, nothing, except perhaps after the event, can serve as the pretext to the anecdote. The theme expresses, demonstrates – one could call it the demonstrator – exhibits what could be called *ideological motif*. In this particular case the motif is inherited from the eighteenth century: it is the theme of origin. The theme is not a neat setting, to be read in an instant: on the contrary, it is perpetually allusive, animated by a kind of discursiveness, a sign unfurling in the wake of a history; it is not created for itself, arising from its visible form, but concealed by a tradition, which also gives the history of its meaning.

Verne takes up the theme of the island to demonstrate its profoundly historical significance: it is not taken for its mere content; it is simply an implement with the power to change its meaning (its value derives from the history of its meanings).

The theme is like a tool which no longer has its finished form, or which is no longer suited to its function, and which must be remade to meet new requirements. The island is first of all a privileged object which can clarify the implications of an *ideological* series. The theme is both the form of and the reason for the series: its visible image and the law of its succession. It is both at once, in a strict concordance: the law of its succession because it is also the visible image, and reciprocally. To go back to the distinctions previously established, we see that it thus realises the union of the signs and the fable, the composition of the work. Unless it were to contain the secret of their disunity, and thus of the defect of the work.

The island is a way of showing, linking and ordering ideological objects (that is to say, a material common to several ideological ensembles, *elements*, which only have their meaning within a specific organisation): nature, industry, science, society work, and even, to some extent, destiny. (This systematic character of Defoe's novel is demonstrated in the appendix to this chapter.) Verne displays his mysterious island in order to relate the appropriate themes to a representation – a representation recorded by the history of ideas and by history, a representation of origins which gives them a determinate form. Thus he suggests that this representation itself carries, once and for all, the mark of a historical period. Thus it is not origin itself which is in question: the motif is not taken up for its permanence, or for the possible identity of its content through time, but because it can serve as the term of a relationship, because it distinguishes even more than it reconciles, because it makes possible a comparison of two ideological realities, with regard to a common obsession.

Thus the instrumental function of a thematic, at a given moment, determines the value of the theme from its beginning. The true Robinson Crusoe, the 'first', could pass along the true corridors of the true origins. The new Robinson Crusoes, appearing later, whether they judge, contest, or imitate, show that the *other* was there only for them, for them to be assessed; or at least that he was there for the same purpose, equally representative within the framework of a common function. If the image of the island can be taken up again and again as the site of a variation, this is because it contains the same *fictive* value at all moments of its history. Because Verne uses the image as a stratagem, as though the better to mark the date, without explicit emphasis, without needing to propose the theory of its use, Verne makes the favoured eighteenth-century representation of the island seem identical to his own.

The island as a theme is an ideological implement (one could say that the theme, in relation to ideological or representative work, has the same value as the concept in relation to theoretical work), an instrument like all the other symbolic representations of origin: the child, the savage, the statue, the first man, the blind man. The presentation of origins also implies the special moment of rupture, the moment of *loss* of origins: the contract, the education of the senses, education. Properly psychological motifs can also fill this role in the philosophical symbology of the eighteenth century:

the feat of appropriation as Rousseau describes it, or, as with Marivaux, the surprise which restores human nature to its first condition, and gives it, though late, the seeds of a true conscience, an initial stimulus to progress.

In the image of these motifs, the original theme, the one which Verne began from, has not initially been exploited more for itself than it is in its repetition. *Robinson Crusoe* was not a narrated history: behind certain contingencies remained the idea of origin as the *revelation of an order*. And behind this idea, which is also representative, or rather allusive, there was a privileged model of reasoning, according to which genesis and analysis are linked in the unity of a single movement: Condillac gives this reasoning its definitive form. It is not because there really was an origin that there is then a genesis from this origin, and then analysis of this genesis: but it is because a genesis must be analysed, and because the object of this analysis must be generated, that there is an origin. And this is why the idea of origin was an irreplaceable *theoretical instrument*, at least to resolve the problem which those who had made it posed themselves. It is also interesting to know (a point which cannot be developed here) that this motif is the instrument of a theory which, even at its moment of perfection, already carries in itself, by an irony of analysis, the elements of its own criticism: with Defoe as later with Rousseau.

Attention must accordingly be called to the implicit and perhaps blind perspicacity of Jules Verne: he sees clearly that origin is not a way of showing the absolute or the beginning, but a way of determinating the genesis of order, of succession. The island is indeed the place of origin, but the origin is not a neat beginning: it is immediately elaborated in a narrative which is a figuration of genesis – it could be said that it has no status independent of this transformation. Thus the island is the place of adventure: its forms, and even its shape, its appearance, in themselves already imply the movement of a plot.

It is not necessary to enumerate or to study in detail all the variations which Verne works out on the theme of the island; it is enough to note that he envisaged all the possibilities: *The School of Crusoes, Two Years' Holiday, The Mysterious Island*, and even that strange posthumous book which is perhaps not by Jules

Verne – *Les Naufragés du Jonathan* (The Shipwrecked of the Jonathan). It is more important to recall that the obviously symbolic *character* of Crusoe constitutes a permanent obsession in all his work. In fact, Verne never fails to emphasise the distinction between the doings of the characters of his novels, and those of the former, the other Crusoe, an almost historical character. On this issue we find, for example, in *The Children of Captain Grant:*

> 'So there are Crusoes everywhere?' asked Lady Helena.
> 'Truly, madame,' answered Paganel, 'I know of few islands which cannot boast of such exploits, and chance had already produced long before him the novel of your immortal compatriot, Daniel Defoe.'
> 'Monsieur Paganel,' said Mary Grant, 'Can I ask you a question?'
> 'Ask me two, my dear, and I promise to give you an answer.'
> 'Well,' said the girl, 'are you afraid of the idea of being cast away on a desert island?'
> 'Me!' shouted Paganel.
> 'Really, old chap,' said the Major, 'don't tell us that it is your favourite wish.'
> 'I wouldn't say that,' said the geographer, 'but really an adventure would not entirely displease me. I would make a new life for myself. I would hunt and fish, live in a cave in the winter and in a tree in the summer; I would store my crops and eventually colonise my island.'
> 'All alone?'
> 'All alone, if necessary. But is one ever alone in the world? Animals could be my friends, a tame young goat, a talking parrot, a playful monkey. And if chance sends you a companion, like the trusty Friday, what more do you need to be happy? Two friends on a rock, that's happiness! What if the Major and myself were . . .'
> 'Thank you,' said the Major, 'but I have no taste for the role of Crusoe, I wouldn't be very good at it.'
> 'Dear Paganel,' said Lady Helena, 'your imagination is carrying you away again. I think that the reality would be

very different from your dreams. You have only considered imaginary Crusoes, carefully dropped on their well-chosen islands, the favourite sons of Mother Nature. You can only see the fine side of things!'

'What? Madame, don't you think it possible to be happy on a desert island?'

'I don't think it is. Man is made for society, not for isolation. Solitude can only lead to despair. It's a question of time. At first, perhaps, material cares and the struggle to survive would divert the wretch just saved from the sea, and present necessities might hide the threats of the future. But later, when he begins to feel lonely, far from his kind, with no hope of ever seeing his home and his family, what must he think, what must he suffer? His island is the whole world. He is the whole human race, and when he dies, so horribly alone, he is like the last man on the last day of the world. Believe me, Monsieur Paganel, it is better not to be such a man!' (*The Children of Captain Grant*, part II, ch. 3)

Everything that follows constitutes a kind of commentary upon this passage: it is enough to point out that here we can read the important motifs of Verne's reflection upon the relations of man and nature; we pick up in passing the theme of colonisation. The idea can be put in two words: Crusoe has become an anachronistic character; in order to dream we now need other images.

For present-day travellers Crusoe is a new incarnation of the *predecessor*, a new father figure: to such an extent that the father is here made fun of; his failure precedes their success. We will even see that he embodies the essential form of the father, the *ideological father*: the debate between the past and the present, which gives consistency to the mutation of the present into the future, is also articulated between ideological forms; it is this new debate which gives Verne's book its *expressive* and revealing reality. The crucial question will now be whether this old, discarded father can be formally eliminated, whether the past can be suppressed in order for the future to establish itself.

2 *The new narrative*

The shape of the departure. The motif of the island endows both states of the narrative, the old and the new, with the same surface form. But the internal organisation of the narrative, which is defined by its *variability*, is profoundly modified from the first: it enables us to define a shape, or, in novelistic terms, a new situation, within the bounds of which a present-day history can be enacted. From the first, Verne's island must signify an absolute destitution, whereas for Defoe the island is already a kind of plenitude, since it expresses the methodical circularity of origins:

> The imaginary heroes of Daniel Defoe were never in such absolute destitution. Either they had abundant resources from their stranded vessels . . . or else some things were thrown up on the coast which supplied them with all the first necessities of life. But here not a single tool, not a utensil. From nothing, they must supply themselves with everything. (*The Mysterious Island*)

(And here we should bring to mind the famous criticisms which Marx and Engels frequently made of the Robinsonians, though it should be remembered that they are aimed at the fictional reveries of the economists rather than at *Robinson Crusoe* itself. We have seen that Crusoe was the last person to let himself be caught in the trap of true beginnings, he who was already so well established in the circularity of an already begotten world. It is not Defoe's fault if certain readers, Ricardo amongst them, fell into this very trap.)

The fictive genesis which the ideology of the eighteenth century acquiesced in is a botched genesis: from the initial good fortune of the shipwreck Crusoe receives all society as though in embryo. This is because Crusoe regards society as an attribute, a 'possession': it is impossible for him to achieve a total reconstruction of society. On the other hand, a new period of history, a new society, which Verne's contemporaries were elaborating, seems able to think (and have writers narrate) its own absolute beginning, and thus to completely master its own evolution:

> These colonists would really have to begin at the beginning. They did not even possess tools, and they were not in that

state of nature which affords a certain leisure. They did not have time. . . . (Ibid.)

Thus they are going to retrace – and this is what their future best illustrates – the whole process of the conquest of nature, which has actually already been achieved: they are going to show that they possess their future in so far as they are the masters of their past. They will travel again over this road from its beginning, from the beginning rather than from nothing, as we will see later, otherwise the fiction would have been as gratuitous as a daydream (and nothing was further from Verne's intentions).

We see that the initial trajectory of the adventure – by means of a contrast between several possible images – seems to restore the ideological project to its purity, and also its coherence: the characters launched on an assault upon nature, in so far as they are radically different from former heroes, adopt the programme of the conquering bourgeoisie, and eliminate all its ambiguities. Origin, as it had been represented, was a false origin. The time had arrived to show origin as it was. This beginning apparently contradicts all that has just been said concerning the instrumental value of the theme: Verne denounces the artificiality of the Robinsonians in order to put in their place the true narrative of origins, varying the theme only to fall more thoroughly into the image. But we are at the beginning of the book, and who is to say whether that is its real beginning?

We have just seen, in the last quotation, that a lack of goods is also a lack of time. Now one is no longer allowed to shirk the moment of origin; the development of the adventure will tolerate no further delay. Thus the opposition between the two 'forms' of origin – embodied in the common form of the island – has a psychological equivalent in the confrontation of speed and slowness. Robinson Crusoe has all the time in the world, and his labours are only made possible by using those long delays which replace the tools he has not got; whatever he undertakes, he can always choose the longest way; his lack of technical resources is balanced by an inexhaustible fund of *time*. In one sense, *Robinson Crusoe* is the novel of passing time. Verne's characters, on the other hand, are always in a hurry: we have noticed that the theme of haste is a psychological translation of the general idea of industry; his characters are all like Lindenbrock, who pulls the leaves of the plants in his garden to make them grow more quickly. They are compelled to follow as quickly as they can, and sometimes even more quickly, the path already followed by nature. This is the condition on which they deserve to be considered as the masters of the world, as the masters of tomorrow, on the model of their common master whose motto is *mobilis in mobili*. Thus their haste is not an elementary psychological image. Impatience is an eloquent sign: with Verne we are witnessing an abrupt *acceleration of the adventure* which completely reverses its meaning; in relation to the old man it is not only the intention or the form of the enterprise which has changed, but its very conditions. The acceleration of the adventure expresses an acceleration of history and, with it, the apparition of the new.

At the same time, the nature of the hero is inevitably and profoundly modified. If the characters on the mysterious island are different from Robinson Crusoe, who has the use of the products of social labour, it is not because they are absolutely destitute of all resources. The definition of resources has simply changed: there is indeed absolute destitution, but in one area alone.

In fact, the subject of the enterprise is no longer the solitary hero confronting nature directly; even the presence of a minimum of technical objects bequeathed by the vanished society introduces a mediation into the scheme. From the first, there is now a real society: the hero is replaced by a group. The problem is thus completely reversed: Robinson Crusoe had to reconstitute society single-handed; and this situation was indeed the sign of his necessary impotence. But in this case, it is only a question of showing that society, or the group which represents it, is capable of completely mastering the curve of its previous activity. (Naturally it must be said that this situation, clearly stated at the beginning – and taken up again on other occasions: see *Two Years' Holiday* – differentiates *The Mysterious Island* not only from Defoe's novel but also from other novels by Verne, which are organised around a solitary and wretched hero (Hatteras, Nemo, Robur). Thus one could divide Verne's work into two main groups: on the one hand the adventure is lived in solitude and secrecy, on the other hand it is lived by a real collectivity. As well as *The Mysterious Island* we find amongst this second kind *A Journey to the Centre of the Earth* – in which the collectivity is presented in a very simple form; the servant, the son and the father, who in this instance is an uncle, but this is to show that we are dealing as always with a false father, an adopted rather than a natural father – and also *The Children of Captain Grant*. In all these books the same structure is infinitely varied, a certain number of fixed moments. In the same way, the travellers who, instead of going 'from the earth to the moon', are doomed to orbit their goal eternally, also form the microcosm of a society:

> Indeed, I know them, they are the ingenious men. Between the three of them they carry all the resources of art, science and industry into space. With such skills they can do anything, and you will see that they will bring it off.

One important detail recurs: the father figure in the group is always an approximate father, one who is always finally usurped by a natural father, or at least by one more natural; in this sense, the novels of the 'family' (since the family can only build itself around an *other* father) generally deal with failure and deception: with one exception which confirms the rule, *The Children of Captain Grant*. This detail is central, because it constitutes the structural hinge of this series of works: it finally shows that the novel in which a group tries to appropriate its future (in a way that is also a quest for nature), is only a variation on the other category of novel, in which the isolated hero shows the others that he is the master of their past. Thus it is not a question of two independent or contradictory series, but of an authentic implication. The second category, in which the group finally encounters nature in the paternal form of the hero, is probably not a simple derivative: it is more important because it is a way of reflecting upon the novels of the first type. These novels, animated by a real collectivity, are also the only ones which can be defined by the concept of expression or revelation, and not just of figuration.)

We see that Verne has not fallen into the image of an absolute beginning: for an illegitimate image of origin he simply substitutes a complete theme, from which the adventure can take its true meaning, that is to say, a *contemporary* meaning, a meaning which is also historical. The solitary outlaw of the past could not embody modernity. We are dealing with a group of individuals presented in the form of a structured human material.

From the very first: the family, certainly not the biological family but a family of men. (It would be too laborious to attempt an explanation of the fact that women are almost entirely absent from Verne's novels. Indeed, this does not concern the specific question which is dealt with here. Verne explained himself, though with obvious naivety, on this issue in an interview with *Strand Magazine* in February 1895. This statement can be considered both as a screen and a confession:

> Love is an absorbing passion which leaves very little room for other things in the hearts of men. My heroes need all their faculties, all their energy, and the presence of a charming young woman in their midst would have prevented them from realising their gigantic projects.

And the 'chivalrous' Michael Arden absolutely refuses to go to the moon with a woman:

> It was not his intention to found a family on the moon, and to transplant there a mixed race of French and Americans. So he refused: 'Go and play the role of Adam with a daughter of Eve up there, no thanks! I would only need to come up against a few serpents.' (*From the Earth to The Moon*, ch. 22).

It must be said that if the demanding woman is not represented, this is obviously due first of all to the nature of the public to which these books were addressed: small boys who had to be furnished with gigantic dreams, rather than improprieties. It must also be said that woman is not, for all that, absent from Verne's work: on the contrary, her transparent presence is indispensable, not for the sake of a few minor characters (Captain Grant's daughter, the unexpected fiancée of Phileas Fogg . . .), but because it is she upon whom, in the last instance, the destiny of man depends.

Think of *Carpathian Castle*, the only real novel of love that Verne wrote, if we exclude *The Black Indies*. The woman only plays an important part in this novel because she is invested with the attributes of a future Eve: she is the product of man's industry, the ultimate expression of his powers of reconstitution. The woman thus represents the astonishing power of science, its most perfect product; but, in so far as science is nature in motion, she is also the most perfect image of nature. Reciprocally, in all Verne's novels the roles not taken by women characters are played by nature and its transformations: the sea, the interior of the earth and its surface. The machine, as we have seen, is the body which clothes man: nature, the woman, is the domain which he explores or surrounds.) This family of men is generally comprised – with several obvious variations – of a father, a son, and a servant who is directly associated with them. The father is a modern father, a new father; this is why he is also a replacement father, in opposition both to the mythological ancestors (Crusoe) and to the natural father, who is given and not acquired: see *Journey to the Centre of the Earth* and *The Children of Captain Grant*. (This last novel is much more complex than the others. Firstly because the role of the father is doubled between an affective solemn father (Glenarvan) and a scholarly comical father (Paganel) and then because the true father is also revealed as the result and the object of the conquest. In so far as the subject of the book is exclusively the search for the father, the novel concludes with a recognition of the mastery of nature, and it is certainly the only example of its kind; however, this conquest is accomplished in several important stages, in particular the Ayrton episode, which leads up to *The Mysterious Island*, and corrects this over-simple structure by restoring the distance and the discord between nature and the work of man.)

In *The Mysterious Island* the initial group, a distinct élite in relation to the other inhabitants of the island, comprises an adopted father who is also an engineer (the one who makes things); the reporter, the one who observes, who remembers and also cares; and the young man, who possesses a knowledge in the form of recognition (which is properly miraculous) of virgin nature (plants and animals). This is not a gathering of separate individuals but a true collectivity, organised according to the distribution of important functions.

By the side of this initial group, and clearly distinct, there are the performers and the entertainers, inferior beings. (This separation between the two sub-groups clearly shows that if the group, the social element, is symbolic, it does not relate to the abstract idea of society (a collection of individuals), but to a precise form of society, to a state of society, society at the moment when Verne was writing. This division shows that the distribution of individuals within this 'basic element' is not only arranged in a functionalist perspective. The place devolved upon function must be previously determinable from a more fundamental division. This is Comte's distinction between 'entrepreneurs' and 'operators', which he elaborated in 1844 in his *Discours sur l'esprit positive*, (Discourse on the Positive Mind), thirty years before Verne had begun to write, and just contemporary with the *Communist Party Manifesto*. In Verne's conception, society even in its minimum state retains a proletariat.) This second group comprises: the sailor, the one who categorises things according to their edibility (he is thus a caricature of true knowledge, not because he subordinates it to self-interest, but because the norm which he privileges is derisory). There is also the negro, the one who obeys; the monkey, superior to the two preceding figures because he is defined by both his docility and his voracity; and finally the dog, who is a magnificent instrument of transmission, the authentic equivalent of what will be at the end of the novel a natural object – electricity. He alone can ensure certain links, he can create certain forebodings which will become important thereafter: from the beginning, he knows Nemo – at least, he recognises his presence – but obviously this knowledge can only be communicated by mysterious signs.

Later a new element will be added, clearly distinct from the first group: Ayrton, who remains outside the opposition because he has another role to play. There is also Nemo, invisible to the end: for the moment, we can say that he is the personification of the island.

Along with this model of society we are also given what for Verne constituted society's cohesion, knowledge, ingenuity, that is to say, a certain *state of scientific knowledge*. Not an arrested science, a static science, to be passed along like an object; but the knowledge incarnated in the man who uses it – an engineer, or rather *the* engineer, for Cyrus Smith is not a specialist, confined to one kind of activity:

> The engineer was to them a microcosm, a compound of every science, a possessor of all human knowledge. It was better to be with Cyrus on a desert island, than without him in the most flourishing town in the United States. (*The Mysterious Island*, part I, p. 83)

Thus he is 'more than a man', since all social history is focused in his person. He makes a further difference between the modern adventure and that of Robinson Crusoe, for whom 'everything was a miracle to be achieved'. The entire promise of *exploitation* contained in this know-how rests not upon the work of the fiction or the work of the mystery, but upon a historical certainty. Cyrus Smith is so confident only because he knows that he, as it were, embodies the most important aspects of history.

To this is naturally added the object to be transformed, the material of the adventure, virgin nature: 'this island which they would ask to provide for all their needs'. But they are not two different things: nature is only the other side of science since they correspond exactly, following the lines of an obvious harmony. The task of the new Robinson Crusoe will be to rediscover this harmony, to bring it to light:

> The engineer felt confident because he knew himself capable of seizing from this savage nature everything that would be necessary to his life and that of his companions.

At no point, accordingly, do we relapse into the fallacy of a nature which is hostile to man. On the contrary, nature is man's collaborator: nature is in fact already informed by science, and is an inexhaustible reservoir of laboratory products. (In the same way that elsewhere it constitutes an inexhaustible reservoir of artefacts: see particularly, *Twenty Thousand Leagues Under the Sea*. Here too, in a simple profusion, in a natural syncretism which reunites all the styles, the island presents in advance the museum of all those works yet to be made (remember, in a text already quoted, the 'ruins which are eternally young'): 'this vault offered a picturesque mixture of all that Byzantine, Roman and Gothic architecture had produced at the hand of man. And yet this was only the work of nature! She alone had excavated this fairy Alhambra in a massif of granite.')

> My friends, this is iron ore, this is pyrites, this is clay, this is chalk, this is coal. Look at what nature gives us, this is her part in the common labour.

However, this nature which is the true raw material of the adventure also conceals the *mystery*. The island is, in fact, curiously *complete*. All of nature is to be discovered there, in the same way that all the reserves of scientific knowledge are at the disposition of the engineer. This plenitude of means, which gives the adventure its demonstrative simplicity, also requires a demonstration of its own, however; it cannot be merely given and acknowledged as a fact, as was remarked by Cyril Andreev in his preface to the complete Russian edition of the work of Jules Verne (see *Europe*, April 1955, p. 33):

> Lincoln Island, as the colonists called it, is truly a mysterious, extraordinary island. It seems to have been created deliberately for those adventure novels in which the heroes are shipwrecked, unless it were for those critics who have chosen to 'denounce' Verne's scientific errors. In the Pacific Islands there are not and there cannot be either ourangutangs, nor the wild ass, nor the kangaroo. The mineral wealth of the island is no more probable. The colonists find, almost on the surface of the island, clay, chalk, pyrites, sulphur and saltpetre. Jules Verne knew of the imprecisions of his novels, rather, he introduced them with full awareness. The Mysterious Island is the symbol of the universe, the allegory of our terrestrial globe given over to human domination. The Mysterious Island is the novel of an ideal human society face to face with nature.

The regularity of this power, which fills the island as though all nature were there, can only be surprising. Indeed, this *symbolisation* does not only mark the content of the novel: it extends even to the inhabitants of the island. When, from a summit, they manage to observe the contours of the island, they are struck by the already *worked* form of their too obvious irregularities. For them this is the first hint of the mystery. The island resembles nature too closely, which appears to them as the island resembling an island too closely.

We are thus given, once and for all, nature, society (reduced to its most simple expression), and science. Only work remains to be added to the combination, to show what human activity can achieve when it has these *elements* at its disposal. The theme of origins is obviously not being used mythically; the demonstration is perfectly adjusted to the conditions in which the problem is posed, for the real society that Verne represents. At least the narrative will be faithful to the problem as it arises in the consciousness of a society. The imaginative fiction has to serve as the perfect expression of the *real* construction of the future. And those for whom Verne's teaching is intended (we must remember the project of an educational library, realised by Hetzel) will have to undertake an analogous task, they think they will have to undertake an analogous task.

What must be built? A new America. We are thus very far from a new Robinsonnade, in the ordinary sense of the word (which has little to do with the novel actually written by Defoe): Verne compelled himself to *reduce* all possible forms of exoticism; his readers are not supposed to discover the new but to annex it. When the islanders decide to name its important features they choose *old names* which make the new land into a reflection of the one they have just left: they use names which 'recall America' – 'Little Ontario' for example. Thus the problem is to reconstitute from a norm, by an effort of identification: to innovate is to repeat. For Verne this is what defines the theme of colonisation.

> We will make this island into a little America! Here we will build towns, here we will establish railways, here we will erect telegraph systems, and one fine day, when it has been entirely transformed, well fitted out and properly civilised, we will offer it to the government of the Union.

Thus it is not at all a question of inventing, or even of making something new, but of reproducing the possible from its conditions (and not, like Robinson Crusoe, from possibilities already realised). And this programme is the exemplary bourgeois illustration of the theme of the master and possessor of nature.

From these beginnings, already visible as though packed in the seed, will be developed the fictional plot, the contrived narrative. There is no longer any distance – though perhaps there are certain ambiguities, which, when the moment comes, will resolve themselves in an unexpected way – and thus no possibility of discord can arise between the decision to represent an ideological project and the work which gives it shape: this is why we can speak correctly of an expressive theme.

It is easy to follow the successive realisations which, by the mediation of industry, transform nature. 'The clearing was transformed into a factory'. We move from a pottery kiln, then to metallurgy (from the most primitive techniques), and then reach the final stage: the use of electricity, the making of the telegraph, with which, as we shall see, the sequence is broken at the very moment when the adventure undergoes a qualitative change. (In fact this perfected invention will put the colonists in relation to *something else* (this is how Nemo will summon them): it diverts them from the simple line of science-nature and imposes a decisive test upon them. It is interesting to remember that electricity is one of the central images in Verne's work, just like the volcano, which will also play a cathartic role. Certain images involve an exact revelation of the inevitable distance between the project and its realisation. At the moment when they give rise to a crucial image which is the space of a problem, the other images are no longer so predictably docile; they can no longer be used for just any purpose.) Thus a gap is finally filled – at the level of premises there is no distance between the terms to be linked – since nature lends itself to the adventure of its transformation, just as the animals submit to their domestication. 'Decidedly, Pencroff has razed the word impossible from the vocabulary of Lincoln Island.'

The test of the fiction. The book acquires its true subject, and also its meaning, from the fact that, as it develops, this scheme is overturned and even reversed. The line of ideological realisations is broken the moment it crosses the development of another plot, which seems *more real*, in so far as it compels it to acknowledge the persistence of another form of the fiction. It is significant that, at this moment, this apparently independent book remakes a link with other books which it had apparently broken. The relation between the new fiction and the fiction of the past becomes more than simply a critical relation; it becomes a real conflict.

In fact, the presentation of the beginning, of the initial terms of the adventure, is progressively questioned. The colonists do not confront a *new* nature – which would be the equivalent or the complement of the knowledge of the engineer – but, paradoxically, without knowing it, they find themselves on the surface of a 'mysterious island'. The assumptions behind the problem must now be completely re-examined.

The idea of this new beginning is given by the artful form of the island: this is obvious when the colonists can sketch it from the summit of the central mountain, which is also a volcano. It is precisely the presence of the volcano which betrays the fact that this fragment of nature is only an artificial product. The island is not the site of a beginning, but of an ending. (This theme, present from the beginning, will take on its full meaning only at the end of the book.) The island is the last trace of a vanished continent, which explains the richness of its resources: it presents in a reduced and condensed form all that remains of a continent. This seems to explain the mystery: the theme of the volcano is an image of the unusualness of the island.

But it soon appears that the island is not deserted: if it has not been touched, profaned by the hand of man – if then it can serve as the means of testing, really testing, productively testing, initiating the 'shipwrecked from the air' – it is nevertheless inhabited by an invisible form, 'an unknown force'. This force shows itself very early, at the moment of arrival on the island: see the episode of the combat beneath the surface of the lake. It becomes indisputable when a grain of lead is discovered inside the pig killed in the forest: in a way that clearly recalls the thematic of Defoe's novel, this piece of metal seems to imply the existence of the whole of humanity, in so far as man alone produces technical objects.

Then there is the sequence of indecipherable signs, the 'inexplicable facts' which are always surprisingly useful to the colonists. At this moment the novel nearly succumbs to the temptation of an imagery of the miraculous. 'The engineer did not know what to think, and could not help dreaming of bizarre complications,' and the colonists actually begin to have thoughts of a religious providence. But they are not seduced by this facile solution, and seek to establish the relations between this problem and that which they thought they were solving:

> Alone, Cyrus Smith waited with his usual patience, although his stubborn reason was exasperated to feel itself faced with an absolutely inexplicable fact, and he became indignant at the thought that around him, perhaps beneath him, there was some new power to which he could not give a name.

It very quickly becomes obvious that the experience is entirely *faked*: the savage bare island is merely a decor, a device which gathers together the dramatis personae on one of those *trompe-l'oeil* islands of the eighteenth century. The mysterious 'force' pushes them back to the condition of Robinson Crusoe, from which we thought they had been finally delivered; and at a crucial moment this force puts in their hands the shipwrecked chest which contains, in miniature, all the panoply of the perfect Robinson Crusoe: 'nothing was missing'. Their adventure now becomes identical with the motif which, by contrast, had served to differentiate it.

Thus it is not by chance that the wreck, this time, was not *given* from the start: it is precisely this delay which underlines the facticity of the *ideological beginning*. The emergence of this new datum completely obliterates the idea of a conquest. Moreover, the chest also contains, in the guise of a message, a book, the Bible, open as though by chance at a passage marked by a cross: 'For every one that asketh receiveth; and he that seeketh findeth.' This was exactly the theme of the bourgeois industrial transformation of nature, but now its meaning has completely changed: the quest is no longer understood as a relation between the one who gives and those who receive. Thus the problem of man's relation to nature finds a new formulation.

This is where we find the allegorical history of Ayrton: the episode of the abandoned man appears as the irrefutable sign of the mutation of meaning. On another island, close to their own, the colonists discover the actual site of *Robinson Crusoe*: there Captain Grant has undergone an experience similar to that of the great ancestor, and it is thither that the convict Ayrton has been banished, to punish him for his treachery, with the promise that they will come and find him again at the indefinable moment when his crime has been expiated. Ayrton too had considerable resources at the beginning – all that had been bequeathed to him by Captain Grant; but he could not bear solitude and he gradually regressed to an animal state. When the colonists find him again he has lost the power of speech, and his return to civilisation (to being an exploiter and a colonist) will involve a slow and difficult re-education. This is an interesting variation on the motif of isolation, for it reveals to the colonists the secret of their situation: their success is measured on the scale of Ayrton's failure; indeed, they face the same problems.

It is not a natural task which has been imposed upon them (such as a real conquest of nature); it is a symbolic opportunity to display certain *capabilities*, not a real enterprise of transformation. Ayrton was destroyed (morally, of course) and he vanished into nature. Thus an ethical redemption can serve as an illustration for the industrial quest. Both are a test of values in which the real labour is of little importance: at most it has a merely pedagogic function, since for the adolescent of the group it can be the occasion of an initiation. In the same way – as Rousseau intended with *Robinson Crusoe* – the book itself is instructive for its readers. Indeed, the enterprise as it seemed initially was a distortion: the island is not virgin nature but a site prepared for a trial or experiment; any progress is like the illusory progress through a labyrinth, in search of a beginning.

Likewise, the idea of an adequation between nature and science is also called into question; not because it would be less real than a mere dream, but because the image of a laboratory which it implies is ambiguous (remember that for Verne nature is a 'natural laboratory'). The application of knowledge to a natural material is only the consequence of an application of nature to this knowledge, and this second sort of application, which becomes first in authority, is a historical mystery:

> [Pencroff]: 'Monsieur Cyrus, do you believe that there are islands with castaways? Islands specially for being comfortably shipwrecked upon, where the poor devils could always get by?'
>
> 'It's possible,' said the engineer smiling.
>
> 'It's certain, monsieur,' answered Pencroff, 'and it is equally certain that Lincoln Island is one such.'

There is obvious interest in this gradual transformation of the colonists' conception of their activities: for now they encounter *fiction* itself, and the novel which was a contradictory commentary on another novel begins to reflect upon itself. The fiction is no longer in the representation of reality but in the represented reality itself.

> From that day onwards, Pencroff seemed to be anxious. This island, *which he had made his own private property*, no longer seemed to belong entirely to him, and he seemed to be sharing it with another who was stronger than he.

The help of the one 'who does for us everything that we cannot do for ourselves' is precisely double-edged, and thus provokes a double reaction of admiration and rejection; the first reaction indicates the renunciation of the initial goal and the second reaction indicates its permanence: 'That invisible protection which made their own actions as nothing, left the engineer feeling both vexed and moved.'

For this superfluous assistance crucially demonstrates to the conquerors that they are the *objects* of an action and not its subjects (on the same level as nature). Thus the initial problem is now meaningless, and their adventure becomes precisely analogous to Ayrton's symbolic ordeal for reasons which are *apparently* different: he too had been sent to redeem himself by means of an assimilation into nature.

If the island is faked and artificial this is because it is actually only the visible form of the wishes of Nemo, who is hidden in the crater of the volcano, the secret stage-manager. And this is why, when Nemo dies, the island has no choice but to disappear with him back into the sea from which they came. When the ordeal of the colonists is over, when Captain Grant's ship arrives to put an end to the castaway's penance, with this illusory nature vanishes all that had been founded upon it: there is not a trace of the work accomplished; the colonists can determine nothing concerning the object of their quest. They are no longer what they had taken themselves to be: the agents of a real transformation. The attempt at colonisation has failed.

The meaning of this deviation remains to be established; we have yet to grasp how the intervention (*irruption*) of the form of the book in the process of narration has been able to place everything in question, and *why the questioning of the fiction is accomplished by the fiction itself.* We still have to decipher some new signs.

Nemo's mistake. Through the intervention of the mysterious and powerful 'force' the narrative is brought back to its point of departure, since the very conditions of the adventure are placed in question: what now seems an index requires a new interpretation. The colonists were not at grips with nature itself, but with another reality which must now be identified. It is this identification which gives the fable its new subject: now that it is no longer a question of the theme 'work in order to know', we must seek the reasons behind a spurious success. 'Natural' nature did not pose any problems of this sort: as a true source of power, as a reservoir of true fulfilment, it produced both the knowledge of its power and thus the explanation of an inevitable fatality; in that instance, nature was its own science, as the principle of all the rationalities, and did not need to have recourse to external reasons in order to justify its power. But when we are dealing with a 'mysterious' nature in which work is too easy, in which a just effort is no longer the guarantee of conquest, then the exigence of *another knowledge* makes itself felt – a knowledge which is no longer the emanation of nature, but an extrinsic key by which a supernatural power will be revealed. Thus, as in so many other novels by Verne, history is told by means of an experience of decipherment. The falsely natural initial data must be translated into another language in order to reabsorb the trick which has endangered the adventure.

This search for a new rationality could well culminate in a supernatural imagery: we have already met with this possibility at least once before. And a conclusion of this kind would perhaps not be surprising when we consider that in the spring of 1884 Verne went to Rome to seek the blessing of Pope Leo XIII; we are told that there he was 'congratulated on the purity and the moral and spiritual value of his works' (Madame Allote de la Fuye, *Jules Verne, sa vie, son oeuvre* (Jules Verne, His Life and Works), Kra, 1928, ch. 18). And *The Mysterious Island* – which shows the relative failure of human labour, or has it depend upon a providence which does not accommodate itself to historical progress except in so far as it has nurtured this progress – could well be considered a Catholic novel, obeying the orthodoxy of the Church's educational principles: the disparagement of all scientific knowledge of the world. Verne reminding engineers of the necessary subordination of their knowledge to revealed mysteries, struggling by the side of Huysmans, of Drumont, of Leo Taxil, adding a new weapon to those which they had already collected together (aestheticism, fraud, fanaticism), in order to remind men of the supernatural which they were beginning to neglect – would have been a fine token of 'moral value' for the bourgeois pope, and one more splendid contradiction in a work consecrated to 'progress', a contradiction which is now scarcely enigmatic.

This was not Verne's purpose. In his book, Moré demonstrates convincingly that Verne's life and entire work exclude the possibility of such conformism. If Verne remains inevitably discreet on this point, and frequently offers only a negative defence of his lay status, it is nevertheless true that his implicit opponents were not deceived in this matter. At the beginning of 1868, fifteen years before the visit to the pope, Veuillot wrote to Hetzel:

I have not read the extraordinary journeys of Jules Verne.

> Our friend Aubineau tells me that they are charming, except for one oversight which doubtless spoils nothing, but which disfigures everything, and leaves the miracles of the world as enigmas. It is beautiful but it is inanimate. Someone is missing. . . . (Quoted in Parménie and Bonnier de la Chapelle, *Histoire d'un éditeur et de ses auteurs, Hetzel* (An Editor and His Authors, Hetzel), Albin Michel, 1953, p. 489)

This is well said, and certainly very shrewd. And it is also rather significant that in this 'judgment' we find the very terms of the problem which has just been posed: What mediates between the *enigma* and the *miracles*? Verne agrees with Veuillot in what he rejects – the structure of the novel has adequately demonstrated this – leaving the mediating role to science; but for all that he does not give the expected reply, and it is this double refusal which gives the novel its true meaning and, certainly, its *educative* value.

Moreover, the supernatural solution is invoked only in passing and with a deftly sustained triviality:

> 'I am not inquisitive but I would give my right arm to see him face to face! In my opinion he should be handsome, tall, strong, with a fine beard, and hair like sunbeams, and he should be sleeping on the clouds, a large ball in his hand!'
>
> 'But Pencroff,' said Gideon Spillet, 'that's God the Father that you have just described to us.'
>
> 'Possibly, Mr Spillet, but that is how I imagine him.'

Nemo, an absent but active presence, a hidden and efficient god, is a fake god, in the same way that he is a false father, as he will appear: though not a caricature, at least the image of a failure, half respected. He has superior powers at his command but he remains a man. Also, his enormous power can be measured by analogy:

> Though it is evidently the intervention of a human being I agree that he commands powers beyond those of ordinary

> humanity. That is still a mystery, but if we discover the man, the mystery will also be discovered.

Accordingly the sign can be deciphered; a brief encounter will suffice. There is no point in trying to say what has already been said so well:

> Although there are certain men endowed with advantages which nature has denied to others, it is not said that these men are raised above human nature; because, for this, it were necessary that they possessed qualities in peculiar, which are not comprised in the essence or definition of humanity. The stature of a giant, for example, is exceptional but human. The ability to compose poetry is not given to all men, and yet it is human. Human also is the ability to imagine different objects; with eyes staring as though they were actually present. On the other hand, if any man possessed the means of grasping the ideas and principles of knowledge denied to other men, he would no longer remain within the boundaries of human nature. (Spinoza, *Tractatus theologico-politicus*, marginal note to ch. 1)

Nemo is characterised by the fact that he does not possess these gifts but has nevertheless been able to use the 'natural advantages' of humanity in order to achieve prodigies of invention and conquest; more than any other, he has known how to use the power to *form new images*.

But such a description is inadequate because it remains merely negative: we must still answer the question of identity. Who is Nemo? Indeed, the first real answer to this question will be given by the analogy with the status of Ayrton, the man cast-out who must redeem himself by submitting to the conditions of a symbolic solitude. Nemo, too, as though he were undergoing some test, needs to be judged, and this is precisely what he asks of the colonists in the last pages of the book: 'What do you think of me? Am I wrong? Am I right?'

This is how the novel is in fact decentred in relation to what initially seemed its essential preoccupation: the theme of conquest masks that of the test, the ordeal. And it must certainly not be thought that there was no conquest because the enterprise was preceded by an anticipated conquest. Nemo is no more of a conqueror than are the colonists: he is in exactly the same situation as the men he wanted to deceive.

This is how the supernatural is expelled. Nemo has simply transferred his appointed ordeal on to others. He is Crusoe as much as they, and may even be the most Crusoe-like of them all. He is the true Crusoe which the others merely imitate.

He is both Crusoe and a false god: he has appropriated only the setting and the solitude of deity. 'I am dying from having believed that one could live alone.' If Nemo has turned the work of the colonists into something spurious, what Marx, like Jules Verne, called a 'Robinsonnade', this is because he is a retrograde power – and at the same time miraculously prospective: he has made perverted use of his vast knowledge, not in order to build a better society, but in order to facilitate a solitary journey of some 20,000 leagues. He has strolled along the paths of a conquest of nature, and thus he will, until the end of his enterprise, remain an amateur, who needs other amateurs to appreciate his work, even if they must depreciate their own, which is then only the reflection of it. He is obliged, in order to see the future which he gives humanity, to make an image of it that is already retrospective, i.e. to make progress appear in the guise of the useless.

Thus, far from being the condition and the precocious image of the human future, Nemo remains tied to the form of the past. He is the very image of yesterday, instead of that of tomorrow. Indeed, Cyrus Smith judges him thus: 'Captain, your mistake is to have believed that one could resurrect the past, and you have fought necessary progress.'

These words would have a particular meaning, since they directly evoke Nemo's incessant struggle against the English policy of oppressing colonial peoples; it is interesting to note how unrevolutionary such a struggle could appear to the avant-garde bourgeois that Verne nevertheless was. But it is very important to be able to generalise this judgment, which is also a judgment of the novel itself, and to see in it the condemnation of a form of activity that is in other respects totally *reactionary*, even if in some respects it seems progressive. What he pronounced is a condemnation of utopia, i.e. of the future seen through the father's eyes.

Like the novelist, Nemo needs to give something to see, to give himself the spectacle of reality. This explains the ineluctable return to a fictional model which seems obsolete: the Robinson Crusoe of legend, as Defoe had not wanted to depict him. The results of the Industrial Revolution – and the island colonists are both the agents and the products of this revolution – are *applied* to a typically pre-revolutionary ideological representation. In relation to the grandiose ideological figure of the solitary hero, Nemo is in the same situation as are the colonists in relation to him: he can only express the meaning of this work by identifying himself with this hero. But he thereby renounces his project of a real conquest to become (not only in the representation which he gives of himself, but in the representation of others which he imposes, in his actions and even in his decisions) the *fictive subject* of an obsolete adventure. This is why he can only save himself by resort to a factitious experience: the ordeal which he forces upon others. It is by the mediation of these others that he can 'reconcile himself with the rest of humanity', which they are assumed to represent in an *abridged* form (in the way that the island was a miniature version of nature itself; and just as Nemo resumes all the fictions); by virtue of the *role* which has devolved upon them they are merely the ambassadors of an imaginary humanity, dispossessed of their power, which is no longer defined by their knowledge and their labour.

The lesson of the novel is obvious. If a literary work succeeds in showing how the earth will turn into a copy of paradise, this is not accomplished by presenting this transformation as the result of human labour, but by insinuating that the result has already been achieved, by an anticipation: certainly not with the suggestion of some external agency but by the action of a *single* man, on condition that this action is applied by inverse. That is to say that the novel of work, of labour, has reached in Verne's work – whether or not this was his intention – a point at which it must necessarily invent new forms of expression, forms which will allow it to dispense specifically with the degenerate figure of the solitary hero. Verne does not invent these forms, but he does play upon past forms, with great virtuosity, in a way that exposes the reality of their obstructive, retarding, retrograde qualities.

The final secret which the characters in the book have to decipher – and this is also the ultimate meaning of the expressive motif of the island adventure – is that instead of having to settle their score with nature, as they had expected, they find themselves settling someone else's score with the fiction, showing that a certain fictional mode is henceforth historically finished. Thus their enterprise is not as absurd as it might seem. Although it does not evince a reality, it is thoroughly conclusive, against the grain of Nemo's project, since it betrays the vanity of that project. It does thus have a meaning. Similarly Verne's work, far from being illusory, locates the mythology that it constitutes firmly *in* history.

The island and all trace of the colonists is to disappear with Nemo:

> Their immediate reaction was a deep anguish! They had no thought for the immediate danger which threatened them, but rather for the destruction of this ground which had been their sanctuary, for this island which they had made fertile, this island which they had loved, which they had one day hoped to see flourishing! So many efforts in vain, so much work wasted.

The fable indeed culminates in an instance of the *precarious*: and this episode is not adventitious, since Verne takes it up again in his final novel, *The Adventures of the Barsac Mission*, in which the scientist's setting fire to Blackland, his creation, obviously recalls the disappearance of Nemo with all his works.

The book accordingly finishes with a destruction rather than a conquest: it describes a dispossession rather than an appropriation, a dispossession in work and adventure. The possible short cuts into the future, as well as the detours into the past, vanish with Nemo. The book succeeds in showing up the position of literature in relation to the history which it claims to describe: the images which it tries to preserve are not vain illusions, but are worthy of proper commemoration:

> Never would they forget this island on which they had arrived destitute and naked, this island which had supplied their needs for four years, of which there now remained only an outcrop of granite pounded by the waves of the Pacific, the tomb of the man who had been Captain Nemo.

That is the last sentence in the book.

It is interesting to know that the colonists will subsequently have only to *reproduce* the adventure of their fictive initiation in order to found a real colony, in America: still with the posthumous assistance of Captain Nemo, who has left them a casket of precious stones. This implies that fiction can, if only by contrast, serve as an initiation, an introduction to real work. It is an inverted reflection of this reality, and yet its sole image, to the extent that a description of the real work which follows after can be dispensed with. In itself, the repetition would be uninteresting; the evocation will suffice. Verne's work thus reveals a recurrent meaning, in presenting the fiction itself as a precarious instance of the real, but also as its anachronistic and immoderate prefiguration, a form which is inevitably preceded.

III The function of the novel

> This much seems certain, this sea contains only fossil species, amongst which both the fish and the reptiles are all the more perfect for the antiquity of their creation. (*Journey to the Centre of the Earth*)

Mobilis in mobili: this, as we know, is Nemo's call-sign; it is also the basic maxim for a historical reverie about destiny. Through it we can penetrate easily to the general principle which Verne wanted to illustrate. It abruptly discloses all the ideological implications which are the necessary condition for the novel as Verne conceived it: like the still vague perception of a historical event, it involves the notion that science is the essential instrument of a transformation of nature. *Mobilis in mobili* – this is the position of science, and thus the position of man in his relation to nature; this is Axel, who rediscovers a unity with the original sea while bathing near the centre of the earth. Science is in nature, the future is in the present, just as the *Nautilus* is in its element, where the real can no longer be distinguished from the symbolic. The unknown bathes in the known: it is precisely this intimate liaison, this conjunction which is also a conjuncture (that of the modern itself), this adequation, which best characterises Verne's work, *from within*. It tells us what he has done; it is the very heart of his project. It could well serve as its general title.

But it is most important that this same idea can serve to designate the insufficiencies or, rather, the limits of the work; it instigates a revelation of the confusion which obscures the relation between science and nature, and it discloses the impossible work which is the inevitable and illusory complement of the realised work. The principle of an imaginary fidelity to the future is itself inevitably fictive: this fidelity announces itself in a contradiction, in the words of infidelity. Voyages and encounters are both merely returnings and rediscoveries.

Thus what we are obliged to call *the reverse of the work* begins to take shape: the conditions of its possibility which enable us to read it against the grain of its intended meaning.

Similarly, the imagined identity between science and nature is not an absolute identification, because it is elaborated within that indeterminate space between reality and fiction, in that interval which betrays the obsolescence of all forms of anticipation. As we have just seen, Verne seems to have reached one of the limits of the aesthetic consciousness, to have travelled to the very frontier of his own knowledge, in so far as he took upon himself the task of this revelation.

Moreover, this is why a certain caution is seemly in asserting, as Michel Butor has done, that Verne's attitude to science became pessimistic. It was never Verne's intention to argue *a* belief in the power of science, nor was it his intention to argue against such a belief. That was not his theme. Not a complacent representation, then, but an interrogation of the *image of science*. Obviously Verne's work must be grasped in relation to the notion of progress and industry, but these notions are not the centre or direct content of that work. Verne's problem is this: How is it possible to figure that *ideological project which is the self-consciousness of an industrial society*? Through this singular problematic he successfully reveals the true meaning of this historical project. Far from devising a poetic celebration of the scientist-expert, making him into a solitary exile, he wishes to demonstrate the distance between this kind of representation and the reality of human labour. Verne's originality is to have made this distance apparent *within* this representation.

For this reason it is not enough to say that Verne is the representative of a particular ideological moment or of a certain social class, unless we first question the notion of representation itself. There is a too ready tendency to interpret the idea of representation in a retrospective sense: a work, once it is finished, would be representative *because it had been made* – that would be the dubious reward for this accomplishment, just as an elected candidate becomes (by definition) a representative. But, before the work is finished, before the votes are cast, is there or is there not representation? In any case, it is there that we must seek out the roots, the meaning of all representativity: in the conditions for the emergence of the work, for example, conditions which do not necessarily belong to the movement of the work. The problem of representation must be posed at the moment when the work takes form (*se fait*), for it is this decisive moment which articulates both what the author intended to or had to represent and what he in fact represents. Thus the purpose of Verne's work is not to translate or illustrate an idea or programme, but to realise the *combination* of the thematic figures and the fable. The interest of Verne's work resides in the discovery of an object which indicates this very combination: the island, the juncture of the thematic figure with the events, of a certain plot-form which derives from the collision of two possible narratives which also symbolise two forms of fiction. This makes the island irreducibly different from all the other thematic figures.

An attempt to represent is not to be confused with a gesture of assimilation: an individual represents a social class and its ideology in so far as he situates himself in relation to this ideological 'climate'; otherwise, in the case of the writer, he would write nothing. The novel is only a *work* in so far as it is an apt contribution, in so far as it admits innovation in relation to the 'spirit' (*esprit*) on which it depends. ('Spirit', 'climate': both unsatisfactory expressions in that they attempt to define the indefinite, though let us not attribute any mystical value to this 'indefinite', impoverished as it is.)

Firstly it is impossible for a specific work to reproduce the totality of an ideology: a partial apprehension is all that is possible; thus there is a choice, a choice which is significant in so far as it is more or less representative. The contradictions which inhabit the work cannot be the same, term for term, as those contradictions upon which the work depends, even if we should discover these same contradictions in the life of the author: in the history of Verne's life we find, simultaneously, Veuillot and Leo XIII, the 'red platform' candidate in the Amiens municipal elections, and the correspondent of the student Aristide Briand in Nantes. The work can be described as the reflection of these real contradictions, in so far as it is an authentic *production* rather than a reproduction. And finally, an ideology is only *made* from the totality of these productions, or at least it is only made *from* them. Ideology is not, prior to the work, like a system which can be reproduced: it is resumed, elaborated by the work; it has no independent value.

The *act* of the writer is fundamental: he realises a particular crystallisation, a restructuration, and even a structuration of the data upon which he works: all that which was no more than a collective foreboding, project, aspiration, *precipitates* abruptly in an image which rapidly becomes familiar, becomes the real itself, the flesh of these projects. Verne's work furnishes a unique example of this process; it endows the ideological with a new form but also, more important, a visible form. This visible form is not shadowed by any ideal reality, any invisible form, but it does display the signs of its modification, without there being any substance there to support it. The work exists on the reverse side (*envers*) of what it would like to be, the reverse of itself. Where is this reverse?

Until this moment we have been describing the *treatment* to which an ideological project is subjected at the moment in which it is made readable. And as we have already seen, this description could be systematised working from the image of the father (a fluctuating image in Verne): the father is one of the significant characters in the work, an obsessive theme which finally acquires a general value (there are natural and artificial fathers; there is Nemo, the father of the fiction and the fiction of the father; there is also the volcano, the father of nature); the father constitutes a privileged fictional object which seems almost to offer a key to all the other objects. But at the same time, it informs the narrative itself as it constantly returns to its moment of origin: thus posing the question, the riddle of birth, to history itself, and not, as elsewhere, to the individual subject. Finally, the continuing presence of the image of the father, further multiplied by the number of roles it is called upon to play, relates back to more than a material figure or the form of an interrogation: it evokes the reality of the father at the level of the work itself. The literary father, the father of the book: Robinson Crusoe, a thematic ancestor rather than a determinate ideological model; the symbolic figures and the direction of the narrative are deduced from him; this father gives meaning to the work by making it the term of a historical relationship. This relationship, beyond the history of the works and their themes, beyond any history *of* language, alludes to history *tout court*, with which Verne, like so many others, had aspired to struggle.

The project, no longer just ideological but belonging to the domain of literary ideology, this project of making a modern Robinson Crusoe, expresses that necessity without which there would be no writers: new works for a new era. And would the works be related, by analogy with the relations between historical eras? For Verne, Crusoe the ancestor can seem only imaginary, purely fictional: and thus he has to invent a true Crusoe, this being the programme of the anticipatory work. To outline a new Crusoe, intended as a symbol of reality, is to pose the problem of fiction and its reality, and consequently the problem of its mistaken irreality: all these problems in a single necessary moment.

But we see that the new Crusoe exists only thanks to the survival of his predecessor; the new *prolongs* the old, affirms its persistence, which may well be weakened by this disavowal. The motif of the island, no longer just in the reality of its content, but its reality *tout court*, that which gives it a history: this motif reveals the regressive form of the narrative, because it is a borrowed theme, and has hardly any meaning beyond this fact which expresses an ideological confrontation. Verne's literary project cannot be simple, original, self-begotten; it is inexorably linked to other projects which lend it substance and meaning. This is the only way that the problematic of a work is constructed: around this argument, whose real setting is a library rather than an island. Consider the frontispiece which Grandville so delicately chose for Defoe's work. It does not show Robinson Crusoe in his true setting, the setting which has all the versimilitude of artifice, a virgin nature, cultivated with all that sentimentality which the bourgeoisie lavishes on the purity of its young brides. By a subtle displacement, he places him in that paradise of illusion in which the truth is simply correct behaviour: in a public garden. A motionless statue, watching unnoticed.

Crusoe is indeed this apparition which judges us by our appearances and gives the key to many historical dreams: this phantasm, its shape so precise and complete, which fixes definitively the limits of certain representations, of a certain knowledge which is coherent only by virtue of not straying beyond its boundaries, by sustaining its incompleteness. It is no longer just a question of ideology but of an ideological form.

The fact that this form is obsolete, and that Verne should pick on precisely this form to express his supposedly progressive project, does not mean that the project is invalid. It means that it is only possible to link themes within a specific work by at the same time situating them, implicitly or explicitly (extraordinarily, Verne chose the latter), within the historical sequence of themes, a sequence in which no single theme can properly be isolated.

Indeed, this sequence only unfolds, this history only progresses, in its own singular fashion, not necessarily that of the projected work. (There are certain works which, unlike those of Verne, develop without understanding their situation in literary (or any other) history. They may even take their beginning from this incomprehension. And because of this *misunderstanding* they show an apparent internal disunity.) Paradoxically, and almost inevitably, history lags behind the project of describing it, and this delay contaminates the narrative itself: the 'reservoir of symbols' does not furnish Verne with the means of representing a total conquest, as seems to have been his intention.

But this hindrance is not due solely to a technical reluctance. The discord between the representation and the expression derives from the structure of the project itself as much as from the means employed in its realisation. It would be too easy to blame the writer's difficulties on the distance which separates the work from reality; we are concerned with a flaw common to both, neither of which can be explained by simple ideological contradictions.

Above all, let us not say that the book is stronger than reality, or vice versa; that the eighteenth-century *Robinson Crusoe* is still vital enough, or even dead enough, to be appropriated by a later work, to contribute to the new reality by supplying its reverse. The problem would then be too simple; it would be enough to say that Verne, through the project of a realist stylisation of the ideological vocation of his epoch, encounters an obstacle, an impediment to his work, in the manipulation of the ideological means. It is rather that he meets with difficulties in trying to use them as simple instruments. Precisely because it is expressive and not just figurative, the expressive motif is not as manageable as it might seem, not to be subsumed in a simple opposition: an irresistible impulse displaces the character of Crusoe from its convenient background position as a piece of scenery which is particularly useful for the contrast between the new and the old which it establishes. Crusoe, who had played the role of the fictional within the fiction itself, now reappears as a real hero, the true hero of the story, who, in his various embodiments, Nemo and Ayrton, ranged against Cyrus Smith and Captain Grant, against the two typical representatives of the contemporary entrepreneur, suggests the two possible forms of solitude. This fiction within the fiction becomes an instance of the real, denying the reality of the fiction.

Does this mean that the validity of the ideological project is challenged – or even challenges itself – at the very moment of its realisation? Does contradiction break forth in the passage from a form of consciousness to a form of writing? Emphatically, if there really is a contradiction, if contradiction is to mean anything at all, it is not *there* that it emerges or takes place. Jules Verne the bourgeois, and the bourgeoisie of Jules Verne, duly takes one step forward and three steps back. But this procrastination involves two realms: on this side of the book, in the historical relation which links the works in a specific sequence; and beyond the book, in the play of historical relations without which there would be no book. Within the book something else is happening.

This effort to grasp a contemporary form, modernity, through an obsolete form, by the expedient of this contrast, is a failure. A writing of reality, a writing which deploys all the possibilities preserved by the entire history of writing, does not exist: there is finally a writing of writing, since, in this enterprise, it is the intermediate form which captures the most reality. The contours of allusion are more significant than the content, their supposed plenitude: they are the very object of writing.

If the old book manages anyway to emerge at the moment when the representation of a new world is being composed, this is because that old book is not just the mobile screen, not just a passive implement in the process of representation: it is also part of a reality which it does not merely help to describe. If the weight of 'literature', of writing, prevails over the conscious will to transform, this is because there is more than a form, a pretext, a simple figure, in the expressive motif; a decisive allusion to the potential work, a new book, a new world. The former man *profoundly* defines the new man, even if he seems momentarily to endanger his enterprise.

It must not be thought that this has defined a necessary form of the writer's work, the general progression, as though determined in advance, of all literary projects, wherever they are situated in the history of works. But the book which we have just been engaged with could only appear in this form. For the appeal from book to book, culminating in the victory of antique representation, ultimately signifies the dependence of the present upon the past, of the contemporary upon the history *which constitutes it.* The flaws in Verne's project are the index of this dependence. The conquering bourgeoisie, whose fictional potential image Verne wanted to draw, was not a traveller from nowhere: the new man, as Verne manages actually and positively to describe him, is not a solitary, the conqueror of an absolute, the appropriator of virgin nature, but simply the master of a certain number of relations. His most essential feature is that he has *companions*; he is accompanied not only by other men but also by that which both gives meaning to his project and simultaneously presents the first challenge to it: all that history in which they are ineluctably involved. And this involvement is not only lived, directly perceived as the consequence of a conscious choice; it is a conflict, a trauma, burdened with secret repressions. This bourgeoisie which cannot abolish its history feels inarticulately that it is permanently bound to that history, that it will be history's consummation, that it will never be unburdened, and that this inertia which hinders its intention is also the necessary condition for any enterprise (as it is for the written expression of the project of transformation). It is this viscosity of history which only anchors decisions to their true meaning after passing through the acknowledgment of a necessary delay.

The new world is not so new that the world – as it has been described so meticulously and desultorily by classical political economy and even by classical literature, but with what compromises, what myopia! – can appear once and for all obsolete; in other words, as merely an object-lesson in the old-fashioned. The society which Verne's 'represents' has not yet cast off the fetters which checked the old mercantile society within the circle of a certain historical condition, described, in other respects, scientifically; and thus it is the prisoner of its old dreams. The bourgeoisie has its revolution behind it: it cannot be revived by any kind of technical progress. Consequently bourgeois ideology has become incapable of thinking and representing the future.

This is more or less what happens: Jules Verne wants to represent, to translate, an imperative which is profoundly ideological, that notion of labour and conquest which is at the centre of his work. In relation to the historical reality which it recuperates, this ideal is contradictory; real labour is alienated, perfect conquest is inevitably constrained by the conditions of former colonisation. These are the real limits of bourgeois ideology: but this ideology is emphatically not internally contradictory; for that would presuppose that it gave a complete description of reality, that it ceased to be an ideology, whereas it is precisely its insufficiencies, its incompleteness, which guarantee its flawed coherence. The interest of Verne's work lies in the fact that, through the unity of its project – a unity borrowed from a certain ideological coherence, or incoherence – and by the means which inform this project (or fail in this enterprise), by specifically literary means, it reveals the *limits*, and to some extent the *conditions* of this ideological coherence, which is necessarily built upon a discord in the historical reality, and upon a discord between this reality and its *dominant* representation.

The literary failure of Jules Verne, the fragility of that enterprise which is not his alone, this is what forms the matter of his books: the demonstration of a fundamental *historical defect*, whose most simple historical expression calls itself the *class struggle*. Accordingly it is no coincidence that all Verne's images of reconciliation open out on to the description of a conflict. Today and tomorrow, *mobilis in mobili* – for the novel this involves two things at once: and yet they are not the same thing. An attentive reading will prove this.

Like Balzac, then, though using very different forms, Verne encounters or rather witnesses within his work the encounter of the figures which he has created – figures which determine the real within the limits of the work – and the ideological project which he perhaps wished simply to illustrate. We have seen that there is a conflict between these two instances: the presence and the style of Nemo completely transform the enterprise of the aspiring colonists. Not that the objects of the adventure have been destroyed or replaced, but, crucially, their meaning has changed. Nature is not what one took it for; between that basic reality and human actions there is not only the mediation of labour and science, but also the entire screen of historical myths, factitiously constituted but none the less real, since facticity is its *raison d'être*. *The Mysterious Island* tells the story of just that test of its power which men make. It is indeed the myth which *emerges* with Nemo, and with it all the burden of history, that reticence and that inhibition which make it interminable. Nemo is the exact type of the hero who was thought to have vanished, whereas that disappearance was both the sign and the guarantee of the modern itself.

Nemo is Crusoe, a tragic, condemned Crusoe who does not progress, because he is already an anachronism. He is the recurring fiction. He is that ancestor: the bourgeois future. In this way the notion of mechanical progress is admitted to its role as an ideological representation, to its *place* as a great bourgeois rite, typical of a certain moment in the history of the bourgeoisie. Nemo is the fatal resurgence, the resurrection, not of the son but of the father.

What characterises Verne's novels is that by their structure they encounter this antagonism as an obstacle: and thus the enterprise of a demystification of the book is illusory, or rather it belongs to the makers of mythologies, because the book is itself this demystification. Everything happens as though Verne knew the ideological situation of the epoch whose aspirations he wanted to represent, by giving them the material incarnation of a book. But there is no such thing as an implicit knowledge: the book is not a simple reflection of the contradictions of its time, nor is it a deliberated description of the project of a social class at a given moment. It represents a form of final *perception* of reality, and this is what defines the nature of the book – this rather than the nature of art, for it is not saying much to say that Verne is an artist (it has merely a polemical value and is indeed indisputable, since it comes down to saying that he is no less an artist than others). On the other hand, there is some purpose in showing that Verne is a genuine writer. It is a perception rather than a knowledge in the true sense (a theoretical knowledge), rather than a mechanical (unconscious) reproduction of reality. It is an effort to express its profound nature, to illuminate its recesses, through the arrangement of animated figures and the unfolding of a chosen fable.

Verne's flaw, his defect, relates not to a *historical project* but to a *historical statute*. And this difference is crucial: this is not to offer yet another new 'interpretation' of Verne's work, another translation, another commentary; on the contrary it is an explanation of the discords which connect the work to itself. These discords are not finally the direct reflection of an ideological contradiction, but the symptom of a historical opposition. What may seem no more than a simple literary allusion, the digression via Robinson Crusoe, enables us to reveal a real situation, better than any other form of consciousness (except, of course, a genuine theoretical elaboration, but that is no longer a question of consciousness in the strict sense of the word). In its way, so simple and curiously veiled, perspicacious and deceptive, the book finally shows us – though it may not be in the manner stated – what it proposed to enunciate: the history of its moment.

June 1966

Appendix
The Thematic Ancestor: Robinson Crusoe

1 In 1719, that is to say before his time, Defoe, that brilliant journalist, initiates – in all senses of the word, dynamic, ludic publicising – the theme of the man on an island. (We are not concerned here with immediate antecedents, but it would nevertheless be interesting to discover how Defoe realised this form, by looking at its thematic prehistory and tracing the history of what was not yet a theme. This history would be paradoxical because it seems to involve what was almost always a stage setting, as in Sophocles and Shakespeare, but this is only a hypothesis.) He made the island the indispensable setting, the scene for an ideological motif which was only beginning to emerge: the meditation on origins. In fact the ideological form was not to adopt the precise shape that Defoe had predicted, so that it would be necessary to make a separate historical study of the readings of *Robinson Crusoe*, to show within those readings a completely developed ideology of origins which Defoe had not yet discerned. Briefly, it must be said that Defoe himself never entirely fell into this ideology, in so far as he was the first to give an explicit critique of it. Crusoe's island is thus a genuine *anticipation*, an early form of what is not yet an actuality. Retrospectively, this form is distorted by inaccurate readings which are motivated by the search for a faithful replica of the object. It is thus important to realise that Defoe did not actually say some of the things that Verne and many others before him thought that they had

heard. Defoe is possibly the only author by proxy (*auteur d'anticipation*), in so far as he supplied his successors with images.

2 It must be remembered that *Robinson Crusoe*, in spite of the stubborn legend engendered by these false readings, is not simply an adventure story but is the instrument of an inquiry, the theme around which an ideology has been progressively established (at least, *one* of the themes; there are others which are perhaps of equal importance). This 'story' is an early embodiment, an advance popularisation of the concept of origin. Marx and Engels were not mistaken when they repeatedly cited it as the exemplary specimen of an economic ideology. This is not the moment to document the importance of images of origin in the philosophy of the eighteenth century, images which were eventually systematised into a dictionary and a grammar (by Condillac, Buffon, Diderot, Maupertuis, among others; Rousseau at a later moment, plays a very special role, for he elaborated the final, grand system, which is negative and critical). With his miraculously *innocent* gaze, which surveys the origins of society, art, industry, thought and manners, the man on the island holds a place alongside the child, the savage, the blind man, the statue . . . in the arsenal of 'metaphysical instruments', conceptual images. These presences absent to themselves, neutral in so far as they accept their meanings, are valuable less for the frank and naive description which they give of qualities than because they systematically elucidate an order: beneath their gaze the necessary sequence of a constitution is revealed, the hierarchy according to which the elements of a genesis are organised. The theme already has this value with Defoe, and it could be said that he gives others a formal model: but with Defoe, more than any other, the revelation of order has a critical value; it must have given him pleasure to introduce, at a late moment within this ideal history, God and the Other. It remains that the 'history', beyond its anecdotal support, has a didactic significance: it is a complete representation, the visible body on which a theory can be inscribed. All those who have wanted to settle their accounts with *Robinson Crusoe* – Jules Verne amongst others – have achieved this in so far as it allowed them to criticise a certain representation of origins. This critique depends on revealing the *circularity of*

origins; on this theme, see *Anti-Dühring* and the work of Jules Verne. From the first moment the origin allots itself what it would like to engender: Crusoe's shipwreck is a good example.

Yet a careful reading of Defoe will show that this critique is already spontaneously there. The origin appears expressly as a false origin, whose function is to display a process rather than explain it. The individual theme must not be too promptly assimilated into its ideological environment: the readings at the margin of the book all replace the object by its horizon. Of course, the theme must be relocated in its ideological field, but without losing its particularity: representations of origin within an ideology of origins are not all necessarily equivalent; each has its different manner of at least stating the question. We should thus proceed methodically from *Robinson Crusoe* to the surrounding ideology, rather than the other way round.

3 Crusoe's gaze is destitute, deprived and impoverished rather than naive. This forsaken gaze confronts the desert island. This is an important characteristic because it places us at once within the limits of an economic system. *Robinson Crusoe* is for classical political economy what the statue, the first man, will be for the theory of knowledge. This gaze encounters the universe for which it was made: a universe of *decay*. It is astonishing to see how in Defoe's narrative exoticism, a dryness of things, is substituted for the expected luxuriance of nature. Nature is posited as a poverty, an absence of goods.

4 The first manifest theme, that of Providence, recurs in the mechanical fashion of an obsession; as a theme it is superficial, perhaps a mere screen. From the prologue dealing with the father, it is this theme of Providence which initiates the narrative and links the episodes. It is linked with the outline of a thematic of fantasy: vague premonitions and the devil. The whole is cemented by a diffuse deism. These pretended themes divert us from the idea of origin, which accordingly remains deeply buried and was perhaps not revealed until after the event. The plot is built on a sequence of 'miracles'; life on the island is a 'tissue of wonders . What is the significance of this apparent attempt to apologise which is so foregrounded, even though the style remains informal? Is it a pretext, a pretence merely for the sake of the audience?

5 In fact the problematic of origins only really appears at the moment when the fantasy themes have been exorcised – themes only rudimentarily developed, with no efforts expended on the marvellous, which is only alluded to as if in passing, even though the method of repetition puts it in the foreground. The exorcism does not even necessarily pass through the moment of interpretation: the 'story' itself puts the devil to flight; it was a cannibal, an old goat . . . and Providence is quickly forgotten. However, this factual exorcism is duplicated by an interpretative critique of the attempted apology: behind the fantastic there also stands nature, the tricks played by nature. The outstanding moment of this critique is the encounter with cannibalism which marks the final defeat of evil and all its ideological consequences. The tolerance accorded to cannibalism as an *equivalent* form of civilisation is based on the fundamental discovery that nature is anthropophagous. Man Friday's question about good and evil – which entirely overthrows the distinction – corresponds to this critical idea of tolerance. In passing, via the critique of religion, there is a glance at the colonial methods of the Spanish.

Thus, with the critique of the surface ideology, the meditation on the idea of nature makes an appearance.

6 The destitute gaze reveals nature, less by discovering new qualities than by surveying and exploring a sequence, elucidating in the process a hierarchy of determinations: the objects are arrayed in time according to the needs of this impoverished gaze. Naturally the motive of the sequence is critical: the objects have more or less value according to the moment at which they are summoned forth. God is thus no longer in first place, and, in fact, God is when the parrot calls Crusoe's name. The state of nature, then, the moment of birth – the arrival on the island is a rebirth which falls on the same date as Crusoe's actual birthday – functions solely in fixing the scale of the sequence by marking the first gradations, and the sequence is recorded by the notches on the tree trunk which mark off the time of experience.

7 From the destitute gaze to '*my* island', the genesis marks the stages of an appropriation. From an initial absolute poverty, Crusoe becomes a 'king in his kingdom', and he comes to speak of it as 'my estate'. His adventure is indeed a history of economic

development. The island represents the *natural place* of an economic autarchy. 'My kingdom, my island, where I had not allowed corn to grow beyond my need.' The island source reveals a sequence *and* a decorum. In this place of origins is discovered the 'middle station' which is praised by the father at the beginning of the book, and which governs the fluctuations of Providence. Crusoe has found what he was seeking – that equilibrium which restores man to himself – in that very place to which, he believed, Providence had sent him as a punishment; here again we come across the motif of the critique of all prejudices. Crusoe had chosen adventure in the face of decorum: adventure bestowed that very decorum; this might stand as a synopsis of the programme of economic conquest. We encounter a veritable obsession with decorum, as both a moral and an economic doctrine: 'Nature instructs us that it is futile to sow more than we eat.'

The circularity of this process – which keeps it from being more than the mere image of a genesis – is self-evident. Defoe guides Crusoe from his 'riches' – the ship and all that society thereby bestows on him – to his 'estate', which he has acquired by means of this legacy. This transition is a critique of the notion of a 'long series of miracles'. The obvious circularity of this exposition corresponds, as we shall see, to a certain thematic of time.

8 The motor of genesis is *work*. *Robinson Crusoe* is primarily a novel about work, the first of its kind. We witness the reinvention of all the elementary technical processes solely by means of one man's labour:

> So I went to work; and here I must needs observe, that as reason is the substance and original of the mathematicks, so by stating and squaring everything by reason, and by making the most rational judgement of things, every man may be in time master of every mechanick art. I had never handled a tool in my life, and yet in time, by labour, application, and contrivance, I found at last I wanted nothing but I could have made it, especially if I had had tools; however, I made abundance of things, even without tools, and some with no more tools than an adze and a

hatchet, which perhaps were never made that way before, and that with infinite labour.

I was then but a sorry worker; but soon after, time and necessity fashioned a perfect artisan, as they might have done, I believe, for any other . . .

As an example, here is the story of the 'invention' of the mill:

. . . but I was at a great loss about my tools; I had three large axes and abundance of hatchets (for we carried the hatchets for traffick with the Indians), but with much chopping and cutting knotty hard wood, they were all full of notches and dull, and tho' I had a grindstone, I could not turn it and grind my tools too; this cost me as much thought as a statesman would have bestowed upon a grand point of politicks, or a judge upon the life and death of a man. At length I contrived a wheel with a string, to turn it with my foot, that I might have both my hands at liberty. Note, I had never seen any such thing in England, or at least not to take notice how it was done, tho' since I have observed it is very common there: besides that, my grindstone was very large and heavy. This machine cost me a full weeks work to bring it to perfection.

The essentials of technology can thus be reproduced or replaced, a process which – as we have just seen – suggests a meditation on the rational origins of technology.

The narrative of these labours follows a long temporality in order to evoke most effectively the successive overcoming of difficulties. It is leisurely:

No man can judge what a rough task it was for my hands; but labour and patience brought me to the end of it as in so many other affairs; I have only mentioned this detail to show how so great a portion of my time was spent in accomplishing so little; that is to say, that task which can be nothing when you have the use of tools, becomes an enormous labour and demands a prodigious time to execute solely with the hands.

> This lack of implements, I say again, made all operations slow and laborious, but for this there was no remedy. Moreover, having divided up my time, I could not waste it entirely.

Crusoe can only replace the missing tools because he has all the time in the world. Time, long delay, is an equivalent of a long mediation by tools. This is why *Robinson Crusoe* is the novel of duration as well as the novel of work: the twenty years that Crusoe spends on his island, each laboriously unthreaded day after day, in an endlessly chronicled sequence which serves as a formal framework to the novel. The novel is less a reflection on industry than a slow evaluation of *effort*. As well as rationality, time elapsed is presented as the veritable source of technology.

It is also worth emphasising that the time of work obliterates thoughts of God.

> I begin to feel at ease: I set myself to work at my own preservation and subsistence, far from grieving upon my position as a judgement of heaven and thinking that the hand of God was heavy upon me. Such thoughts had become foreign to my mind.

9 In the last episode of the first section, the mutiny, Crusoe's basic attitude throughout his sojourn on the island appears clearly: cunning. He has become exceptionally skilful in the techniques of camouflage: the destitute gaze is afraid of being seen, and concealment becomes a major preoccupation. It is this successful dissimulation which lends a physical meaning to the decision 'not to reveal himself'. But there are many other reasons for the decision: for Crusoe it corresponds to the wish 'not to show himself as he is', as Crusoe, the man; which demonstrates that the problem initially posed and continuously developed is 'the escape from nature'. Crusoe teaches us that there is no state of nature; that the notion belongs with those other myths which have been successively denounced (providence, God, good and evil). There is only an economic development, the acquisition of a kingdom; otherwise, a radical absence of innocence and, in its place, fear and doubt.

A specific temporal organisation corresponds to this: when Crusoe escapes from the island, he discovers other goods, which have multiplied during his absence, derived from the capital he had left behind. He is now entitled to the large financial returns on a Brazilian plantation. For during the genesis, both natural and fictive, nothing has happened; the kingdom has been established, finally, independently of the 'original situation', as though there had been no origin. Those twenty years, the long sojourn on the island, were really no more than an illusion, just like the state of nature. The original island is completely reintegrated into the larger economic process: now it is called 'my new plantation'.

The elaboration of the theme into a complete story effectively divorces the theme from its purpose: the adventure on the island betrays the myth of the island of origins.

10 In confining the argument to *Robinson Crusoe*, it is not implied that this was a lucky accident. Defoe seems indeed to have concentrated on seeking out forms of expression which would bestow specific symbols on the world he knew. Another of his novels, though less renowned, offers an example of almost equal interest. In relation to eighteenth-century English mercantilism Moll Flanders, travelling from London to the American colonies, born in Newgate and familiar with high and low society, reveals as much as Robinson Crusoe: in her path social relations, class conflicts and the growth of capital appear in a cruder light. For this reason it has been called one of the earliest realist novels. Moll Flanders is also poor, economically destitute, though in a less romantic fashion – born in poverty, the daughter of a temporarily reprieved thief; and if her destiny appears instrumental by the mediations of providence, this is because it embodies an absolute authority of explanation or of accusation. A prostitute, a spouse, a pickpocket, a proprietor, always accompanied by continuously catalogued commodities (which have a value whatever their source), she is the eloquent, simple critic of love, commerce and marriage, those basic categories of the society which – by special privilege – she knows only from below. Social relations appear to her as things, because she deals with them directly, and not by intermediaries as others do.

Like Crusoe she *reveals*; but, like him, she escapes from the imaginary to become the site of the only reality.

July 1963

Chapter 22

Borges and the Fictive Narrative

Here something returns upon itself, something coils around itself, and yet does not enclose itself, but frees itself in its very coils. (Heidegger, *The Essence of Reasons*)

Borges is essentially preoccupied by problems of narrative: but he poses these problems idiosyncratically, fictively (one of his collections is entitled, significantly, *Fictions*). He offers a fictive theory of narrative, and thereby runs the risk of being taken too seriously, or taken too far.

The obsessional idea which shapes the book (*Fictions*) is that of necessity and duplication realised to the fullest in the Library (see the story 'The Library of Babel'); here each book is in its exact place as an element in a sequence. The book (the narrative, in fact) only exists in its recognisable form because it is implicitly related to the totality of all possible books. It exists, it has its allotted place in the universe of books, because it is an element in a totality. Around this theme Borges weaves all the paradoxes of the infinite. The book exists only by its possible multiplication: externally, in relation to other books, but also internally, as it is itself structured like a library. The substance of the book is its self-identity; but identity is only ever a limit-form of variation. One of the principles of the library, which lends it an almost Leibnizian character, is that no two books are identical. This may be transposed and used to define the book as a 'unity': there are not two identical books in the same book. Each book remains deeply different from itself because it implies an indefinite repertoire of 'bifurcations'. This subtle meditation on the 'same' and the 'other' is the object of the story about Pierre Ménard, who 'writes' two chapters of *Don Quixote*. 'The text of Cervantes and that of Ménard are verbally identical': but the analogy is purely formal; it contains a radical diversity. The stratagem of a new reading, of deliberate anachronism, which consists of reading, for example, the *Imitatio Christi* as though it were the work of Louis-Ferdinand Céline or James Joyce, is not just for the sake of the incidental surprises thus procured; it relates inevitably to a process of *writing*. The meaning of Ménard's apologue is now obvious: reading is in the end only a reflection of the wager of writing (and not vice versa); the hesitations of reading reproduce, perhaps by distortion, *the modifications inscribed in the narrative itself*. The book is always incomplete because it harbours the promise of an inexhaustible variety. 'No book is published without some discrepancy between each copy' (*The Lottery in Babylon*): the slightest material defect evokes the inevitable inadequacy of the narrative to itself; the narrative speaks to us only in so far as time permits itself to be determined by the operations of chance.

The narrative thus exists on the basis of its internal division, which makes it appear in itself as a dissymmetrical relation and as a term in such a relation. Every narrative, even in the moment of utterance, is the revelation of a self-contradictory *reprise*. The investigation of the work of Herbert Quain introduces us to that exemplary problem-novel *The God of the Labyrinth*:

> There is an incomprehensible assassination in the opening pages, a slow discussion in the middle, a solution at the end. Once the mystery has been solved there is a long retrospective paragraph which contains this sentence: 'All the world thought that the meeting between the two chessplayers was fortuitous'. This sentence implies that the solution is incorrect. The anxious reader looks back to the relevant chapters and discovers a different solution, the correct one. The reader of this unusual book is shrewder than the detective.

From a certain moment the narrative begins to turn inside out: any story worthy of the name contains, even if in a concealed form, this retrogression which opens up unsuspected avenues of interpretation. In this Borges belongs with Kafka, who makes the anxieties of interpretation the centre of his work.

The allegory of the labyrinth barely assists our understanding of this theory of narrative; too simple, yielding too readily to the perils of reverie. The labyrinth, rather than the enigma, the unfolding of the narrative, this is the inverted image which the story reflects from its end, in which is crystallised the idea of an inexhaustible division: the labyrinth of the narrative is traversed backwards, with a derisory exit in sight, an exit which leads to nothing, neither a centre nor a content, since one might just as well retreat as advance. The narrative derives its purpose from this dislocation which links it to its double – ever more ineluctable as we realise that it corresponds less with its initial conditions. On this theme, one might quote the detective story 'Death and the Compass', which might well have been written by Herbert Quain: the progress of Lonnrot, the detective, towards a solution announces a meta-problem; the solving of the mystery was in fact one of the terms of the mystery itself; to resolve the problem, to avoid the trap, would have been to have failed, etc. The narrative contains several versions of itself which are all so many predictable failures. Here is a certain affinity with the art of Poe: the narrative is inscribed on its reverse side, begun from the end, but this time in the form of a *radical* art; the story is begun at the end in such a way that we no longer know which is the end and which is the beginning, the story having wound around itself to produce the illusory coherence of an infinite perspective.

But Borges' writing has a value other than that of the riddle. If he seems to make the reader think (and the best specimen of this genre is the story 'The Circular Ruins', in which the man who dreams a man is himself dreamt), it is because he deprives the reader of anything to think about: hence his predilection for the paradoxes of illusion which do not strictly contain any ideas at all (the label on the bottle which shows a label on a bottle which shows . . .). Borges at his simplest, but probably the Borges who tricks us, makes great use of these dots. His best stories are not the ones that open out so easily, but those which are entirely sealed off.

'Readers will witness the execution and all the preliminaries of a crime, the intention of which is known to them, but which they will not understand, it seems to me, until the very last paragraph.' When Borges, in a prologue, thus summarises 'The Garden of Forking Paths' we are obliged to believe his promise. The story is shut in, encompassed, between the problem (no need to pose it) and the solution. And the last paragraph, truthfully announced in the prologue, does in fact give us the key to the mystery. But this is accomplished at the cost of a formidable confusion which is established retrospectively in all that precedes the conclusion. The solution seems just as derisory: only at the cost of a trick, apparently, can it carry the burden of a story. The author is cheating by making a mystery out of insignificance. But the solution is on display; it just runs along the edges of the story's meaning: it is a new fork which closes off the plot at the same moment as it gives notice of its inexhaustible content. A possible exit is blocked, and the narrative is concluded: but where are the other doors? Or is the ending defective? And the story escapes, flies out of the false window, in a vague interruption. The problem seems perfectly clear: either the story has a meaning and the false ending is therefore an allegory, or the story may not have a meaning and the false ending is then an allegory of absurdity. This is how Borges is usually interpreted: he is made to conclude by having attributed to him the appearances of an intelligent scepticism. It is not established that the scepticism is in fact intelligent, or that the deep meanings of his stories lie in their apparent subtlety.

Accordingly, the problem would seem to be wrongly stated. The story certainly has a meaning, but not the one that we think. The meaning does not follow from the possible choice between several interpretations. The meaning is not an interpretation; meaning is not to be sought in a reading, but in the writing: the footnotes, incessant and indiscreet, indicate the great difficulty that the story has in developing at all, as though it were initially arrested. Hence the relatively simple editorial technique of copious allusion. Rather than writing it, Borges *indicates* his story: not only the one that he could write, but those that others could have written. This can be seen in the analysis of *Bouvard et Pécuchet*, which is printed in the Borges special number of *L'Herne*, a fair specimen of the style of Ménard. Instead of tracing the line of the story he indicates its possibility, generally postponed or deferred. This is why his critical essays are fictional even when they are about actual works; and this is also why his stories are told largely for the sake of the explicit self-criticism which they embody. This is the culmination and the fulfilment of Valéry's hollow project: to watch what one does when one is writing or thinking. Borges has found the authentic method of achieving this. How to write the most simple story, when it implies an infinite possibility of variations, when its chosen form will always lack those other forms which might have clothed it? Borges' art is to answer this question with a story: by choosing from amongst these forms precisely that which best preserves the question, by its instability, its obvious artificiality and its contradictions. There is a great distance between these efficacious fictions and the complacently annotated delayings of the sinister academic poetician: the distance which separates the lips from the cup.

Before we return to the forking paths, we can take another example, more transparent (not that it is to be condemned for that, if in spite of appearances there really is something in what Borges has written), 'The Shape of the Sword'. Using a technique from the detective novel, as made famous by Agatha Christie in *The Murder of Roger Ackroyd*, the story is told in the third person by the protagonist (I tell that he; he tells that I: the 'I' is not the same; only the 'he' is the common term which makes the narrative possible.) A man tells the story of a betrayal but does not discover until the end that he is the betrayer. This revelation is effected by the deciphering of a sign; the narrator has a scar on his face, and when the same scar appears in the story the identity is revealed. All explanation is thus superfluous: the presence of this eloquent token (the story is its discourse) serves the purpose. But the token itself has to be used in a discourse, otherwise its significance would remain hidden. It is sufficient for the token to reappear at a privileged moment of the story in order to assume its full meaning. This is rather like Racine's *Phèdre*, when the queen announces at the opening of the play that she is going to die, that her robes are stifling her . . . and then actually dies at the end of Act 5. Nothing seems to have happened: fifteen hundred lines have been needed to charge this decisive gesture with its meaning, to give it its truth in language, its literary truth. Evidently the function of the discourse of the narrative is to deliver *the truth*. But this is done at the cost of a very long detour, a cost which must be met. The discourse shapes a truth only by bringing itself into question, only by adopting the appearance of pure artifice. It only progresses inevitably towards its end by elaborating its own futility (since everything was given in advance); its episodes are freely improvised only in order to deceive the reader (since everything will be given at the end). The discourse winds around its object, enveloping it, so as to combine two narratives in its single movement: a right side and a reverse side. The foreseen is unforeseen because the unforeseen is foreseen. This is the privileged point of view that Borges chooses: the one that precipitates the dissymmetry between a subject (the plot) and the writing which is our access to it. In so far as the story begins to make sense, the narrative diverges, calling attention to all the other possible ways of telling it as well as all the other meanings that it could have.

In fact the story of the *Garden*, which could have been part of a spy story, veers towards a controlled surprise. In the narrative something happens which the initial plot would have done without. The protagonist, a spy, has to solve a problem which is posed in a very confused way. He goes to the house of a certain Albert, and does what had to be done there; when he has done this we are told what it was, and the mystery is solved in the last paragraph, just as promised. The completed story conveys a certain fact, which is nevertheless not very interesting. In order to signal the bombardment of a town called Albert, the spy commits a crime against a man called Albert whose name he has found in a telephone directory. This resolves the mystery, but what of it? This insignificant meaning has migrated to produce another meaning, and even another story which in contrast is more important. In Albert's house, apart from the name of Albert, which will be used as a cipher, there is something else: the labyrinth itself. The spy, whose job is to hunt out other people's secrets, has gone inadvertently to the place of the secret: just when he was not looking for the secret but for the means of communicating one. Albert keeps in his house the most elaborate labyrinth that could be devised by a perversely subtle mind: a book. Not a book in which one is bewildered, but a book which is itself bewildered on every page, 'The Garden of the Forking Paths'. Albert has deciphered this fundamental secret: he has not found the translation (except for a linear translation, one which deciphers without decoding, refrains from interpretation: the motive of the secret is that it is the geometrical place of all interpretations); he has recognised it. He knows that the book is an ultimate labyrinth – to enter it is to be lost; he also knows that this labyrinth is a book in which anything can be read since this is the way it is written (or rather *is not written*, since, as we shall see, such a writing is impossible).

In fact, the labyrinthine novel of the scholarly Ts'ui Pen resolves all the problems of the narrative (though naturally it does so on condition of not existing: in a real narrative, one can only pose a few problems):

> In all fictions, whenever several solutions present themselves, men choose one and eliminate all the others; in the fiction of the almost inextricable Ts'ui Pen they are all chosen simultaneously. (J. L. Borges, *Labyrinths*, ed. Donald A. Yates, and J. E. Irby, Penguin Modern Classics, 1970)

The perfect book is the one which succeeds in eliminating all its doubles, all the simple pathways which pretend to cross it; or rather it has succeeded in absorbing them: for a given event all the interpretations coexist. Let a character knock on a door, and if the narrative is freely improvised we can expect anything and everything. The door may open or may not open, or any other solution (if there are any); the artifice of the labyrinth is founded on an axiom: these solutions form an enumerable whole, finite or infinite. A narrative will ordinarily privilege one of these solutions, which will then seem inevitable, or at least true: the narrative takes sides, moves in a determinate direction. The myth of the labyrinth corresponds to the idea of a completely objective narrative, one which takes all sides at once and develops them to their conclusions: but this ending is impossible, and the narrative only ever gives the *image* of a labyrinth, because, condemned to choose a definite term, it is compelled to conceal all the forkings, and to drown them in the line of a discourse. The labyrinth of the Garden is the analogue of the Library of Babel, but the real book has only the labyrinth of its own incompleteness in which to lose itself. Just as Borges had promised in the prologue, the last paragraph gives us the solution: it gives us, as it were, the key to the labyrinth, by pointing out that the only real traces of the labyrinth will be found in the form of the narrative, precarious and finite, but precisely achieved. Each story discloses the idea of the labyrinth, but it gives us the only *readable* reflection. Borges has been able to conclude his demonstration without falling into the expository gesture of the traditional mystery writers (given that a rhetoric of the mysterious had been elaborated in the eighteenth century): in a story concerned with Melmoth there is someone who tells us a story about Melmoth in which there is . . . and no story could ever finish because of this system of Chinese boxes. The real labyrinth is that there is no longer a labyrinth: to write is to lose the labyrinth.

The real narrative is then determined by the absence of all the other possible narratives from amongst which it could have been chosen: this absence hollows out the form of the book by putting it into endless conflict with itself. Then instead of the ultimately convivial allegory of the Library in which one can be lost, instead of the Garden big enough to wander in, we have now the critical allegory of the lost book which survives only in its traces and insufficiencies, the Encyclopaedia of Tlon:

> Let it suffice for me to recall that the apparent contradictions of the Eleventh Volume are the fundamental basis for the proof that the other volumes exist, so lucid and exact is the order observed in it. (Ibid.)

The incomplete or missing book is present in its fragments. It is not therefore absurd to imagine that, instead of a total book which would regroup all the combinations, it would be possible to write one of such insufficiency that the importance of what had been lost would shine forth from it:

> a vast polemic concerning the composition of a novel in the first person, whose narrator would omit or disfigure the facts and indulge in various contradictions which would permit a few readers – very few readers – to perceive an atrocious or banal reality. (Ibid.)

The stratagems of Borges all ultimately lead towards the possibility of such a narrative. The enterprise can be deemed both a success and a failure in so far as Borges manages to show us by means of the insufficiencies of a narrative that we have lost nothing.

December 1964

Chapter 23

Balzac's Les Paysans: *A Disparate Text*

> Large cities need playhouses, and corrupt peoples need novels. I have seen the manners of my time and I have published these letters. Would that I had lived in a century in which I could have thrown them in the fire. (Rousseau, *La Nouvelle Héloise*)

> 'If you stay here for a long time, you will learn many things from the book of nature, you who, they say, write for the newspapers.' (*Les Paysans*)

> the writer . . . who wanted to study the poverty question from the life. (Ibid.)

> It is not enough to observe and to paint, you must observe and paint to some end. (1835 Preface to *La Comédie humaine*)

The novelistic project as conceived by Balzac is not simple but divided, announced simultaneously along several divergent lines. Everything comes about as though Balzac, in making a book, had wanted to say several things at once: as we shall see, he effectively managed to *write* several, not necessarily those which he had intended. The important thing is to know how the work undergoes the test of this diversity: does the dislocation between the several different types of utterance succeed in unmaking the book? Is it not, on the contrary, *made* from their contrast?

We know from the 1842 preface to *La Comédie humaine* (The Human Comedy, uniform edition, trans. K. P. Wormeley, London, The Athenaeum Press, from which all Balzac quotations in this chapter are taken) that the book is supposed to conform to several different models. In a first gesture, the examples of Buffon's natural history and Walter Scott's historical novels are proposed together. The former gives the author his subject (the representation of the social species); the latter indicates the means of its realisation (the sequence of novels). Thus we have a form adapted to a content, and a theoretical juncture between literature (the novel) and reality (men as precisely differentiated by their mutual social relations). In fact, things do not work so simply, and this first opposition is false. Reality, modelled on the form of natural history as the author undertakes to represent it, is not an independent reality, but a reality already elaborated by means of an analogy which is formulated with very little regard for objectivity:

> There is but one animal. The creator works on a single model for every organised being. 'The Animal' is elementary and takes its external form, or, to be more accurate, the differences in its form, from the environment in which it is obliged to develop. Zoological species are the result of these differences . . .
>
> I, for my part, convinced of this scheme of nature long before the discussion to which it has given rise, perceived that in this respect society resembled nature. For does not society modify man, according to the conditions in which he lives and acts, into men as manifold as the species within zoology. (Preface to *La Comédie humaine*)

The transformist novel is not a scientific novel: the myth of science gives only an image of objective reality, and thus lends a form to the writer's general project. The symmetry proposed between science and the novel is obviously false: it serves to justify, by means of whatever theory, a pre-existing anthropological project ('I must paint man'); it does not establish an authentically new content, but provides the means of realising an already given subject – by analogy with the natural sciences to represent human variety. The choice of a scientific model does not introduce science into the novel by adapting objectivity and fiction. The choice merely proposes a novelistic *process* which is allied to what certain formalists have called 'characterisation', which will here be called the process of *differentiation*: to paint man the differences between the various 'species' must be represented; as we shall see, this image borrowed from natural history serves to overturn the traditional technique of the novel by suggesting the use of new techniques to the novelist. Science is not Balzac's path to new realities; rather, it supplies a style, in the most general sense of the word. But this new instrument implies that the novel has been penetrated by a *doctrine*, an unscientific doctrine which will eventually be inverted: the process of variation is used to portray a certain conception of *man*.

In the second instance, there is a new form of duality which is even more characteristic; Balzac claims to create a new genre, half-way between political ideology and literature. In innumerable texts he defines himself first as a political thinker and only afterwards as a novelist. Paraphrasing Rousseau, he writes in the dedication to *Les Paysans* (The Peasants) 'I study the movement of my epoch, *and* I publish this work'; the construction of the sentence reveals an effort to join together two different undertakings which were independent from the beginning. The scheme of the ethical novel is transposed into that of the novel of manners. The production of the literary work is subordinated to a 'study', which may use the novel in which to formulate its results, but goes largely beyond the novel in its scope. Balzac calls himself a historian of manners rather than a novelist: guided by a great historical thought, he only thought of giving this a literary form after the event: as we know, the actual order of events was a precise inversion of this account. If we are to credit the author's declared intentions, it seems to be the political content which is most important, which gives the work both unity and originality. To read correctly, according to these instructions, is to ascend from the provisional form to the basic content, to hear the lesson which is uttered on the edges of the story. For the writer can only be a novelist and a historian if he is also an ideologue: a master and a judge.

> The law of the writer, by virtue of which he is a writer, and which I do not hesitate to say makes him the equal, or perhaps the superior of the statesman, is his judgment, whatever it may be, on human affairs, and his absolute devotion to certain principles . . . 'A writer ought to have settled opinions on morals and politics; he should regard himself as a tutor of men; for men need no masters to teach them to doubt,' says Bonald. I took these noble words as my guide long ago; they are the written law of the monarchical writer just as much as that of the democratic writer. (Preface to *La Comédie humaine*)

After Buffon and Scott, Bonald determines the third model which will shape the work. It is not enough to have a knowledge of men, as the analogy with the natural sciences might have led one to believe; they have to be instructed, inculcated with the principles which are supposed to guide the work of the novelist. Engels, who knew Balzac's work well, was to say that the writer asks questions but does not answer them. According to Balzac, however, the writer must ask questions in order to be able to answer them. Perhaps, in fact, these two propositions are compatible: the one defines the novelistic *project*, while the other defines its real *product*; Balzac compels himself to 'give answers' though perhaps he does something entirely different. However, it is altogether remarkable to find announced in the preface to the *Comédie humaine* a *universal* law, one which applies not only to Balzac but to the monarchist writer as well as to the democratic writer. It is a matter of an objective necessity rather than a novel constraint: it is not a question of forcibly inserting ideology into literature, any more than was the case with science. All literary works are determined by their relation to an ideology. A good novelist without an ideology is inconceivable: the excellence of the novelist lies not in his ideology but in the fact that he confronts *an* ideological utterance with *a* fictional utterance. According to Balzac himself, then, it appears that ideology does not have a distinct independent form in relation to the work:

it realises a *literary* function at its own autonomous level; without ideology there could be no fictional lesson, and probably no novel either.

In relation to the novel, ideology does not play the same role as science: it does not offer the global image of a style which can be copied, but produces specific utterances which can be inserted into the tissue of the novel; meanwhile, in their different ways, both are internalised, taken up in the work of the writer, for which they are not distant models but immediate transformable material. The relation between the novel and ideology, no more than the relation between the novel and science, as it appears explicitly in Balzac's project, is not a real relation between independently existing terms: it is a matter of a double analogical implication which defines the very movement of the novelistic undertaking. Ideology is to be used (and thus modified), science is to be imitated; the novelist draws on them only to serve his own ends. We will not be asking, in an aside: Which science does Balzac borrow from? What is his ideology? Each time, in a different form, we are asking the same question: What kind of novel did he want to write? To put it simply, the study of Balzac's doctrine ought to contribute to a definition of the novelist rather than the propagandist. Balzac's 'thought' is of interest only as an element of literary production: caught up in a text whose importance is not to be measured by its ideological quality. We should forswear this negative and reductive reading which, claiming to eliminate an inessential and deceptive surface, goes directly to the depth of the work, doubly destroying it by decomposing it and extracting that which gives it value. If Balzac's 'thought' had a meaning in itself, the work would simply be a translation of the thought, simply a reading and a commentary on the thought, lacking any objective necessity. Indeed, any such thought runs the risk of a superficial originality: it is essentially borrowed, and, in so far as it has an independent existence, it does not define the enterprise of literary production. The understanding of the work does not involve unmaking it and studying separately the elements of which it is composed. At this point we meet with a formidable problem of method: these elements are not to be isolated, but neither must they be confused, otherwise the real complexity of the work is lost. In writing a novel, Balzac undertakes to say *two things at once* which cannot be taken for each other: on the one hand, he must tell the truth, he must know and he must display this knowledge; on the other hand, he must select and propagate a decorous fiction (*vérité de convenance*), that Monarchy and Catholicism alone can ensure the future of French society. These two intentions could be co-extensive: the statements of principle relying on the analysis of fact (objective description of a situation and a nature), the principles eliciting the meaning from the facts. In fact, there is nothing of the sort: there are two different movements which are opposed rather than complementary, mutually conflicting rather than converging. The author wants to *know* and to *judge*: in the work, two types of utterance correspond to these two projects, utterances dislocated in their relation because the one expresses the lucid and the other the confused. A knowledge of the Balzacian novel must begin from a grasp of the manner in which these two utterances are *fused* together. Balzac's work is the site of a contrast which is its defining principle; the text is not simple and unified, it is uneven, disparate.

If Balzac has indeed written two things at once, and if the novel is the product of this encounter, to read one of his novels is to read twice, to read two books which are neither separate nor mingled but united. The text offers not one but several meanings. This possibility of a double reading is most clearly announced in the dedication to *Les Paysans*:

> The object of this particular study – startling in its truth so long as society makes philanthropy a principle instead of regarding it as an accident – is to bring to sight the leading characters of a class too long unheeded by the pens of writers who seek novelty as their chief object. Perhaps this forgetfulness is only prudent in these days when the people are heirs of all the sycophants of royalty. We make criminals poetic, we commiserate with hanged men, we have all but deified the proletariat. Sects have arisen, and cry by every pen, 'Rise, working men!' just as formerly they cried, 'arise arise!' to the third estate. None of these

> Erostrates, however, have dared to face the country solitudes and study the unceasing conspiracy of those whom we term the weak against those others who fancy themselves strong, that of the peasant against the proprietor. It is necessary to enlighten not only the legislator of today but him of tomorrow. In the midst of the present democratic ferment into which so many of our writers blindly rush it becomes an urgent duty to exhibit the peasant who renders Law inapplicable, and who has made the ownership of land to be a thing that is, and that is not. You are now to behold that indefatigable mole, that rodent which undermines and disintegrates the soil, parcels it out and devours an acre into a hundred fragments – ever spurred on to his banquet by the lower middle classes who make him at once their auxiliary and their prey. This essentially unsocial element, created by the Revolution, will some day absorb the middle classes, just as the middle classes have destroyed the nobility. Lifted above the law by its own insignificance, this Robespierre with one head and twenty million arms is at work perpetually; crouching in country districts, entrenched in the municipal councils, under arms in the national guard in every canton in France, – one result of the year 1830, which failed to remember that Napoleon preferred the chances of defeat to the danger of arming the masses.

To the careful reader, this text offers precisely two meanings. There is a simple and unequivocal intention, and yet through its formulation it appears – though untainted with ambiguity – *other than it is*; rather than being uttered, it is displayed, indicated from a distance, and thus stripped of any immediate presence, given up to its *remoteness*. What is actually at issue here – the communication of an 'appalling truth'?: doubly appalling, first because it is unconscious and secret; second because, with regard to the political choice advertised here by Balzac, it announces the advent of a *danger*. Accordingly, a double rupture has to be brought about by the novel: at the level of knowledge, and at the level of judgment. In a single movement (but is it really one?) the author intends to inform and to disquiet. The ideological proposition is the most apparent; but it is easy to reveal by its side, as the condition of its realisation, the utterance of the fact which contests it. Balzac writes *against* the people: it is impossible to be unaware of this decision, to pay no attention to it by assimilating the author of *Les Paysans* to the 'democratic' writers, Victor Hugo and George Sand, precisely those with whom he does not want to be associated. This decision in principle, which in itself does not directly affect the writer's work (it is not enough to be against the people or with them in order to write) receives its real meaning when, to support his denunciation, it imposes the preliminary or the correlative of an analysis. If one is going to speak against the people, effectively, one must speak *of* the people: they must be seen, given form, *allowed to speak*. Like eulogy, condemnation is not in itself enough: the ideological claim inevitably requires a presentation and a disclosure; then the argumentation turns into style. In proportion to its double meaning, this text makes possible a double reading: the reductive reading attends only to the explicit; a different reading will try to extricate the conditions which make its utterance possible. Without separating the utterance from the project, without making them independent of each other, this reading will see them in their relative autonomy, which is also their contrast. In showing a workers' rising, or how it is prevented, though he does not summon them to rise, Balzac is nearer to Marx than was Victor Hugo for example: for does he not say, even if it is in the opposite direction and with different means, the *same thing*?

Thus it must not be thought that ideology, metamorphosed into art, becomes insignificant and effaces itself as ideology: no more than we can isolate doctrine and judge it for itself, aside, should we privilege the art of the writer, and invoke this art to veil that which gives it substance and meaning. Balzac's novels exist because they are rooted in this double project. We should not be trying to evade this duplicity, but to explain it.

In relation to *Les Paysans* we will ask ourselves the question: What is writing a novel? The first answer, given by Balzac himself, is that it is to solve the great question of the hour. 'But what will emerge from this ever more passionate debate, between the rich and the poor? This study is written solely to elucidate this terrible social question.'

Notice that two questions are being asked together, a question of fact and a question of power: the novel has to *show* the rich matched against the poor, and also to protect the rich from the poor, to ensure the junction of (natural) history and (political) ideology. In fact, in a paradox which is in some degree the source of the work, the motive of its writing, *the rich are weak: they need protection*. The question is accordingly an *enigma and a scandal*. Why are the rich so weak? This can be understood as a harmony of two notes. We observe the initial junction of the judgment of fact and the judgment of value: the novel undertakes an inspired ideological vindication, and also an exact knowledge; this initial paradox must be explained and subdued.

The scandal is affirmed, acknowledged from the beginning: thus it cannot establish a true progression. The novel moves forward by exploring the enigma: since the ideological purpose is already an answer, passing itself off as a question, the endeavour to know should resolve a real difficulty; this image of *resolution* affords the possibility of constructing the novel. The rich are weak: thus there is another rich class, hidden, stronger than the former. Thus the novel is elaborated in two periods: the first shows the confrontation of the rich and the poor in its most extreme (and scandalous) form: represented by the encounter between the cottage and the castle.

> Have you now taken in all the many details of this hovel, planted about five hundred feet away from the pretty gate of Les Aigues? Do you see it crouching there, like a beggar beside a palace? Well, its roof covered with velvet mosses, its clacking hens, its grunting pig, its straying heifer, all its rural graces have a horrible meaning. (*Les Paysans*, vol. I, ch. 3)

We are dealing with a special secret: the cottage ('this fatal cottage' built on the ruins of the castle) is a tavern, which is to say, by definition, an unsavoury place. It is foretold that behind the poetic pastoral façade there is a chance of finding something 'horrible' and unexpected. This insignificant secret is the allegory of the great secret which supplies the subject of the work.

Across the great gap which separates the two powers, their debate seems hollow, insoluble and artificial; and from this situation, which on its own terms seems to be a false situation, there gradually emerges a *boundless anxiety* which lends a secretly dramatic tone to the first chapters of the novel. By means of this contrast, the question is exhibited in all its acuteness. In the second period, much more extensively, we are progressively given the missing link, which explains everything: the bourgeois community, the 'mediocracy', presented in its fissured complexity: eager for the same prize, they are temporary allies but they are not united. Then the tone changes, and throughout the description of the mediocrity of this intermediate world (which is not the *demi-monde*) Balzac recovers a certain victorious gaiety. The infinite untenable gap which separates the extremes of the cottage and the castle, the poor and the rich, is now *filled*: here is to be played out the decisive event, of which the episodes of the plot are merely an *effect*.

> From the peasant sphere this drama will now raise itself to the high region of the middle classes of Soulanges and of La-Ville-aux-Fayes, curious figures whose appearance in the narrative, far from arresting its development, will accelerate it, like the villages engulfed in an avalanche which make its passage the more swift. (Ibid., vol. I, ch. 13)

This progression is gratifying, in so far as it satisfies a curiosity, but it is also disquieting, it justifies a galloping indignation: the narrative, as expected, moves in two opposite directions.

This first, very rudimentary analysis shows that, like so many other novels by Balzac, *Les Paysans* is a prophetic meditation on the events of 1830 (the action is set in 1823): it deals with the period in which the bourgeoisie appears on the surface of history to take charge in its own name, to take history as its private property. This accession, this arousal, has to be not only evoked but *reproduced* by the whole of the novel, furnishing an equivalent rather than an image. At this point the historical purpose is accompanied by a properly novelistic exigency: to display the *thing* as it is (the triumph of the bourgeoisie) it is not enough to show it, since, precisely, it is not there (on the one hand it is hidden; and on the other hand, in the presence of reality itself, the novel would lose its *raison d'être*): by appropriate means a substitute must be supplied. Accordingly, behind the historical project and the ideological project, or rather in between them, assuring their connection and their separation, there emerges, in its specificity, a literary project which no longer consists in knowing or judging. It is a matter of *writing a book which shall be like a world*. This new problem – it is a problem, since the means of realising this intention must be found – is the real origin of the novel.

Two complementary solutions are adopted together: the one is external to this particular novel, the other organises it internally. The novel is initially situated in a network of books which replaces the complexity of real relations by which a world is effectively constituted. Located within the totality of a corpus, within a complex system of relationships, the novel is, in its very letter, allusion, repetition and resumption of an object which now begins to resemble an inexhaustible world. Conceived according to this principle, the work is a combination of elements which together have a substance and a complexity analogous to that of reality. The imaginary universe is not a reflection of the real universe: it constitutes a system of reality; whence we realise how inevitably remote is the project of writing a novel from that of telling the truth: it is not enough 'to study poverty from the life', it must still be communicated by the elaboration of an imaginary object. The technique of 'reappearances', of the recurring character, corresponds to this wish to *situate* the novel in relation to the external. But we must not narrow our definition of this technique to the mere fact that the same characters pass through different plots; it is important that these characters (as well as places and situations) are also playing an *analogical* role, that they are always, explicitly or implicitly, one term in a comparison. Because they are defined by their relations to one another, they manifest their unity within a unique world whose existence they accordingly assure: 'This miller, a Sarcus-Taupin, was the Nucingen of the valley.' Thus the totality of the work is like a vast ground upon which each individual element appears. This is why, to read a Balzac novel adequately, you must read two at once – any two if necessary. In this way one discovers the necessary redoubling of meaning which takes the place of an absent reality. The work itself is vast enough for each of its moments to suggest a multiplicity of possible relations and itineraries. The order of the work tends to produce this illusion of diversity: these dimensions have to be such that no memory can grasp the work in its entirety. This is why Balzac worked so much, at such speed. Michel Butor has demonstrated in *Répertoire I* that an essential component of the *Comédie humaine* is this possibility which it offers of being read in more than one direction, of being conscientiously and thoroughly explored or rearranged in a different sequence on each occasion. It thus has a bulk which is more than the mere sum of its parts. For a knowledge of Balzac the writer, all beginnings are valid, in the knowledge that they are only ever one beginning among others.

However, this first definition of the novel is not in itself enough: the relation to the whole work, which displaces the individual novel and endows it with a movement analogous to that of reality, must have an equivalent in the novel's relation to itself, in its internal organisation. To the principle of *combination*, which makes the novel one novel among others, there corresponds a principle of *distinction* which effects a separation and a reunification of the novelistic elements in a way that replaces the world of history. The content of a novel is thus inevitably determined: to show an object, any object, is to present it in its difference, in its specificity, to forestall any confusion with other objects even if they are spoken at the same time. The novel advances by the internal production of an allegorical *diversity*.

To construct a novel is to produce a certain number of discrete elements in confrontation. This is why, in its internal organisation, the book is, as it were, quartered (*écartelé*): because it produces this encounter of opposed terms it is inevitably unbalanced, it has a number of fulcrums. In this respect *Un Début dans la vie* (A Start in Life) offers an especially significant example: in a single place (triply individualised: it is enclosed; it is typical of the 'social material of an era'; finally, it is only appropriate to certain of its occupants: the others, according to a process which we will often encounter, are displaced), a public carriage, for the duration of the journey, a variety of representative characters are united (they are doubly individualised: by the conflicts and multiple alliances which 'unite' them; by their likeness to or their difference from those of the same type, or a different type, depicted in the other novels). Sitting side by side we have the following: a rich farmer (old Leger); an adolescent from the *petite bourgeoisie* (Oscar Husson); two artists (G. Bridau and Mistigris); a notary's clerk (G. Marest); a senior state official (Count Sérizy).

From the space of the social the novel borrows elements from different regions, and constitutes a new space in which these elements meet. These are the differences and the contrasts between all its elements (places and people) which form the subject of the novel: but it must not be forgotten that this differentiation is only possible because all these elements belong to the same world, the world of the *Comédie humaine*, whic hencloses them and gives them their meaning. Thus, in *Honorine*, when the consul of Genoa mentions a certain Count Octave, he specifies: 'He led a life rather like that of the Count Sérizy, who I think you all know; but less well-known because he lived in the Marais, rue Payenne, and never received guests'.

Based on this system of differences, the novel will inevitably have several centres of interest, and will require a multiple attention. *Un Début dans la vie* seems, in fact, to be made from two novels placed end to end: one deals with Count Sérizy and his relations with his bailiff Moreau (he will function as the point of reference in *Les Paysans*, which elucidates the relations between General Montcornet and his bailiffs: analogous, and yet distinct, since the action is now set in the country and not in Paris where conditions are essentially different); the other story, barely hinted at in the beginning, a novel of education, tells of Oscar Husson, who finally has only a very remote connection with what has been previously narrated. A 'purposeful' conclusion, which brings back the same characters, now altered, emphasises the *contrived incoherence* of the narrative: the necessity which shapes the novel compounds it of gathered fragments. To realise his settled project, Balzac cannot content himself with *writing well*, building his novel harmoniously around a central theme: the *delineation* of the project requires that there should not be a foreground which establishes a perspective on successive backgrounds, but that there should be several abruptly discontinuous foregrounds. It has hardly been noticed that Balzac's compositional principles are those adopted in another domain by Brecht. Balzac puts the world into his work as Brecht puts the dialectic on the stage: both culminate in a *broken plot*.

These same principles are at work, though on a vaster scale, in *Les Paysans*. Its population is recruited from all parts of society, and there are more than two foregrounds. We find: Montcornet, a general and imperial count, a great land-owner from among the artisans of Paris; Mme de Montcornet, née Troisville, a woman of the world, a Parisian, born of a legitimist family, more or less ruined; Blondet, a Parisian journalist; abbé Brossette, a legitimist priest; the provincial bourgeoisie, gathered in the departmental capital around Gaubertin; the *petite bourgeoisie* of the sub-prefecture (divided into the upper world of Soulanges, gathered around Mme Soudry, and the lower gathered around Mme Plissoud); Rigou, the village bourgeois; and the whole hierarchy of the peasantry.

This lists only the main characters who occasionally hold the stage. But there are also: the provincial administration (the bishop, the prefect, the attorney-general: Bourlac . . .); the legitimist land-owners (Soulanges . . .); the opera singer, mistress of the farmer-general, former landowner of Les Aigues (Mlle Laguerre); the demobilised soldiers now turned foresters.

Some of these categories, in particular the peasantry, should certainly be broken down into further elements. Naturally each individual is represented in relation to the appropriate place (e.g. Rigou to Blangy) or the inappropriate (Montcornet to Les Aigues). Contrary to the accepted idea, Balzac does not always depict the accord, the osmosis between a place and a character. Their dissonance is often even more significant: 'The objects around us do not always harmonise with our souls.'

According to a familiar principle, a geographical division corresponds to defined social types: thus the countryside where the story takes place is not a simple independent place but a complex and divided reality; the chateau, the village and the sub-prefecture are quite distinct.

This multiplicity of constitutive elements poses a peculiarly complex problem of composition: the narrative will also be inevitably divided between several divergent centres of interest which are constantly proliferating. A novelistic diversity corresponds to the plurality of places, situations and interests:

> After that remark some persons will expect to see the flashing of the cuirasse of the former colonel of the Imperial Guard, and the raging of his anger as it falls like a waterspout on his little wife; so that the end of this present history may be like the end of all modern dramas – a tragedy of the bedchamber. Perhaps the fatal scene will take place in that charming room with the blue monochrome where beautiful ideal birds are painted on the ceiling and the shutters, where Chinese monsters laugh with open jaws on the mantle-shelf, and dragons, green and gold, twist their tales in curious convolutions around rich vases, and Japanese fantasy embroiders its designs of many colours; where sofas and reclining chairs and consoles and what-nots invite to that contemplative idleness which forbids all action. No; the drama here to be developed is not one of private life; it concerns things higher or lower. Expect no scenes of passion; the truth of this history is only too dramatic. And remember, the historian should never forget that his mission is to do justice to all; the poor and the prosperous are equals before his pen; to him the peasant appears in the grandeur of his misery and the rich in the pettiness of his folly. Moreover, the rich man has passions, the peasant only wants. The peasant is therefore doubly poor; and if, politically, his aggressions must be pitilessly repressed, to the eyes of humanity and religion he is sacred. (*Les Paysans*, vol. I, ch. 1)

The narrative will be composed of several 'rays of light': in other words it will admit of several kinds of illumination. It will not be a novel of private life, nor a novel of the outdoors, but, simultaneously, the story of a discrete passion and a monumental conspiracy, a story of the rich and the poor, and of *that which separates them*. The novelist, because he is also a historian, must 'give everyone a go', one by one; thus the only form of equality that Balzac can acknowledge is made manifest, equality in contrast, secured by fictional means, which allows the protagonists to meet on the stage as though in a world. *Les Paysans*, in contrast with, for example, *Le Médecin de campagne* (The Country Doctor), is a complete novel in which a diverse world is diversely presented.

> The peasants who, in this drama, are supernumeraries so essential to its action that it may be doubted whether they are not in fact its leading actors. (*Les Paysans*, vol. I, ch. 2)

There is only a single stage for two, indeed several actions: the illusion of a real world is created from the encounter of several worlds, or spheres, which are closed and independent. The problem of composition comes down finally to a problem of casting (since we are dealing with a play or a stage). The problem can be formulated most simply: Who plays the leading part? The reply to this question is not, however, simple.

Let us look more closely at the solution offered in the first chapters of the novel. The movement from one sphere to another is effected by means of an internal imbalance appropriate to the presentation of each sphere. The narrative begins by reproducing a letter from Blondet to Nathan describing life in the country. The narrator comments on this quotation by emphasising its extreme importance:

> If this letter, dashed off by the idlest pen of the century, had not by some lucky chance been preserved, it would have been almost impossible to describe Les Aigues; and without this description the history of the horrible events that occurred there would certainly have been less interesting. (Ibid., vol. I, ch. 1)

What is there in this letter that makes it more than just a way to begin? It shows the scene of the action, the countryside, not from the perspective of a rightful inhabitant (which Montcornet is not anyway) but from outside, in a way that is even more revealing than distorting: Blondet does not see nature as it is (and how should that be?) but as a stage setting, as the scenery for an opera.

> At last I have seen a landscape in which art is blended with nature in such a way that neither of them spoils the other; the art is natural, and the nature artistic. I have found the oasis that you and I have dreamed of when reading novels. (Ibid.)

> . . . an opera setting . . . (Ibid.)

> The village has a primitive air; it is rustic, and has that decorative simplicity which we artists are forever seeking. (Ibid.)

> 'Almost as charming as at the opera,' thought Blondet, making his way along the banks of the Avonne. (Ibid., vol. I, ch. 2)

Blondet does not see the site of peasant life (which, as we shall see, is not nature in its original condition), but a nature which is ordered and embellished. In this he is blinded by the habit of only seeing that which his education has accustomed him to see: the reflection of a painting, a novel or a play. However, at the same time, he is alive to a real component of the landscape; this landscape which has for so long been the setting for the evolution of an actual opera singer, Mlle Laguerre, the former owner of the chateau, who has helped to inscribe there the memory of Piccini. This nature which the opening of the story depicts is emphatically *contrived*: a quality achieved by the use of the point of view of the journalist who sees it as an alien 'sphere'. Yet it is not a question of subjectivity but of objectivity: the countryside is not actually nature in its simple virgin state, first because it is furrowed by a 'horrible secret', and also because it is the site of social relationships (the countryside is above all the place of Property: the capital letter is Balzac's own). Nature as a setting: this is not the product of a direct vision of reality (which would be a pure reflection), but neither is it an illusion; the distortion implied by

Blondet's specific point of view is, after several detours, doubly revealing. We are taught to recognise the 'sphere' of the journalist, and also the sphere which will remain definitively closed to him (in front of the Peasant he will say only 'O Rus!'): in both cases the revelation occurs without the knowledge of the subject of this vision.

The first chapter, accordingly, gives the narrative a true point of departure (and not simply a beginning): it establishes a novelistic perspective, both particular and complex. Far from being limited and static, this perspective is the origin of a movement because of the internal imbalance which moves it; it implies the transition to a new perspective. Thus the character of Blondet (and he plays a relatively secondary role in the plot), determines the construction of the narrative: here the novelistic element precedes and defines the reality of which it has to produce the illusion. Significantly, this same Blondet has the task of bringing the novel to its conclusion.

The novelistic system attains an effect of reality, not by means of descriptions (that is to say, direct imitations of reality, pure visions), but by means of contrasts and discords. The function of Balzac's descriptions, one which has hardly been grasped, is always to *produce a difference*. But to recognise this it is obviously not enough to duplicate these descriptions, making them the *object* of a description, projecting on to them what one imagines is there. Literary analysis is commonly stuck in an *ideology of description*, finding everywhere texts that describe or texts to be described.

We can now understand how it will be possible to pass from the point of view of Blondet to that of Fourchon, the initiator of the peasant world, and then, by a *swerve*, from the chateau to the cottage. This new point of view will obviously be communicated in a different way: one cannot produce a letter from Fourchon. (Not that he is unable to write, since he has been a schoolmaster, but to whom could he write? In the system Fourchon's special place is marked by the fact that he has no answering Nathan.) But note that Fourchon, in relation to the rural world, is in a situation analogous to that of Blondet in relation to the world of property: he is not entirely at home (a failed farmer, fallen from his class, he is a close companion of the peasants but he remains at the edges of their universe); thus another sliding will be possible, moving the story to another level. Just as Blondet is not altogether an owner, because he has nothing, but above all because he writes, so Fourchon is not altogether a peasant, because he is a spokesman. But also, just as the works of the journalist or the writer do not belong entirely to him – this theme is generally developed in *Les Illusions perdues* (Lost Illusions) – so Fourchon's words *escape* from their owner, and finish by representing something entirely different from the social realm to which he directly belongs.

> Let it be the law of public necessity or the tyranny of the old lords, it is all the same; we are condemned to dig the soil for ever. There, where we are born, there we dig it, that earth! and spade it, and manure it, and delve in it, for you who are born rich just as we are born poor. The masses will always be what they are, and stay what they are. The number of us who manage to rise is nothing like the number of you who topple down! We know that well enough though we have no education! We let you alone, and you must let us alone. If not, and things get worse, you will have to feed us in your prisons, where we'd be much better off than in our homes. You want to remain our masters, and we shall always be enemies, as much as we were thirty years ago. You have everything, we have nothing; you can't expect we should ever be friends.
> (*Les Paysans*, vol. I, ch. 5)

Listening to this astonishing speech one may well ask why Balzac has been taken for a realistic writer in the narrow sense. In fact, all the possible improbabilities seem to be gathered on this page. Improbability of situation: although this theme is mentioned in the title of the chapter ('The Enemies Face Each Other') it is rather unlikely that such a direct confrontation should bring together the heroes of the contradiction, the rich and the poor; this encounter is essentially unreal, largely symbolic. Improbability of tone: in spite of the rags of peasant idiom in which the speech is clothed, a sort of emphasis raises it and carries it beyond its immediately representative character; by a formal augmentation, the expression is adapted to an unusual situation. Improbability of content: 'Nailed by the law of necessity' – to depict the limits of his condition, this untypical peasant has access to a borrowed knowledge; it remains to be seen whether these limits are real limits or the limits of a form of knowledge (particular or general). In short, the clarity and extremity with which the conflict is presented reveals a transposition which belongs to the novelistic rather than the real.

We are even more surprised to hear this speech when we remember that we have already heard it in analogous (at least convergent) form from the abbé Brossette, a character from an entirely different realm. It is important to note, in passing, that this same Brossette will appear, transformed, in another sphere: he will be the wordly confessor of Beatrix.

> And thus it was that the abbé Brossette, after studying the morals of his parishioners, made this pregnant remark to his bishop: 'Monseigneur, when I observe the stress that the peasantry lay on their poverty, I know how they fear to lose that excuse for their immorality.' (Ibid., vol. I, ch. 2)

> 'Madame la Comtesse,' said the abbé, 'in this district we have none but voluntary paupers. Monsieur le comte does all he can; but we have to do with a class of persons who are without religion and who have but one idea, that of living at your expense.' (Ibid., vol. I, ch. 5)

Formulated differently, taken in an opposite sense, the same idea appears: for Brossette as for Fourchon, the peasant is marked by his condition to the point of being imprisoned in it. And thus his struggle against the rich is not spontaneous, episodic and individual, but is inevitably determined by a class conflict. This idea essential to the development of the novel (it supplies its title) is presented at least *twice*: it derives its meaning from the difference which the duplication establishes. What appears to Fourchon as a law is for the priest the fact of deliberate sinfulness, a subjective system of theft and debauchery. Whether fatality or perversity, the situation is thus presented, partially in the discourse of the two privileged observers, as a form of knowledge. This is not an expression of the author's beliefs. In opposition to Brossette, Balzac thinks that the system of poverty is objective and does not depend on the individual will (which is why charity to individuals is denounced in this novel as futile); but in opposition to Fourchon, Balzac does not believe that it is a destiny. The world of the poor is not eternally fixed; on the contrary, it *evolves* historically (this gives weight to the threat against the bourgeoisie; soon the poor will lay the blame directly on you), and it can be *modified* (this is the meaning of the great social novels: *Le Médecin de campagne*, and *Le Curé de village* (The Village Priest)).

We have seen that the novel is not mechanically constructed as a simple reflection or description of reality. Before describing, we must show, explain, establish: a new and significant world is revealed by a system of tilted mirrors which produce broken, deformed, fragmented images. Blondet, Fourchon, Brossette – these *observers*, slightly out of alignment in relation to the centre where others are enacting the drama, are neither full characters nor authorial spokesmen; but the novel is shaped by being projected on to the triangle of their discourse.

It is not by their positive individuality, but by the displacement which separates them from themselves, from their situation and from others, that the characters of the novel make possible the advent of a reality, of an equivalent for reality. One could obviously perform the same analysis for the places, and the situations, for all the fictional elements. The basic problem of novelistic writing is encountered in an identical form at all levels; it is a question of *producing a difference*. It is by the variation which displaces them, both within and without, that things and beings ultimately become demonstrative. Balzac's enterprise could be defined by this obsession with discriminations which shapes all his choices.

> Guided by the genius of observation, he visited the lowlands and the social heights, like Lavater, he studies the stigmata which the passions or the vices imprint on every face. He collected his types in the great human bazaar like an antiquary choosing his treasures, he evoked these types

> when they came in useful, placed them in the foreground or the background, according to their value, placing them in light or shade with the magic of the great artist who knows the value of contrasts, finally endowing each of these creations with names, features, ideas, a language and an appropriate character which gave them such individuality that, in this enormous crowd, no one could be mistaken for any other.

In her biographical sketch of 1858, Laure de Surville went straight to the main point, with this important exception: she ascribed to a 'genius for observation' what is in fact the *product* of the work of the *writer*; she reduced what was actually an innovation to mere accuracy. Had Balzac been content to observe a given reality accurately, very probably he would not have written: in the works there is nothing given; and, with regard to the enterprise of writing, reality is only *initial* in so far as it is necessary to move away from it and to substitute something else for it, which, having chosen the project of conformity, remains to be done.

It also seems that the novelist's most useful tool is that which allows him to imitate real distinctions by producing equivalent distinctions (we will deal with this point at greater length at a later stage). However, it is worth making two immediate remarks about this operation: it is not employed in isolation, but with others which have just been mentioned; it does not duplicate term for term a pre-existing natural reality which it would have merely to reproduce, to repeat, in furnishing an image which is at once general and concrete. The type obviously implies a resemblance.

> If the portraits of Tonsard, his inn, and his father-in-law, take a prominent place in this history, it is because that place belongs to him and to the inn and to the family. In the first place, their existence, so minutely described, is the type of a hundred other households in the valley of Les Aigues. (*Les Paysans*, vol. I, ch. 3)

But this resemblance is only significant against the background of a difference: if Tonsard is the same as a certain number of people, this is because, in alliance with them, he is opposed to other groups.

The homology between the universe of history and the universe of the novel is not realised at the level of specific *elements* but at the level of *systems: it is the novelistic system as a whole which produces a reality effect.* The social type, in becoming a character in a novel, if he is broadly representative, does not, however, fill the role of a generality: he is not individualised merely by a name or by the detail of the plot, but by the relations into which he enters with other typical characters, equally representative and yet distinct, characters who define his function. For the sake of simplification, let us say that there is never one single type and one single character for a given generality, but several which exist only through their differences. Thus the figure of the steward passes through a certain number of novels and is thereby diversified:

> Hence the social nomenclature and natural history of land-stewards as defined by a great Polish noble.
>
> 'There are,' he said, 'two kinds of steward, he that thinks only of himself, and he that thinks of himself and of us; happy the land owner who lays his hands on the latter! As for the steward who thinks only of us, he is not to be met with.'
>
> Elsewhere can be found a steward who thought only of his master's interests as well as of his own [See *Un Début dans la vie; Scènes de la vie privée* (Scenes of Private Life)]. Gaubertin is the steward who thinks of himself only. To represent the third figure of the problem would be to hold up to public admiration a very unlikely personage yet one that was not unknown to the old nobility, though it has, alas! disappeared with them [see *Le Cabinet des antiques*; *Scènes de la vie de province* (Scenes of Provincial Life)].
>
> Through the endless subdivision of fortunes, aristocratic habits and customs are inevitably changed. If there be not now in France twenty great fortunes managed by intendants, in fifty years from now there will not be a hundred estates in the hands of stewards, unless a great

> change is made in the law. Every land owner will be brought in time to look after his own interests. (*Les Paysans*, vol. I, ch. 7)

Here we encounter once again the comparison with natural history, a comparison now being put to work. It serves to establish that fictional multiplicity which has a double value since, in a synchronic sense, it distributes and balances the elements of the work, whilst in a diachronic sense it alludes to a historical evolution. In the same way, though this new example is even more significant, there is not a general type of the Miser, but a differentiated universe of avarice:

> Perhaps you will remember certain masters of avarice pictured in former scenes of this comedy of human life: in the first place the provincial miser, old Grandet of Saumur, miserly as a tiger is cruel; next, Gobsek the usurer, that Jesuit of gold, delighting only in its power, and relishing the tears of the unfortunate because gold produced them; then Baron Nucingen, lifting base and fraudulent money transactions to the level of state policy. Then, too, you may remember that portrait of domestic parsimony, old Hochon of Issoudun, and that other miser in behalf of family interests, little La Baudraye of Sancerre. Well, human emotions – above all, those of avarice – take on so many diverse shapes in the diverse centres of social existence that there still remains upon the stage of our comedy another miser to be studied: namely, Rigou, – Rigou, the miser-egoist; full of tenderness for his own gratifications, cold and hard to others; the ecclesiastical miser; the monk still a monk so far as he could squeeze the juice of the fruit called good living, and become a secular only to put a paw upon the public money. (Ibid., vol. I, ch. 13)

The miser of Blangy takes shape only against the background that Sancerre, Issoudun, Saumur and Paris compose for him. It is this dissection of temperaments, separating and opposing them, which makes the work: but this division is not the product of a finesse of psychological observation, no more than the basic means for the elaboration of the work is a simple mechanical fidelity to the real, a fidelity which would suggest passive reception rather than the enterprise of production. And this psychology only has meaning in the texture of the novel, or rather, as establishing the textures of a novel: its true function is indeed to realise this coherence.

The novel now appears in its true pedagogic function: it is not the product of a lesson, a content to which it would merely give form, but the very condition for this lesson; but now it is no longer the same thing. The novel, rather than being founded on an empirical generalisation, of which it would be the particular expression, makes possible a didactic generalisation, on the basis of its specific constitution (a few elements of which have just been pointed out):

> Some minds, eager after mere amusement, will complain that these various explanations are far too long; but we once more call attention to the fact that the historian of manners, customs, and morals of his time, must obey a law far more stringent than that imposed upon the historian of mere facts. He must show the probability of everything, even the truth; whereas, in the domain of history, properly so called, the impossible must be accepted for the sole reason that it did happen. The vicissitudes of a social or private life are brought about by a crowd of little causes derived from a thousand conditions. The man of science is forced to clear away the avalanche under which whole villages lie buried, to show you the pebbles brought down from the summit which alone can tell you the formation of the mountain. If the historian of human life were simply telling you of a suicide, five hundred of which occur yearly in Paris, the melodrama is so commonplace that brief reasons and explanations are all that need be given; but how shall he make you see that the self-destruction of an estate could happen in these days when property is reckoned of more value than life? *De re vestra agitur*, said a maker of fables; this tale concerns the affairs and interests of all those, no matter who they be, who possess anything.

> Remember that this coalition of a whole canton and of a little town against a general who, in spite of his rash courage, had escaped the dangers of actual war, is going on in our districts against other men who seek only to do what is right by those districts. It is a coalition which today threatens every man, the man of genius, the statesman, the modern agriculturalist, – in short, all innovators.
>
> This last explanation not only gives a true presentation of the personnages of this drama, and a serious meaning even to its petty details, but it also throws a vivid light on the scene where so many social interests are now marshalling. (Ibid., vol. I, ch. 9)

Thus the wish to diversify the novel as much as possible does not trap it in an absolute particularity: on the contrary, all the singular figures finally converge in the expression of a general theme, the 'Suicide of Property'. Thus this novelistic diversity makes itself felt, a diversity which 'gives weight to the smallest detail'. 'Here it is a question of': by means of a kind of internal multiplication, the narrative achieves, within its exact internal limits, a new breadth: by a collusion between the most circumstantial and the most significant, demonstrating that each element belongs to a system, the novel *instigates* a political lesson. *De re vestra agitur*: the novel is also a petition, which, as it is constructing a world, says: This world is not any world, it is *your* world.

But note that this generalisation does not imply confusion: it intervenes only after the event; the novel produces a politics, but is not itself the product of politics. How could politics become directly fictional? The generality is evoked from the diversity, not as a reduction, but as an explanation: it is not a substitute, but it does endow it with its significance. The fact that '*all* social interests' are in play does not imply a confusion, but precisely the opposite – a very exact identification. The novel has not been diverted: its movement has simply been accentuated, emphasised and simplified.

To summarise: the institution of a fictional reality is accomplished by the complex arrangement of differential elements. The wish to know the social world and to present a substitute for it is realised in the production of a diversity.

'Reread this kaleidoscopic work, here you will find that no two garments, no two heads are the same' – thus the 1835 preface (signed Félix Darvin).

It might be thought that this is merely a question of a trick (*procédé*); of a neutral technique, serving only to realise, to translate an intention already worked out. As we shall see, this is not so. The process constitutes the intention itself; it is, in fact, open to so many variations that it seems impossible to conceive of it as a purely material instrument. Whether it is the instrument of two very different intentions, or whether it can only be used in the vicinity of many different intentions, or whether it can only be used in the vicinity of a different opposing intention, it appears to be caught up in the movement of the novel as one of its constitutive elements, perhaps even as its real subject.

Indeed, the work thus constituted in its systematic unity seems to be coherent and full, finished. To such an extent that one might ask: Why this unity rather than another? For the work to have consistency, it is not enough for it to be a system: the system itself must be determined, must not be simply any system. This is why it is not enough to analyse the mechanism of the novel in order to understand, or rather, to explore it: we must see how this mechanism actually functions, whether it is utilised directly, naturally, or whether it does not undergo a characteristic modification whereby it becomes the *object of the novel*.

Once in operation, the system has a life of its own, and produces an unexpected effect. The instrument which, in theory, enables us to make distinctions (to know and to display reality) will in fact serve to confuse (to judge). This is because one means can be adapted to several different incompatible uses: as though it possessed a power of its own, a power to produce a meaning or meanings, that multiplicity of meanings which constitutes it.

We must now return to the ideological project, temporarily forgotten. The narrative as conceived by Balzac must, we remember, realise two requirements at once. It must take the place of two narratives at once. By means of the narrative we can see and we can judge: each of these attitudes implies a different partition of reality. The problem faced by the writer is thus how to reconcile, how to connect and adapt these two shapes? Balzac's solution is disconcertingly simple: it is enough to superimpose them, to compel one means to serve the production of its opposing meaning, reconciling confusion and clarity in the coincidence of meanings.

Thus, to take an immediate and elementary example, if there is a description it must, in principle and from the first, be distinct; but it must also corroborate an accusation. Thus the man of the people, not as a general idea but as a real plea in the novel, is, as already announced in the preface to *Les Paysans*, the *savage*. This metaphor obviously implies the idea of distance; the peasant is not a man like any other.

> 'What can be the ideas, the morals, the habits of such a being? What is he thinking of?' thought Blondet, seized with curiosity. 'Is he my fellow-creature? We have nothing in common but shape, and even that!' (*Les Paysans*, vol. I, ch. 2)

The image will recur endlessly. It is introduced by Blondet:

> 'Here's one of Cooper's redskins,' thought Blondet; 'one needn't go to America to study savages.' (Ibid.)

> 'Well, well!' cried Blondet, laughing, 'so here we are, like Cooper's heroes in the forests of America, in the midst of traps and savages.' (Ibid., vol. I, ch. 5)

and it is taken up again by the abbé Brossette (whose place in the novelistic system is symmetrical with that occupied by Blondet):

> By the nature of their social functions, the peasants live a purely material life which approximates to that of the savages, and their constant union with nature tends to foster it. (Ibid., vol. I, ch. 3)

> My bishop sent me here as if on a mission to savages; but, as I had the honour of telling him, the savages of France cannot be reached. They make it a law unto themselves not to listen to us; whereas the church does get some hold on the savages of America. (Ibid., vol. I, ch. 5)

Used differently in each particular case, the image is not only representative of a particular point of view. It is used anonymously, from that point of view, outside the flow of the narrative which is that of the author:

> The savage, and the peasant who is much like a savage, seldom speak unless to deceive an enemy. (Ibid., vol. I, ch. 6)

It even shapes the narrative at its most anecdotal:

> This piercing scream echoed through the woods like a savage war-cry. (Ibid., vol. I, ch. 10)

In its multiple uses, the image finally acquires, to some extent, an autonomous value. It characterises the peasant by demonstrating his original relationship to nature; but in this case it is allegorical, that is to say, inadequate. The peasant is not a true savage; the nature which he inhabits is unnatural – diversified and permeated by the different modes of appropriation. It presupposes the existence of a society. But the comparison has an exotic value, above all in its remote displaced character: it does not correspond exactly to a reality which it represents by distortion. The artificiality becomes clearer when we find it being used very differently, applied by Mme Soudry to Rigou:

> The tall, stiff usurer always had an imposing effect upon Madame Soudry's company, who instinctively recognised in his nature the cruelty of the tiger with steel claws, the craft of a savage. (Ibid., vol. II, ch. 2)

Clearly, now, the comparison with the savage signifies a profound *misunderstanding*: by its incoherence, this is what Balzac's text itself is saying. To see a savage within the peasant, as do Blondet or Brossette, is not to see the peasant entirely as he is: the image is significant principally because of the gap which paradoxically links it to its model.

Les Paysans is a novel in the style of Fenimore Cooper, because it describes the same 'primitive' violence. The landscapes of Morvan, 'countryside', are not pastoral; they show the image (even before the appearance of the inhabitants) of a disquieting virgin nature, the very same which is supposedly inhabited by the American Indians.

But if there are savages, and if the peasant is indeed a savage, there is nowhere in a savage state: every place shown in the *Comédie humaine* is the setting in front of which a social relationship is enacted. Thus we see a very primitive discord between the place and its occupant, which will be the focus of novelistic curiosity. This importance of the *place*, which is the first object of the analysis of manners, ought to be remembered: the conception of the relation between man and the surrounding nature is a specifically literary means – not a datum but the product of the work of the writer. But this instrument has a double value: it shapes the novel and determines its content. That the forests of Morvan should be described in the same terms as the forests of America, and this with an explicit reference to the writer who popularised this setting, is initially an artifice of writing: the same artifice which will, for example, make Rigou a 'Heliogabalus', a 'Louis XV without a throne', the 'Tiberius of the Avonne valley', the 'Lucullus of Blangy', a 'village Sardanapolis'; but that the 'man of the woods' should be, because of this metaphor, the same here and there, is a historical, critical and polemical thesis which, using the same means, produces a meaning radically opposed to that which the system (as it has been analysed) produced. Far from a distinction, it seems, it is now a question of a mingling and a confusion. As we shall see, this coexistence of two kinds of statement is typical of the work of Balzac the writer: it is this which, in the juncture (*rencontre*) which it establishes between a knowledge which is distinct and an ideology which is confused, makes the work literary (and not, as Balzac sometimes says, historical or political). This is why, from a theoretical point of view, nothing prevents our making a special study of the *form of the work:* we are certain to find implied there the reality principle which fills it.

The form which organises the fictional debate – a real historical debate, and an artificial debate (because it derives from a technique of literary composition) – also endows this debate with content: a study of the process of writing is inadequate in so far as it inevitably encounters the object of history itself.

Balzac resolves the technical problem posed by this *double game*, but by emphasising and giving new life to a traditional form, the fictional *type*, which has already been discussed. Let us say, rather, that he *encounters* the solution to this problem, because this time it does not depend on the conscious control of a technical means: he encounters it in the ordeal of that change of meaning which unforeseen functions confer on a system of representation.

The choice of typical objects (characters, places, situations, periods . . .) is an initial response to the necessity of describing: it makes possible an identification of reality as such, a representation of each element of a situation. It would be easy to show how in *Les Paysans* the diversity of the characters, which has a indistinctly psychological and sociological function, catches precisely, because it involves discrimination, the complexity of the bourgeois world, its demultiplication into different spheres, spheres temporarily and precariously in relation. This difference and mobility of 'characters' makes it possible to show all aspects of the bourgeoisie in its complex reality. By means of the 'type', ever more accurate identifications of social categories can be made. But the use of fictional types eventually produces a very different effect: the initially constituted reality is now judged according to a theory of society. Thus the literary instrument receives its true meaning, not from the necessity of reflecting reality itself, but from its place in the novelistic system, conceived as the best vantage point on this reality.

If the novel involves the use of 'types', this is because these types have between them relations other than real (the real relations between types are determined by the real existence of the social groups of which they give a fictional image), relations determined by their very nature as types, ideal relations: in which case the function of the type will be to confuse rather than to clarify.

It is this double nature of the fictional object which gives reality and even matter to Balzac's project, which makes this project into a work. The two meanings are each affirmed in turn, and there is an endless sliding from the one to the other.

This can be more easily explained by means of an example. We know of the importance of place in the development of a novel: it must be shown that this typical function is ambiguous. The opening of *Les Petits Bourgeois* provides an excellent example of the first conception of the fictional object: a long description of *things* (a house, furniture) in the form of an exploration (so characteristic of the Balzac exposition) exhibiting what *Un Début dans la vie* called 'the social material of an epoch': all the details of the house serve to show how the *petite bourgeoisie* is determined in relation to the bourgeoisie, both by it and against it. This very complex relation is *constituted* by the articulation of the novelistic description: the typically 'petit-bourgeois' furniture is positioned in front of 'bourgeois' walls, which it both conceals and reveals; it is this material occultation which gives an image of reality. All of Balzac's descriptions obey such norms; thus, in *Les Paysans*, three of the important locations are characterised by a system of oppositions:

> We ask those who really know France, if these houses – those of Rigou, Soudry and Gaubertin – are not a perfect presentation of the village, the little town, and the seat of a sub-prefecture? (*Les Paysans*, vol. II, ch. 4)

Each of these locations is typical of a specific social unit, in which the relations between the social groups are formed in a singular way: the three important forms of the bourgeois coalition in the provinces are thus changed into novelistic objects. It is extraordinary that Balzac is never satisfied with the truth of the realised type, that he refuses to accept it as definitive. From one novel to another the type undergoes a variation: if Soudry's house represents perfectly *the* small town, and Gaubertin's the departmental capital, the provincial village is just as much Saumur as it is Issoudun, just as much Angoulême as it is Bayeux, or equally those imaginary places in *Les Paysans*. This variation is not dictated by anecdotal requirements (for example, an attention to the picturesque), a mere geographical colouring appropriate to the setting: it answers the desire to *fill* this frame by diversification. Only Paris has the right to be unique, because it is multiplicity itself: but the small town, if it is to retain its identity, requires the description of other small towns, which are finally so many aspects of it; the total conception of the *Comédie humaine* resolves this problem of interminable description. Contrary to any initial beliefs, the type is all the more representative in that it partakes of several specimens, unique and original.

But, as we have said, the function of the type is interrupted, becomes ambiguous, when it is related to other types, not in a real relationship of difference, but in a relation of analogy obviously fantastic. With regard to the same example, this is what happens when Balzac says that the provincial town is Paris at a slower pace, as he does in *Les Illusions perdues*. In the same way, in *Les Petits Bourgeois*, in contradiction with the initial precision of the décor, the bourgeois salon is later presented as a reduction of the Faubourg Saint-Germain. These comparisons between types no longer simply diverse, but really opposed, are not made in passing: they are on the contrary one of the constants of Balzac's style. The type loses its function of reality to become a troubled image: it is no longer representative in the strict sense of the word, but the term of a systematic identity.

In order to understand this sliding, the system which determines the organisation of the narrative must be constructed in its entirety. With Balzac, the novel takes the *scene* for its general frame – a scene which is neither a unity of place nor a unity of time, but a fictional element, defined by the light of a theory of society, independently of the differential method which elsewhere sufficed to describe it. We meet again with a feature of the Balzac novel which has already been described, though now it has a different meaning: an essentially *unbalanced* construction. The rhythm of the narrative is broken, the succession of episodes is abrupt and discontinuous. This answers to a demand for progression which defined the nature of the scene. *La Rabouilleuse* (The Fisherwoman) offers a good example of these formal ruptures: after a static and very extended account of life in Issoudun, which forms a complete narrative unit, the sudden entry of Philippe Bridau into the village, on the initiative of Desroches, is related. Nothing enabled us to foresee this event: abruptly the narrative takes on a new dimension, is played out at an entirely different level. Always the novel is shaped by the same structure: very long, isolated elements of description are brutally cut short by an unexpected event, an event in relation to which the description seems insufficient, and thereby arises the need for a new description; thus a progression is established within a demonstrative system. The event is the appearance of an individual, previously described in a portrait. The narrative model, the scene, is the infinitely varied and renewed encounter of a situation and a portrait, from which emerges a dynamic individuality, what Balzac calls 'moral power': in the wake of this encounter the situation is changed and a new narrative element impels the scene.

This extremely simple narrative organisation depends on a systematic representation of the plot: the plot is derived from the impact of a 'moral force' on a real situation, which produces displacements and readjustments. The 'moral world' is always confronted with the real world, but is always autonomously determined. The situation and the individual 'force' are reciprocal though never mingled. Thus we see that the important theme of the work is that of *success* and of *depravity*. This theme is both 'moral' and 'social': through this theme we shall discover that articulation which is the characteristic object of the scene. There is depravity whenever the gap between the force and the situation is such that their confrontation is indecisive. This is what happens to Maxence Gilet, as it is described at the end of *La Rabouilleuse*:

> Thus perished one of those men destined to do great things, had they remained in their proper sphere; a man who was nature's favourite child, for she gave him courage, composure and the political acumen of a Cesare Borgia. But education had not endowed him with that nobility of thought and conduct without which nothing is possible in any career. (*La Rabouilleuse*, ch. 1)

Education is obviously the only feature linking the 'situation' and the 'force': and this is why all Balzac's novels will deal with either an education or a decline.

Un Début dans la vie is the supreme example of the novel of adaptation; *Les Illusions perdues* that of a novel of maladaptation:

> We can expect anything from Lucien, good as well as evil. (Arthez' letter)

> Ah! his is a nature which is splendid only in its setting, only in its sphere, its climate. (David Séchard)

The encounter can culminate in a reconciliation or can produce aberrant results which deform the situation (see *La Rabouilleuse*) or the individual (Rubempré): in which case the initial force expands in the form of a vice.

> The superimposition of the character of Rastignac, who triumphs, on that of Lucien, who fails, is simply a large-scale representation of a capital fact of our epoch: the ambition which succeeds, the ambition which is thwarted, the ambition of the first steps in life. (David Séchard, preface to the first edition)

'A capital fact of our epoch': with this fact, the analysis of manners takes fictional form. Adaptation and maladaptation are *generalities*, typical elements which persist whatever the variety of the situations.

This is all therefore both very coherent and very simple, so that the coherence is not that which has previously been identified. Every man carries with him a 'moral world': the question is whether, placed in contact with one or several situations, this world will succeed in realising itself, and in what direction; in fact, a moral world can develop in contradictory directions:

> All the laws of nature have a double action, each in an opposite direction. (*Les Illusions perdues*)

The ideal programme of the *Comédie humaine* consists in realising all the possible encounters between moral forces and real situations, and in representing all the forms of 'moral' adaptation.

We find the 'theory' of this adaptation in its simplest form in *Les Illusions perdues*:

> The organisation of modern society, infinitely more complicated in its machinery than in the ancient world, has produced a subdivision in man's faculties. Previously eminent men, compelled to be universal, appeared in small numbers like torches in the midst of the ancient nations. More recently, though the faculties may have specialised, excellence was achieved in a wide sphere. Thus a man of supreme cunning, as Louis XI was considered to be, could

> apply his skill to everything; but nowadays the accomplishment has subdivided itself. For example, there are as many tricks as there are professions. A clever diplomat may well be deceived in some provincial matter by a lowly attorney or by a peasant. The craftiest journalist may find that he is a complete simpleton in commercial matters.

and a great novelist may not succeed in business. The problem of adaptation is posed when a kind of technical division establishes a diversity, this time within the moral world. To hold up the edifice of the scene a new kind of type now becomes necessary: the moral type.

All these speculations, which are of an ideological nature, could be explained by reference to a tradition (Swedenborg, St Martin, the philosophical novel). It seems more significant to interpret them in relation to a problematic of literary forms. The scene, the composition of the narrative (situation-explosion), the type, are not initially ideas about the world and man, but fictional objects, which Balzac has chosen or established less because they may have seemed to him to be true or real than because they were the vehicles, *par excellence*, of the fiction. Thus we see that it is the problem of literature itself which is posed by the articulation of two conceptions of the type (the real type, the moral type).

With Balzac, as the preface informs us, the novel ceases to represent individual relations, encounters in the anecdotal sense of the word. These relations are only objects for the new novel because they are capable of extension: the individual has a place in the novel only because he is the term in a series. But Balzac's entire work is built upon a double characterisation of this extension. The individual exists in relation to a situation, but this situation is only apparently simple: in fact, it results from an intersection, which produces a coincidence between the real milieu, the real setting (represented by means of diversity: Balzac's first system), and the moral world (represented by means of confusion: Balzac's second system). The fictional element is doubly representative because of this double inscription. Individual encounters, which form the very substance of the plot, are significant because the individual is himself the product of an encounter (he is doubly determined).

The 'moral type' is a literary means equal in status to the 'real type': in fact, in the development of fictional discourse, they are even usually confused; the same type can be both moral and real. The difference emerges when the question of the relations between the two different types is posed. Two connections are in fact possible: a relation of difference and opposition which expresses a real relation; an ideal unity which evokes an absolute universality. We have already given sufficient examples of this first type of connection. For its part, the moral universe is a Leibnizian world, where 'it is always and everywhere the same, almost to perfection': concierges in this world are like duchesses, priests are like all the other kinds of celibate; the rich and the poor can no longer be distinguished:

> The wit of a peasant or labourer is very Attic; it consists in speaking out his mind and giving it a grotesque expression. We find the same thing in a drawing-room. Delicacy of wit takes the place of picturesque vulgarity, and that is really all the difference. (*Les Paysans*, vol. I, ch. 4)

Ornamental language in all its generality is characteristic, typical: in this case differences are secondary. Comparing and uniting, literature in this case takes no notice of real relations, real limits, and discovers everywhere the confused identity which joins man to man, *beyond* social differences: a single individual relates to a real series and to a moral series (Mme Soudry is typical of the small provincial town, but she is also typical of certain aspects of human nature).

> Is not this a picture of life as it is at all stages of what we agree to call society? Change the style, and you will find that nothing more and nothing less is said in the gilded salons of Paris. (Ibid., vol. I, ch. 2)

Le Curé de Tours (The Vicar of Tours) gives an example of this new lesson which has insinuated itself into the novel: a lesson via identification, and no longer by differentiation.

> This history is commonplace: it would suffice to enlarge slightly the narrow circle within which these characters will act in order to find the coefficient reason for happenings in even the highest levels of society.

The scene itself is typical, since it is that element of literature, both the most simple and the most determinate, in which are reflected all the varieties of the moral world. The scene, lacking in doors or windows on to the diversity of the real world, carries in itself the infinity of the moral universe:

> Perhaps the crudity of this portrait will be criticised, the brightness of the character of the fisherwoman deemed to have been borrowed from that truth which the painter ought to leave in shadow. Oh, well! this scene, endlessly repeated, with appalling variants, is, in its rough form and its horrible veracity, the very type of those which all women play out, at whatever rung of the social ladder they may find themselves, whenever any kind of interest has diverted them from the path of obedience and they have seized power. As with great politicians, in their eyes, all means are justified by the end. Between Flore Brazier and the duchess, between the duchess and the richest citizen, between the citizen and the most lavishly kept woman, there are no differences other than those due to the education they have had and the circles in which they have lived.

and it does not seem that these differences are really important.

However, whilst it is thus formulating, in the confusion of the universal, the 'coefficient reasons', the scene establishes the combination of a world analogous to the real world, and the same instruments assist in the realisation of these contradictory and complementary operations: distinction and confusion. Everywhere in *Le Curé de Tours*, the types which had been used for an ideal demultiplication also serve to clarify real relations by showing a play of conflicts and alliances. At the beginning, the abbé Birotteau, and with him the Listomere clan, represents the old aristocracy in a provincial town; Troubert, on the other hand, with the friends of Mlle Gamard, is the advance troop of the bourgeoisie. The novel progresses only because these determinations seem retrospectively precarious and temporary. Behind Troubert, the Congregation is seen in profile; Birotteau, progressively deprived of his 'traditional resources', finally has recourse to the services of a liberal lawyer. Thus a historical contradiction explodes, the very contradiction which made 1830: it shows the decomposition of the old ruling class under the Restoration, and the help which, if it is to survive, it must seek from the bourgeoisie, who are revealed as the true leaders of reaction. Mlle Gamard is one of the terms of this subtle and precise historical analysis, but she is also 'one of those typical old maids'. The type serves to describe, but it also serves to interpret and to judge, within the framework of a false universality.

The disproportion between the real world and the moral world is simultaneously produced and reduced by the work: outside the work this disproportion has no status, no existence; yet this gap establishes it only after the event through a kind of reversal of the fictional machine; it is a question of a second effect, not a product of chance but determined and constitutive of the work. This enables us better to understand the place of ideology in a *literary work*: it is unimportant whether the author is the partisan of an ideology which is by definition external to the enterprise of writing; what is important is that the operation of a fictional system ultimately produces an ideological effect (confusion). Thus ideology is part of the system, not independent of it. Following the model of other analyses one could say that this ideological surge denotes the presence of a gap, a defect in the work, a complexity which makes it *meaningful*. Balzac's work is the best example of this obligation which every writer discovers, that in order to say one thing he must also say several others at the same time. The constitution of Balzac's narrative is open to two explanations: this narrative tends to realise simultaneously two forms of generalisation. Must we choose between the two explanations, must say we that the one is more profound than the other, must we then emphasise this explanation? It seems that we ought rather to preserve the play of this double explanation which establishes simultaneously two meanings and the gap between them. Balzac is not more of an artist than he is a politician: he is both together, one against the other, one with the other. Separately, the artistic reading and the political reading are false readings: it is their inevitable companionship which must be remembered.

One could, in a very general way, distinguish two types of utterance in the Balzacian narrative: certain utterances are directly linked to the functioning of the fictional system; other utterances are 'detachable' – they seem to have been taken as they are from ideology and inserted into the texture of the novel (and could probably return just as easily to their place of origin). If, in many cases, they are not distinguishable, they are indissociable: the novel is made from their contrast. The literary text does not constitute a homogeneous whole: it does not inhabit a single place prepared in advance to receive it. However, these detachable utterances are not detached utterances: they are in the work not as real utterances, but as fictional objects; in the work they are the term of a designation, of a demonstration; in spite of appearances their status is not directly ideological; the mode of their presence is that of a *presentation* which hollows them, exhibits a fundamental disparity in them. Thus, they are not in the text as intruders, but as *effects*: they have meaning only by that metamorphosis which makes of them elements among others in the process of fictional production.

In his course upon fictional subjectivity (given at the Ecole normale supérieure in 1965–6; the relevant section has been published in *Cahiers marxistes-léninistes* of October 1966), A. Badiou has clearly posed the problem of the relations between ideological utterances and properly fictional utterances. He has shown that in the novel one cannot isolate ideological utterances and consider them as independent realities, as enclaves: ideology is so caught in the tissue of the work that it there takes on a new status, its immediate nature is transformed. One could say, to take up a vocabulary already familiar: from the illusion that it was, it becomes fictive.

We now understand why to forget political ideology in Balzac's work (to pretend that it does not exist, to excuse or condemn it) is to misunderstand it as a literary work. To read the

Comédie humaine indignantly is to reduce it to its ideological process, to see it as no more than the work of a historian or a journalist. To dissociate something derived from pure art as though the rest were unimportant is to be unaware of its necessary complexity.

June 1966

Appendix

Lenin's Articles on Tolstoy

Leo Tolstoy
as the Mirror of the Russian Revolution

To identify the great artist with the revolution which he has obviously failed to understand, and from which he obviously stands aloof, may at first sight seem strange and artificial. A mirror which does not reflect things correctly could hardly be called a mirror. Our revolution, however, is an extremely complicated thing. Among the mass of those who are directly making and participating in it there are many social elements which have also obviously not understood what is taking place and which also stand aloof from the real historical tasks with which the course of events has confronted them. And if we have before us a really great artist, he must have reflected in his work at least some of the essential aspects of the revolution.

The legal Russian press, though its pages teem with articles, letters and comments on Tolstoy's eightieth birthday, is least of all interested in analysing his works from the standpoint of the character of the Russian revolution and its motive forces. The whole of this press is steeped to nausea in hypocrisy, hypocrisy of a double kind: official and liberal. The former is the crude hypocrisy of the venal hack who was ordered yesterday to hound Leo Tolstoy, and today to show that Tolstoy is a patriot, and to try to observe the decencies before the eyes of Europe.

That the hacks of this kind have been paid for their screeds is common knowledge and they cannot deceive anybody. Much more refined and, therefore, much more pernicious and dangerous is liberal hypocrisy. To listen to the Cadet Balalaikins of *Rech*, one would think that their sympathy for Tolstoy is of the most complete and ardent kind. Actually, their calculated declamations and pompous phrases about the 'great seeker after God' are false from beginning to end, for no Russian liberal believes in Tolstoy's God, or sympathises with Tolstoy's criticism of the existing social order. He associates himself with a popular name in order to increase his political capital, in order to pose as a leader of the nation-wide opposition; he seeks, with the din and thunder of claptrap, to *drown* the demand for a straight and clear answer to the question: what are the glaring contradictions of 'Tolstoyism' due to, and what shortcomings and weaknesses of our revolution do they express?

The contradictions in Tolstoy's works, views, doctrines, in his school, are indeed glaring. On the one hand, we have the great artist, the genius who has not only drawn incomparable pictures of Russian life but has made first-class contributions to world literature. On the other hand, we have the landlord obsessed with Christ. On the one hand, the remarkably powerful, forthright, and sincere protest against social falsehood and hypocrisy: and on the other, the 'Tolstoyan', i.e., the jaded, hysterical sniveller called the Russian intellectual, who publicly beats his breast and wails: 'I am a bad wicked man, but I am practising moral self-perfection; I don't eat meat any more, I now eat rice cutlets.' On the one hand, merciless criticism of capitalist exploitation, exposure of government outrages, the farcical courts and the state administration, and unmasking of the profound contradictions between the growth of poverty, degradation and misery among the working masses. On the other, the crackpot preaching of submission, 'resist not evil' with violence. On the one hand, the most sober realism, the tearing away of all and sundry masks; on the other, the preaching of one of the most odious things on earth, namely, religion, the striving to replace officially appointed priests by priests who will serve from moral conviction, i.e., to cultivate the most refined and, therefore, particularly disgusting clericalism. Verily:

Thou art a pauper, yet thou art abundant,
Thou art mighty, yet thou art impotent—
—Mother Russia!

That Tolstoy, owing to these contradictions, could not possibly understand either the working-class movement and its role in the struggle for socialism, or the Russian revolution, goes without saying. But the contradictions in Tolstoy's views and doctrines are not accidental; they express the contradictory conditions of Russian life in the last third of the nineteenth century. The patriarchal countryside, only recently emancipated from serfdom, was literally given over to the capitalist and the tax-collector to be fleeced and plundered. The ancient foundations of peasant economy and peasant life, foundations that had really held for centuries, were broken up for scrap with extraordinary rapidity. And the contradictions in Tolstoy's views must be appraised not from the standpoint of the present-day working-class movement and present-day socialism (such an appraisal is, of course, needed, but it is not enough), but from the standpoint of protest against advancing capitalism, against the ruining of the masses, who are being dispossessed of their land – a protest which had to arise from the patriarchal Russian countryside. Tolstoy is absurd as a prophet who has discovered new nostrums for the salvation of mankind – and therefore the foreign and Russian 'Tolstoyans' who have sought to convert the weakest side of his doctrine into a dogma, are not worth speaking of. Tolstoy is great as the spokesman of the ideas and sentiments that emerged among the millions of Russian peasants at the time the bourgeois revolution was approaching in Russia. Tolstoy is original, because the sum total of his views, taken as a whole, happens to express the specific features of our revolution as a *peasant* bourgeois revolution. From this point of view, the contradictions in Tolstoy's views are indeed a mirror of those contradictory conditions in which the peasantry had to play their historical part in our revolution. On the one hand, centuries of feudal oppression and decades of accelerated post-Reform pauperisation piled up mountains of hate, resentment, and desperate determination.

The striving to sweep away completely the official church, the landlords and the landlord government, to destroy all the old forms and ways of landownership, to clear the land, to replace the police-class state by a community of free and equal small peasants – this striving is the keynote of every historical step the peasantry has taken in our revolution; and undoubtedly, the message of Tolstoy's writings conforms to this peasant striving far more than it does to abstract 'Christian Anarchism', as his 'system' of views is sometimes appraised.

On the other hand, the peasantry, striving towards new ways of life, had a very crude, patriarchal, semi-religious idea of what kind of life this should be; by what struggle could liberty be won, what leaders it could have in this struggle, what was the attitude of the bourgeoisie and the bourgeois intelligentsia towards the interests of peasant revolution, why the forcible overthrow of tsarist rule was needed in order to abolish landlordism. The whole past life of the peasantry had taught it to hate the landowner and the official, but it did not, and could not, teach it where to seek an answer to all these questions. In our revolution a minor part of the peasantry really did fight, did organise to some extent for this purpose; and a very small part indeed rose up in arms to exterminate its enemies, to destroy the tsar's servants and protectors of the landlords. Most of the peasantry wept and prayed, moralised and dreamed, wrote petitions and sent 'pleaders' – quite in the vein of Leo Tolstoy! And, as always happens in such cases, the effect of this Tolstoyan abstention from politics, this Tolstoyan renunciation of politics, this lack of interest in and understanding of politics, was that only a minority followed the lead of the class-conscious revolutionary proletariat, while the majority became the prey of those unprincipled, servile, bourgeois intellectuals who under the name of Cadets hastened from a meeting of Trudoviks to Stolypin's ante-room, and begged, haggled, reconciled and promised to reconcile – until they were kicked out with a military jackboot. Tolstoy's ideas are a mirror of the weakness, the shortcomings of our peasant revolt, a reflection of the flabbiness of the patriarchal countryside and of the hidebound cowardice of the 'enterprising muzhik'.

Take the soldiers' insurrections in 1905–06. In social composition these men who fought in our revolution were partly peasants and partly proletarians. The proletarians were in the minority; therefore the movement in the armed forces does not even approximately show the same nation-wide solidarity, the same party consciousness, as were displayed by the proletariat, which became Social-Democratic as if by the wave of a hand. Yet there is nothing more mistaken than the view that the insurrections in the armed forces failed because no officers had led them. On the contrary, the enormous progress the revolution had made since the time of the Narodnaya Volya was shown precisely by the fact that the 'grey herd' rose in arms against their superiors, and it was this self-dependency of theirs that so frightened the liberal landlords and the liberal officers. The common soldier fully sympathised with the peasants' cause; his eyes lit up at the very mention of land. There was more than one case when authority in the armed forces passed to the mass of the rank and file, but determined use of this authority was hardly made at all; the soldiers wavered; after a couple of days, in some cases a few hours, after killing some hated officer, they released the others who had been arrested, parleyed with the authorities and then faced the firing squad, or bared their backs for the birch, or put on the yoke again – quite in the vein of Leo Tolstoy!

Tolstoy reflected the pent-up hatred, the ripened striving for a better lot, the desire to get rid of the past – and also the immature dreaming, the political inexperience, the revolutionary flabbiness. Historical and economic conditions explain both the inevitable beginning of the revolutionary struggle of the masses and their unpreparedness for the struggle, their Tolstoyan non-resistance to evil, which was a most serious cause of the defeat of the first revolutionary campaign.

It is said that beaten armies learn well. Of course, revolutionary classes can be compared with armies only in a very limited sense. The development of capitalism is hourly changing and intensifying the conditions which roused the millions of peasants – united by their hatred for the feudalist landlords and their government – for the revolutionary-democratic struggle. Among the peasantry themselves the growth of exchange, of the rule of the market and the power of money is steadily ousting old-fashioned patriarchalism and patriarchal Tolstoyan ideology. But there is one gain from the first years of the revolution and the first reverses in mass revolutionary struggle about which there can be no doubt. It is the mortal blow struck at the former softness and flabbiness of the masses. The lines of demarcation have become more distinct. The cleavage of classes and parties has taken place. Under the hammer blows of the lessons taught by Stolypin, and with undeviating and consistent agitation by the revolutionary Social-Democrats not only the socialist proletariat but also the democratic masses of the peasantry will inevitably advance from their midst more and more steeled fighters who will be less capable of falling into our historical sin of Tolstoyism!

First published in *Proletary*, No. 35, September 11 (24), 1908, and subsequently in Lenin's *Collected Works*, Vol. 15, pp. 202–9, Reprinted from Lenin, *On Literature and Art*, Moscow, Progress Publishers, 1967, pp. 28–33.

L. N. Tolstoy

Leo Tolstoy is dead. His universal significance as an artist and his universal fame as a thinker and preacher reflect, each in its own way, the universal significance of the Russian revolution.

L. N. Tolstoy emerged as a great artist when serfdom still held sway in the land. In a series of great works, which he produced during the more than half a century of his literary activity, he depicted mainly the old, pre-revolutionary Russia which remained in a state of semi-serfdom even after 1861 – rural Russia of the landlord and the peasant. In depicting this period in Russia's history, Tolstoy succeeded in raising so many great problems and succeeded in rising to such heights of artistic power that his works rank among the greatest in world literature. The epoch of preparation for revolution in one of the countries under the heel of the serf owners became, thanks to its brilliant illumination by Tolstoy, a step forward in the artistic development of humanity as a whole.

Tolstoy the artist is known to an infinitesimal minority even in Russia. If his great works are really to be made the possession of *all*, a struggle must be waged against the system of society which condemns millions and scores of millions to ignorance, benightedness, drudgery and poverty – a socialist revolution must be accomplished.

Tolstoy not only produced artistic works which will always be appreciated and read by the masses, once they have created human conditions of life for themselves after overthrowing the yoke of the landlords and capitalists; he succeeded in conveying with remarkable force the moods of the large masses that are oppressed by the present system, in depicting their condition and expressing their spontaneous feelings of protest and anger. Belonging, as he did, primarily to the era of 1861–1904, Tolstoy in his works – both as an artist and as a thinker and preacher – embodied in amazingly bold relief the specific historical features of the entire first Russian revolution, its strength and its weakness.

One of the principal distinguishing features of our revolution is that it was a *peasant* bourgeois revolution in the era of the very advanced development of capitalism throughout the world and of its comparatively advanced development in Russia. It was a bourgeois revolution because its immediate aim was to overthrow the tsarist autocracy, the tsarist monarchy, and to abolish landlordism, but not to overthrow the domination of the bourgeoisie. The peasantry in particular was not aware of the latter aim, it was not aware of the distinction between this aim and the closer and more immediate aims of the struggle. It was a peasant bourgeois revolution because the objective conditions put in the forefront the problem of changing the basic conditions of life for the peasantry, of breaking up the old, medieval system of landownership, of 'clearing the ground' for capitalism; the objective conditions were responsible for the appearance of the peasant masses on the arena of more or less independent historic action.

Tolstoy's works express both the strength and the weakness, the might and the limitations, precisely of the peasant mass movement. His heated, passionate, and often ruthlessly sharp protest against the state and the official church that was in alliance with the police conveys the sentiments of the primitive peasant democratic masses, among whom centuries of serfdom, of official tyranny and robbery, and of church Jesuitism, deception and chicanery had piled up mountains of anger and hatred. His unbending opposition to private property in land conveys the psychology of the peasant masses during that historical period in which the old, medieval landownership, both in the form of landed estates and in the form of state 'allotments', definitely became an intolerable obstacle to the further development of the country, and when this old landownership was inevitably bound to be destroyed most summarily and ruthlessly. His unremitting accusations against capitalism – accusations permeated with most profound emotion and most ardent indignation – convey all the horror felt by the patriarchal peasant at the advent of the new, invisible, incomprehensible enemy coming from somewhere in the cities or from somewhere abroad, destroying all the 'pillars' of rural life, bringing in its train unprecedented ruin, poverty, starvation, savagery, prostitution, syphilis – all the calamities attending the 'epoch of primitive accumulation', aggravated a hundredfold by the transplantation into Russian soil of the most modern methods of plunder elaborated by the all powerful Monsieur Coupon.

But the vehement protestant, the passionate accuser, the great critic at the same time manifested in his works a failure to understand the causes of the crisis threatening Russia, and the means of escape from it, that was characteristic only of apatriarchal, naive peasant, but not of a writer with a European education. His struggle against the feudal police state, against the monarchy turned into a repudiation of politics, led to the doctrine of 'non-resistance to evil', and to complete aloofness from the revolutionary struggle of the masses in 1905–7. The fight against the official church was combined with the preaching of a new, purified religion, that is to say, of a new, refined, subtle poison for the oppressed masses. The opposition to private property in land did not lead to concentrating the struggle against the real enemy – landlordism and its political instrument of power, i.e., the monarchy – but led to dreamy, diffuse and impotent lamentations. The exposure of capitalism and of the calamities it inflicts on the masses was combined with a wholly apathetic attitude to the world-wide struggle for emancipation waged by the international socialist proletariat.

The contradictions in Tolstoy's views are not contradictions inherent in his personal views alone, but are a reflection of the extremely complex, contradictory conditions, social influences and historical traditions which determined the psychology of various classes and various sections of Russian society in the *post*-Reform, but *pre*-revolutionary era.

That is why a correct appraisal of Tolstoy can be made only from the viewpoint of the class which has proved, by its political role and its struggle during the first denouement of these contradictions, at a time of revolution, that it is destined to be the leader in the struggle for the people's liberty and for the emancipation of the masses from exploitation – the class which has proved its selfless devotion to the cause of democracy and its ability to fight against the limitations and inconsistency of bourgeois (including peasant) democracy; such an appraisal is possible only from the viewpoint of the Social-Democratic proletariat.

Look at the estimate of Tolstoy in the government newspapers. They shed crocodile tears, professing their respect for 'the great writer' and at the same time defending the 'Holy' Synod. As for the holy fathers, they have just perpetrated a particularly vile iniquity; they sent priests to the dying man in order to hoodwink the people and say that Tolstoy had 'repented'. The Holy Synod excommunicated Tolstoy. So much the better. It will be reminded of this exploit when the hour comes for the people to settle accounts with the official in cassocks, the gendarmes in Christ, the sinister inquisitors who supported anti-Jewish pogroms and other exploits of the Black-Hundred tsarist gang.

Look at the estimate of Tolstoy in the liberal newspapers. They confine themselves to those hollow, official-liberal, hackneyed professorial phrases about the 'voice of civilised mankind', 'the unanimous response of the world', the 'ideas of truth, good', etc., for which Tolstoy so castigated – and justly castigated – bourgeois science. They *cannot* voice plainly and clearly their opinion of Tolstoy's views on the state, the church, private property in land capitalism – not because they are prevented by the censorship; on the contrary, the censorship is helping them out of an embarrassing position! – but because each proposition in Tolstoy's criticism is a slap in the face of bourgeois liberalism; because the very way in which Tolstoy fearlessly, frankly and ruthlessly *poses* the sorest and most vexatious problems of our day is a *rebuff* to the commonplace phrases, trite quirks and evasive, 'civilised' falsehoods of our liberal (and liberal-Narodnik) publicists. The liberals are all for Tolstoy, they are all against the Synod – and, at the same time, they are for . . . the Vekhists, with whom 'it is possible to disagree', but with whom it is 'necessary' to live in harmony in one party, with whom it is 'necessary' to work together in literature and politics. And yet the Vekhists are greeted with kisses by Anthony, Bishop of Volhynia.

The liberals put in the forefront that Tolstoy is 'the great conscience'. Is not this a hollow phrase which is repeated in a thousand variations both by *Novoye Vremya* and by all such newspapers? Is this not an evasion of the *concrete* problems of democracy and socialism which Tolstoy *posed*? Is this not to put in the forefront the feature that expresses Tolstoy's prejudice, not his intellect, the part of him that belongs to the past and not to the future, his repudiation of politics and his preaching of moral self-perfection, but not his vehement protest against all class domination?

Tolstoy is dead, and the pre-revolutionary Russia whose weakness and impotence found their expression in the philosophy and are depicted in the works of the great artist, has become a thing of the past. But the heritage which he has left includes that which has not become a thing of the past, but belongs to the future. This heritage is accepted and is being worked upon by the Russian proletariat. The Russian proletariat will explain to the masses of the toilers and the exploited the meaning of Tolstoy's criticism of the state, the church, private property in land – not in order that the masses should confine themselves to self-perfection and yearning for a godly life, but in order that they should rise to strike a new blow at the tsarist monarchy and landlordism, which were but slightly damaged in 1905, and which must be destroyed. The Russian proletariat will explain to the masses Tolstoy's criticism of capitalism – not in order that the masses should confine themselves to hurling imprecations at capital and the rule of money, but in order that they should learn to utilise at every step in their life and in their struggle the technical and social achievements of capitalism, that they should learn to weld themselves into a united army of millions of socialist fighters who will overthrow capitalism and create a new society in which the people will not be doomed to poverty, in which there will be no exploitation by man.

First published in *Sotsial-Demokrat*, No. 18, November 16 (29), 1910, and subsequently in Lenin's *Collected Works*, Vol. 16, pp. 323–7. Reprinted from Lenin, *On Literature and Art*, pp. 48–52.

Leo Tolstoy and His Epoch

The epoch to which Leo Tolstoy belongs and which is reflected in such bold relief both in his brilliant literary works and in his teachings began after 1861 and lasted until 1905. True, Tolstoy commenced his literary career earlier and it ended later, but it was during this period, whose transitional nature gave rise to *all* the distinguishing features of Tolstoy's works and of Tolstoyism, that he fully matured both as an artist and as a thinker.

Through Levin, a character in *Anna Karenina*, Tolstoy very vividly expressed the nature of the turn in Russia's history that took place during this half-century.

> . . . Talk about the harvest, hiring labourers, and so forth, which, as Levin knew, it was the custom to regard as something very low . . . now seemed to Levin to be the only important thing. 'This, perhaps, was unimportant under serfdom, or is unimportant in England. In both cases the conditions are definite; but here today, when everything has been turned upside down and is only just taking shape again, the question of how these conditions will shape is the only important question in Russia,' mused Levin. (*Collected Works*, Vol. X, p. 137)

'Here in Russia everything has now been turned upside down and is only just taking shape' – it is difficult to imagine a more apt characterisation of the period 1861–1905. What 'was turned upside down' is familiar, or at least well known, to every Russian. It was serfdom, and the whole of the 'older order' that went with it. What 'is just taking shape' is totally unknown, alien and incomprehensible to the broad masses of the population. Tolstoy conceived this bourgeois order which was 'only just taking shape' vaguely, in the form of a bogey – England. Truly, a bogey, because Tolstoy rejects, on principle, so to speak, any attempt to investigate the features of the social system in this 'England', the connection between this system and the domination of capital, the role played by money, the rise and development of exchange. Like the Narodniks, he refuses to see, he shuts his eyes to, and dismisses the thought that what is 'taking shape' in Russia is none other than the bourgeois system.

It is true that, if not the 'only important' question, then certainly one of the most important from the standpoint of the immediate tasks of all social and political activities in Russia in the period of 1861–1905 (and in our times, too), was that of 'what shape' this system would take, this bourgeois system that had assumed extremely varied forms in 'England', Germany, America, France, and so forth. But such a definite, concretely historical presentation of the question was something absolutely foreign to Tolstoy. He reasons in the abstract, he recognises only the standpoint of the 'eternal' principles of morality, the eternal truths of religion, failing to realise that this standpoint is merely the ideological reflection of the old ('turned upside down') order, the feudal order, the way of the life of the Oriental peoples.

In *Lucerne* (written in 1857), Tolstoy declares that to regard 'civilisation' as a boon is an 'imaginary concept' which 'destroys in human nature the instinctive, most blissful primitive need for good'. 'We have only one infallible guide,' exclaims Tolstoy, 'the Universal Spirit that permeates us.' (*Collected Works*, II, p. 125.)

In *The Slavery of Our Times* (written in 1900), Tolstoy, repeating still more zealously these appeals to the Universal Spirit, declares that political economy is a 'pseudo science' because it takes as the 'pattern' 'little England, where conditions are most exceptional', instead of taking as a pattern 'the conditions of men in the whole world throughout the whole of history'. What this 'whole world' is like is revealed to us in the article 'Progress and the Definition of Education' (1862). Tolstoy counters the opinion of the 'historians' that progress is 'a general law for mankind' by referring to 'the whole of what is known as the Orient' (IV, 162). 'There is no general law of human progress,' says Tolstoy, 'and this is proved by the quiescence of the Oriental peoples.'

Tolstoyism, in its real historical content, is an ideology of an Oriental, an Asiatic order. Hence the asceticism, the non-resistance to evil, the profound notes of pessimism, the conviction that 'everything is nothing, everything is a material nothing' ('The Meaning of Life', p. 52), and faith in the 'Spirit' in 'the beginning of everything', and that man, in his relation to this beginning, is merely a 'labourer . . . allotted the task of saving his own soul', etc. Tolstoy is true to this ideology in his *Creutzer Sonata* too when he says: 'the emancipation of woman lies not in colleges and not in parliaments, but in the bedroom', and in the article written in 1862, in which he says that universities train only 'irritable, debilitated liberals' for whom 'the people have no use at all', who are 'uselessly torn from their former environment', 'find no place in life', and so forth (IV, 136–37).

Pessimism, non-resistance, appeals to the 'Spirit' constitute an ideology inevitable in an epoch when the whole of the old order 'has been turned upside down', and when the masses, who have been brought up under this old order, who imbibed with their mother's milk the principles, the habits, the traditions and beliefs of this order, do not and cannot see *what kind* of a new order is 'taking shape', *what* social forces are 'shaping' it and how, what social forces are *capable* of bringing release from the incalculable and exceptionally acute distress that is characteristic of epochs of 'upheaval'.

The period of 1862–1904 was just such a period of upheaval in Russia, a period in which before everyone's eyes the old order collapsed, never to be restored, in which the new system was only just taking shape; the social forces shaping the new system first manifested themselves on a broad, nation-wide scale, in mass public action in the most varied fields only in 1905. And the 1905 events in Russia were followed by analogous events in a number of countries in that very 'Orient' to the 'quiescence' of which

Tolstoy referred in 1862. The year 1905 marked the beginning of the end of 'Oriental' quiescence. Precisely for this reason that year marked the historical end of Tolstoyism, the end of an epoch that could give rise to Tolstoy's teachings and in which they were inevitable, not as something individual, not as a caprice or a fad, but as the ideology of the conditions of life under which millions and millions actually found themselves for a certain period of time.

Tolstoy's doctrine is certainly utopian and in content is reactionary in the most precise and most profound sense of the word. But that certainly does not mean that the doctrine was not socialistic or that it did not contain critical elements capable of providing valuable material for the enlightenment of the advanced classes.

There are various kinds of socialism. In all countries where the capitalist mode of production prevails there is the socialism which expresses the ideology of the class that is going to take the place of the bourgeoisie; and there is the socialism that expresses the ideology of the classes that are going to be replaced by the bourgeoisie. Feudal socialism, for example, is socialism of the latter type, and the nature of *this* socialism was appraised long ago, over sixty years ago, by Marx, simultaneously with his appraisal of other types of socialism.

Furthermore, critical elements are inherent in Tolstoy's utopian doctrine, just as they are inherent in many utopian systems. But we must not forget Marx's profound observation to the effect that the value of critical elements in utopian socialism 'bears an inverse relation to historical development'. The more the activities of the social forces which are 'shaping' the new Russia and bringing release from present-day social evils develop and assume a definite character, the more rapidly is critical-utopian socialism 'losing all practical value and all theoretical justification'.

A quarter of a century ago, the critical elements in Tolstoy's doctrine might at times have been of practical value for some sections of the population *in spite of* its reactionary and utopian features. This could not have been the case during, say, the last decade, because historical development had made considerable progress between the eighties and the end of the last century. In our days, since the series of events mentioned above has put an end to 'Oriental' quiescence in our days, when the consciously reactionary ideas of *Vekhi* (reactionary in the narrow-class, selfishly-class sense) have become so enormously widespread among the liberal bourgeoisie and when these ideas have infected even a section of those who were almost Marxists and have created a liquidationist trend – in our days, the most direct and most profound harm is caused by every attempt to idealise Tolstoy's doctrine, to justify or to mitigate his 'non-resistance', his appeals to the 'Spirit', his exhortations for 'moral self-perfection', his doctrine of 'conscience' and universal 'love', his preaching of asceticism and quietism, and so forth.

First published in *Zvezda*, No. 6, January 22, 1911, signed: *V. Ilyin*, and subsequently in Lenin's *Collected Works*, Vol. 17, pp. 49–53. Reprinted from Lenin, *On Literature and Art*, pp. 58–62.

L. N. Tolstoy and the Modern Labour Movement

The Russian workers in practically all the large cities of Russia have already made their response in connection with the death of L. N. Tolstoy and, in one way or another, expressed their attitude to the writer who produced a number of most remarkable works of art that put him in the ranks of the great writers of the world, and to the thinker who with immense power, self-confidence and sincerity *raised* a number of questions concerning the basic features of the modern political and social system. All in all, this attitude was expressed in the telegram, printed in the newspapers, which was sent by the labour deputies in the Third Duma.

L. Tolstoy began his literary career when serfdom still existed but at a time when it had already obviously come to the end of its days. Tolstoy's main activity falls in that period of Russian history which lies between two of its turning-points, 1861 and 1905. Throughout this period traces of serfdom, direct survivals of it, permeated the whole economic (particularly in the countryside) and political life of the country. And at the same time this was a period of the accelerated growth of capitalism from below and its implantation from above.

In what were the survivals of serfdom expressed? Most of all and clearest of all in the fact that in Russia, mainly an agricultural country, agriculture at that time was in the hands of a ruined, impoverished peasantry who were working with antiquated, primitive methods on the old feudal allotments which had been cut in 1861 for the benefit of the landlords. And, on the other hand, agriculture was in the hands of the landlords who in Central Russia cultivated the land by the labour, the wooden ploughs, and the horses of the peasants in return for the 'cut-off lands', meadows, access to watering-places, etc. To all intents and purposes this was the old feudal system of economy. Throughout this period the political system of Russia was also permeated with feudalism. This is evident from the constitution of the state prior to the first moves to change it in 1905, from the predominant influence of the landed nobility on state affairs and from the unlimited power of the officials, who also for the most part – especially the higher ranks – came from the landed nobility.

After 1861 this old patriarchal Russia began rapidly to disintegrate under the influence of world capitalism. The peasants were starving, dying off, being ruined as never before, fleeing to the towns and abandoning the soil. There was a boom in the construction of railways, mills and factories, thanks to the 'cheap labour' of the ruined peasants. Big finance capital was developing in Russia together with large-scale commerce and industry.

It was this rapid, painful, drastic demolition of all the old 'pillars' of old Russia that was reflected in the works of Tolstoy the artist, and in the views of Tolstoy the thinker.

Tolstoy had a surpassing knowledge of rural Russia, the mode of life of the landlords and peasants. In his artistic productions he gave descriptions of this life that are numbered among the best productions of world literature. The drastic demolition of all the 'old pillars' of rural Russia sharpened his attention, deepened his interest in what was going on around him, and led to a radical change in his whole world outlook. By birth and education

Tolstoy belonged to the highest landed nobility in Russia – he broke with all the customary views of this environment and in his later works attacked with fierce criticism all the contemporary state, church, social and economic institutions which were based on enslavement of the masses, on their poverty, on the ruin of the peasants and the petty proprietors in general, on the coercion and hypocrisy which permeated all contemporary life from top to bottom.

Tolstoy's criticism was not new. He said nothing that had not been said long before him both in European and in Russian literature by friends of the working people. But the uniqueness of Tolstoy's criticism and its historical significance lie in the fact that it expressed, with a power such as is possessed only by artists of genius, the radical change in the views of the broadest masses of the people in the Russia of this period, namely, rural, peasant Russia. For Tolstoy's criticism of contemporary institutions differs from the criticism of the same institutions by representatives of the modern labour movement in the fact that Tolstoy's point of view was that of the patriarchal, naive peasant, whose psychology Tolstoy introduced into his criticism and his doctrine. Tolstoy's criticism is marked by such emotional power, such passion, convincingness, freshness, sincerity and fearlessness in striving to 'go to the roots', to find the real cause of the afflictions of the masses, just because this criticism really expresses a sharp change in the ideas of millions of peasants, who had only just emerged from feudalism into freedom, and saw that this freedom meant new horrors of ruin, death by starvation, a homeless life among the lower strata of the city population, and so on and so forth. Tolstoy mirrored their sentiments so faithfully that he imported their naiveté into his own doctrine, their alienation from political life, their mysticism, their desire to keep aloof from the world, 'non-resistance to evil', their impotent imprecations against capitalism and the 'power of money'. The protest of millions of peasants and their desperation – these were combined in Tolstoy's doctrine.

The representatives of the modern labour movement find that they have plenty to protest against but nothing to despair about. Despair is typical of the classes which are perishing, but the class of wage-workers is growing inevitably, developing and becoming strong in every capitalist society, Russia included. Despair is typical of those who do not understand the causes of evil, see no way out, and are incapable of struggle. The modern industrial proletariat does not belong to the category of such classes.

First published in *Nash Put*, No. 7, November 28, 1910, signed: *V. I-in*, and subsequently in Lenin, *Collected Works*, Vol. 16, pp. 330–2. Reprinted from Lenin, *On Literature and Art*, pp. 53–5.

Tolstoy and the Proletarian Struggle

Tolstoy's indictment of the ruling classes was made with tremendous power and sincerity; with absolute clearness he laid bare the inner falsity of all those institutions by which modern society is maintained: the church, the law courts, militarism, 'lawful' wedlock, bourgeois science. But his doctrine proved to be in complete contradiction to the life, work and struggle of the grave-digger of the modern social system, the proletariat. Whose then was the point of view reflected in the teachings of Leo Tolstoy? Through his lips there spoke that multitudinous mass of the Russian people who *already* detest the masters of modern life but have not *yet* advanced to the point of intelligent, consistent, thoroughgoing, implacable struggle against them.

The history and the outcome of the great Russian revolution have shown that such precisely was the mass that found itself *between* the class-conscious, socialist proletariat and the out-and-out defenders of the old regime. This mass, consisting mainly of the peasantry, showed in the revolution how great was its hatred of the old, how keenly it felt all the inflictions of the modern regime, how great within it was the spontaneous yearning to be rid of them and to find a better life.

At the same time, however, this mass showed in the revolution that it was not politically conscious enough in its hatred, that it was not consistent in its struggle and that its quest for a better life was confined within narrow bounds.

This great human ocean, agitated to its very depths, with all its weaknesses and all its strong features found its reflection in the doctrine of Tolstoy.

By studying the literary works of Leo Tolstoy the Russian working class will learn to know its enemies better, but in examining the *doctrine* of Tolstoy, the whole Russian people will have to understand where their own weakness lies, the weakness which did not allow them to carry the cause of their emancipation to its conclusion. This must be understood in order to go forward.

This advance is impeded by all those who declare Tolstoy a 'universal conscience', a 'teacher of life'. This is a lie that the liberals are deliberately spreading in their desire to utilise the anti-revolutionary aspect of Tolstoy's doctrine. This lie about Tolstoy as a 'teacher of life' is being repeated after the liberals by some former Social-Democrats.

The Russian people will secure their emancipation only when they realise that it is not from Tolstoy they must learn to win a better life but from the class the significance of which Tolstoy did not understand, and which alone is capable of destroying the old world which Tolstoy hated. That class is the proletariat.

First published in *Rabochaya Gazeta*, No. 2, December 18 (31), 1910, and subsequently in Lenin, *Collected Works*, Vol. 16, pp. 353–4. Reprinted from Lenin, *On Literature and Art*, pp. 56–7.

Heroes of 'Reservation'

The tenth issue of *Nasha Zarya*, the magazine of Mr. Potresov and Co., which we have just received, provides striking examples of carelessness or, rather, unprincipledness in the evaluation of Leo Tolstoy, which need to be dealt with at once, if only in brief.

Here is an article by V. Bazarov, a new warrior in Potresov's ranks. The editors are not in agreement with 'certain propositions' in this article, without of course mentioning which propositions they are. That is so much more convenient for covering up confusion! As for ourselves, we find it difficult to point out any propositions in this article that would not arouse the indignation of anyone who has the least bit of regard for Marxism. 'Our intelligentsia,' V. Bazarov writes, 'beaten and dispirited, turned into a sort of amorphous mental and moral slough, and now at the extreme limit of spiritual demoralisation, has unanimously accepted Tolstoy – the *whole* of Tolstoy – as its conscience.' That is not true. It is mere phrase-mongering. Our intelligentsia in general, and particularly that of *Nasha Zarya*, certainly looks very 'dispirited', but it neither did nor could display any 'unanimity' in its appraisal of Tolstoy, and it never did or could appraise correctly the *whole* of Tolstoy. It is precisely the absence of unanimity that is concealed behind the utterly hypocritical talk about 'conscience', a catchword fully worthy of *Novoye Vremya*. Bazarov does not fight the 'slough' – he encourages the slough.

Bazarov 'would like to recall certain instances of injustice [!!] with regard to Tolstoy, of which the Russian intellectuals in general, and we radicals of various persuasions in particular, are guilty'. The only thing that is true in this statement is that Bazarov, Potresov and Co. are indeed 'radicals of various persuasions', dependent on the universal 'slough' to such an extent that, at a time when the fundamental inconsistencies and weaknesses of Tolstoy's world outlook are being hushed up in the most unpardonable fashion, they rush after 'everybody' in a challenging fashion, yelling about 'injustice' to Tolstoy. They do not want to yield to the intoxication of 'that narcotic particularly widespread among us, which Tolstoy describes as "the virulence of controversy"'. This is the very kind of talk, the kind of tune, that suits the philistines, who turn their backs with supreme contempt on a controversy over principles that are defended consistently and in full.

'The main power of Tolstoy lies in the fact that, having passed through all the stages of demoralisation typical of modern educated men, he succeeded in finding a synthesis. . . .' That is not true. The very thing that Tolstoy did not succeeded in finding, or rather could not find, either in the philosophical foundations of his world outlook or in his social-political doctrine, is a synthesis. 'Tolstoy was the first [!] to objectivise, i.e., to create not only for himself but for others as well, that *genuinely human* [Bazarov's own italics throughout] religion, of which Comte, Feuerbach, and other representatives of modern culture could only dream subjectively [!],' etc., etc.

This kind of talk is worse than common philistinism. It is an attempt to adorn the 'slough' with spurious flowers, capable only of deluding people. More than half a century ago Feuerbach, unable to 'find a synthesis' in his world outlook, which represented in many respects 'the last word' of German classical philosophy, became embroiled in those 'subjective dreams', the negative role of which has long since been appraised by the really progressive 'representatives of modern culture'. To declare now that Tolstoy 'was the first to objectivise' these 'subjective dreams' is to join the camp of the retrograde, to flatter the philistines, to echo the Vekhists.

Bazarov writes:

> It goes without saying that the movement [!?] founded by Tolstoy must undergo a profound change if it is really destined to play a great world-wide historic role: the idealisation of the patriarchal-peasant mode of life, the attraction towards a natural economy, and many other utopian features of Tolstoyism, which loom large [!] at the present time and seem to be its most essential features, are actually nothing but subjective elements not necessarily connected with the basis of Tolstoy's 'religion'.

So it turns out that Tolstoy 'objectivised' Feuerbach's 'subjective dreams', whereas that which Tolstoy reflected both in his brilliant literary works and in his extremely contradictory doctrine, namely, the special economic features of Russia of the past century, noted by Bazarov, are 'nothing but subjective elements' of his doctrine. That is what is called being wide of the mark. But then, there is nothing the 'intelligentsia, beaten and dispirited' (etc., as quoted above), enjoys, desires and likes more, there is nothing that humours its dispiritedness more than this exalting of Feuerbach's 'subjective dreams' which Tolstoy 'objectivised', and this *diversion* of attention from the concrete historical economic and political problems 'which loom large at the present time'!

It is obvious that Bazarov is particularly displeased with the 'sharp criticism' which the doctrine of non-resistance to evil evoked among the 'radical intelligentsia'. To Bazarov it is 'clear that there is no reason to speak here of passivity and quietism'. By way of explaining his thought, Bazarov refers to the well-known tale of 'Ivan the Fool' and suggests that the reader 'imagine that it is not the Tarakan (Cockroach) tsar who sends soldiers against the Fools, but their own ruler Ivan, now become wise; and that Ivan wants to use these soldiers, whom he recruited from the ranks of the Fools themselves and who are therefore akin to the latter by their entire way of thinking, in order to compel his subjects to comply with some unrighteous demands. It is quite obvious that the Fools, practically unarmed and unfamiliar with military formation, cannot even dream of gaining a physical victory over Ivans' troops. Even if they resort to the most vigorous "resistance by force", the Fools cannot defeat Ivan physically, but only by means of moral influence, i.e., only by means of the so-called "demoralisation" of Ivan's troops. . . .' 'The Fools' resistance by force achieves the same result (only worse and at the cost of great sacrifice) as resistance without force. . . .' 'Non-resistance to evil with force or, to use a more general term, harmony of means and ends [!!] is an idea that is by no means characteristic only of moral preachers who live secluded from society. This idea is an essential component part of every integral world outlook.'

Such are the arguments of the new warrior in Potresov's ranks. We cannot stop to analyse them here. It is perhaps sufficient – on this first occasion – just to reproduce his main argument and to add five words: Vekhism of the purest water.

From the final chords of the cantata on the theme that ears do not grow above one's head: 'There is no need to describe our weakness as strength, as superiority over Tolstoy's "quietism" and "narrow rationalism" [and over the inconsistency of his reasoning]? We should not say that, not only because it is at variance with the truth, but also because it hinders us from learning from the greatest man of our times.'

Well, well. But, then, there is no reason why you should be getting angry, gentlemen, and answer with ridiculous bravado and abuse (as Mr. Potresov did in Nos. 8–9 of *Nasha Zarya*) if people like Izgoyev bless, praise and kiss you. Neither the old nor the new warriors in Potresov's ranks can cleanse themselves of these kisses.

The general staff of this host provided Bazarov's article with a 'diplomatic' reservation. But the leading article by Mr. Nevedomsky, printed without any reservations, is not much better. 'While he absorbed,' writes this bard of the present-day intelligentsia, 'and embodied in a consummate form the fundamental aspirations and strivings of the great epoch of the fall of slavery in Russia, Leo Tolstoy proved to be also the purest and most consummate embodiment of the ideological principle of humanity in general – *the principle of conscience.*'

Boom, boom, boom. . . . While he absorbed and embodied in a consummate form the fundamental manner of declamation characteristic of liberal-bourgeois journalism, Mr. Nevedomsky proved to be also the purest and most consummate embodiment of the ideological principle of humanity in general – the principle of rant.

One more – and final – statement:

> All those European admirers of Tolstoy, all those Anatole Frances by whatever name they are called, and the Chambers of Deputies, which recently voted by an enormous majority against the abolition of capital punishment and today pay homage to the great *integral* man – the whole of that kingdom of intermediateness, half-heartedness, reservationism – compared with them, how magnificent, how powerful towers the figure, cast of a single pure metal, of Tolstoy, that living embodiment of an integral principle.

Phew! What eloquence – and not a word of truth. The figure of Tolstoy is cast neither of a single nor a pure metal, nor of metal at all. And it is *precisely* not for his 'integrality', but for his deviation from integrality, that 'all those' bourgeois admirers 'pay homage' to his memory.

There is only one apt word that Mr. Nevedomsky blurted out inadvertently. That is the word 'reservationism', which fits the gentlemen of *Nasha Zarya* just as perfectly as V. Bazarov's above-quoted characterisation of the intelligentsia fits *them*. Throughout it is heroes of 'reservation' that confront us. Potresov makes the reservation that he is not in agreement with the Machists, although he defends them. The editors make the reservation that they are not in agreement with 'certain propositions' of Bazarov's, although it is obvious to everyone that it is not a question here of certain propositions. Potresov makes the reservation that he has been slandered by Izgoyev. Martov makes the reservation that he is not entirely in agreement with Potresov and Levitsky, although they are the very people whom he renders faithful political service. All of them make the reservation that they are not in agreement with Cherevanin, although they approve more of his *second* liquidationist pamphlet, in which the 'spirit' of his first brain-child is greatly increased. Cherevanin makes the reservation that he is not in agreement with Maslov. Maslov makes the reservation that he is not in agreement with Kautsky.

The only thing they all agree on is that they are not in agreement with Plekhanov, and that he slanders them by accusing them of liquidationism, while himself being allegedly unable to explain his present rapprochement with his former opponents.

There is nothing simpler than the explanation of this rapprochement, which is only inexplicable to people with reservations. When we had a locomotive we differed very strongly on the question as to whether the power of that locomotive, the stock of fuel, etc., warranted a speed of, let us say, 25 or 50 miles an hour. The controversy over this question, as over any question which stirs the opponents deeply, was conducted with passion and often with bitterness. That controversy – and this refers to absolutely every question over which it arose – was carried on in the open, in full view of everyone, it was thoroughly thrashed out, without being glossed over by any 'reservations'. And none of us ever thought of retracting anything or of whining over the 'virulence of the controversy'. But today, when the locomotive has broken down, when it is lying in a bog, surrounded by 'reservationist' intellectuals who sneeringly declare that there is 'nothing to liquidate' because there is no longer any locomotive in existence, we, the 'virulent controversionalists' of yesterday, are drawn closer together by our common cause. Without renouncing anything, without forgetting anything, without making any promises about setting aside differences, we are working together for the common cause. We are devoting all our attention and all our efforts to raise the locomotive, to renovate, strengthen and reinforce it, to put it on the rails – as to its speed, or which way to turn one switch or another, we shall discuss that in due time. In these difficult days the immediate task is to create something that will be capable of giving a rebuff to the people 'with reservations' and the 'dispirited intellectuals', who directly or indirectly promote the prevailing 'slough'. The immediate task is to dig – even under the most difficult conditions – for ore, to extract iron, and to cast the steel of the Marxist world outlook and of the superstructures corresponding to this world outlook.

First published in *Mysl*, No. 1, December 1910, signed: *V. I.* Reprinted from Lenin, *Collected Works*, Vol. 16, pp. 368–73.

Index